OFF-TRAIL

howing the important centres

STEVEN—

Seaforth Public Library

—•—

No············

Extracts From Regulations

1. The Library is open every week day, except Wednesday and Holidays, from 2:30 p.m. to 5:30 p.m. and from 7 p.m. to 9 p.m.

2. Members must secure tickets from Librarian, cost ten cents for Adults, and five cents for Juveniles, before books may be issued.

3. No books may be retained longer than two weeks, but may be renewed if no application for the book has been made by another member.

4. Any member who fails to return a book or books within the time marked on it, shall pay two cents per day for each day of such over-detention.

5. No books shall be taken out of the Library for one week previous to first day of January, and all books must be returned to the Library before such first day of January, under a penalty of fifty cents.

6. Members may reserve books upon the payment of five cents, and will be notified by post card when book is in the Library.

7. No member shall lend his or her card or book to anyone not a member of the same household.

8. Any member losing, writing on, or otherwise damaging a book, shall pay the amount of damage, the value of the book, or replace it with one as good.

9. All members will be subject to the Regulations of the Seaforth Public Library, and will be bound thereby.

OFF-TRAIL
in
NOVA
SCOTIA

OFF-TRAIL
in
NOVA SCOTIA

WILL R. BIRD
Author of: *This is Nova Scotia*

The Ryerson Press
TORONTO

Published June, 1956

ACKNOWLEDGMENT NOTE

Grateful acknowledgment is made to
the following for permission to quote:
to Leslie Nelson Jennings and *The
Christian Science Monitor* for "The Par-
lor," to Charles Bruce and The Ryerson
Press for excerpts from *The Flowing
Summer,* to *The Boston Post* for "I Am
Nova Scotia" by Bernie Brennen, to Bar-
low Bird and *The Springhill Record* for
"Sugar Makin'," to Justice L. D. Currie
for extracts from an address.

Acknowledgment is also made to the
Nova Scotia Bureau of Information and
to the Nova Scotia Film Bureau for the
use of photographs.

—W. R. B.

PRINTED AND BOUND IN CANADA
BY THE RYERSON PRESS, TORONTO

AUTHOR'S FOREWORD

ONE OF THE FEW THINGS we might agree upon is that there is a bit of the "gipsy" in nearly all of us. Who doesn't like to explore new and strange places, meet different people and scan, back stage as it were, what goes on in areas away from the popular paved routes? From the beginning Nova Scotia has been influenced by the sea. Pirates and privateers knew the myriad coves along the shore that could be used for hiding places. The majority of our first settlers gained part of their living from the sea. The coast of the province has many bulwarks of grey granite, many ramparts of red stone, and something of the nature of the eternal warfare between rock and tide has crept into the lives of the people and endued them with a sturdiness of character that has won the respect of the rest of Canada.

Salty little villages are spaced in unexpected places along a jigsaw coastline varied by red and white sand beaches, tree-capped islands and rugged headlands. These are remote from the main highways but a visit to them richly repays the explorer for friendliness is there, warm and strong; there are shore paths to stroll, dory rides that are delightful adventure, and there are rare tales to hear in the evening when the day's catch has been put away.

It is well, in most cases, to carry a picnic lunch in your car, and an ancient fish stage dipping stilted feet into the salt tide can provide a unique picnic spot.

Inland, quiet roads lead to the serene solitude of small farm and logging communities, and the mellowness of drowsy summer noons when locusts sing along old fences and swallows chuckle under barn eaves. You'll find the folk who pursue humble rounds incidental to cows and chickens quite willing to chat and help you become acquainted with farm animals. They'll show you pasture trails leading to berry patches in old burntlands, to old beaver meadows where candid snapshots with your camera will stimulate vacation memories when you are back home.

But remember that even in the deep woods you will imagine you can smell the sea, and gulls nest far back in wilderness lakes. A day of it, a week of it, and time loses importance. You lose all hurry, content to explore a little and eat a lot, to sleep at any hour, being friendly with everyone and only hating the day your vacation ends.

No country produces a better crop than its inhabitants and you'll find that Nova Scotians living along the byways in random places have developed a strength of soul to serve in need, a dry humour for conversation, and a philosophy to reinforce cheerfulness that is a precious tonic. Only half of Nova Scotia is known; there is another half lying at the end of narrow ragged shore lanes and hill roads and back settlement reaches. These roads are dusty, often stony, sometimes rutted, and must be driven with care, but the chief compensation is lack of traffic and the pleasure of suddenly finding yourself in a tiny hamlet of saltbox homes that seems part of the landscape, belonging there as truly as the scrubby, thick-trunked trees, deformed by onshore winds, that cling wherever there is sufficient soil. There is only the sound of the sea and the cry of a solitary gull. Sand peeps flit up and down along in flashing silvery wheels. You park the car and prowl along the beach, wondering how far you are from pavement. Then you meet a weathered native who offers a whimsical welcome and in minutes you are wishing you could find lodging and stay a few days.

I must ask my readers to remember one thing. Every person you meet will not have an unusual story to tell, though the way this book reads would make it appear so. Time and again we questioned from ten to twenty persons before finding one who could give us a little story with a flavour all its own. It takes persistence and patience to find them, but the hunting is always sweet.

—W.R.B.

I AM NOVA SCOTIA

I am Nova Scotia.

Named for his beloved land by a proud and prudent Stuart king.

I am a continent's beginning . . . a sea-washed gate to one of History's greatest grounds.

I am the skirling pipes of Edinburgh . . . the neat straight farms of Brittany . . . the ballads born on Shannon's banks.

I am the gypsy flowers of Stratford, blooming where they will, with careless, fire-bright colour.

My three centuries were measured not by Time but by the tides.

Ebb and flow mean more to me than day and night.

My crimson purple seas climb higher here than anywhere on earth, and only God could quiet the harbours of my sheltered jutting shores.

Many a cutlass has been swung . . . and many a deck changed hands before my eyes.

Bold pirates prized the stately ships fashioned from my forests.

Ships of sail-filled grace given to the seas . . . my staunch ally, and yet my ancient enemy.

I am a land where Spring comes softly, bearing a hush of unborn beauty waiting to burst free.

I am Summer, lilac-laden, drowsing deep in new-mown hay and clover.

I am the cry of autumn geese, a plaintive call above the flaming leaves of Fall.

I am the ghost of softly-slipping Micmacs gliding through the snow-wrapped woods, silent as the pines.

I am Nova Scotia.

An ageless, patient land where loveliness has not been forced . . . where Old World beauty lingers still.

My weathered cottages sit among the flowers splashed about their feet, while ox bells turn evening's air to muted music.

I am the pine-topped isles . . . the headlands of granite, grey against the sky.

I am the forest primeval, immortalized for all ages.

I speak in many tongues . . . I go to many churches . . . I am home to those of many lands.

I am history and heartache and happiness . . . I am a quiet corner of the world where there is time to love.

I am Nova Scotia.

—Bernie Brennen in *The Boston Post.*

CONTENTS

LIST OF ILLUSTRATIONS

1

The Unknown Half of Nova Scotia

ON a lovely June day we left Amherst by Highway Two and, three miles out, turned right on a dirt road by a small schoolhouse and drove through an area of marshland, upland risings and quiet farmland. It is known in the locality as the "back road" and few use it save those who reside there. Memories of more than forty years ago brought back a picture of a merry company in a long straw-filled sled, snuggled in rugs and "buffaloes," going to one of the homes for a "donation." In those days Methodist preachers had slim salaries which were augmented by "donations" attended by all the countryside, and by many town folk. Farmers took their sleds to town and offered free "straw rides" to all who wished the outing, the purpose being to get paying guests for the bountiful tables set up at the farmhouse chosen for the occasion.

Members of the preacher's circuit would take in butter that had become too salty, skinny fowl, scabby potatoes, a forequarter of beef, anything that was not considered too great a loss. The provisions would feed the good man and his family for a month, and there were cracked sugar bowls or similar dishes on the table as receptacles for cash donations from those who dined. We used to gaze with awe at the amount of food an average-sized farmer could stow away, and his wife and five or six children had amazing capacity. When they could hold no more the good man would make quite a show of placing a dollar bill in the cash bowl, and would

1

feel he had more than done his part. We from the town would drop a quarter in the dish and feel equally satisfied.

This night I remembered a huge crowd pressed the younger folk to the upstairs part, and someone opened a closed door to reveal a room quite bare of furniture. "Let's have a dance," suggested someone. A dance meant a game we called "Dan Tucker" but the preacher had sternly denounced dancing, card playing and similar evils.

"He'll never know," said a girl, "and Jimmy can play his mouth organ."

But the girl chosen as leader was wearing new shoes that hurt her feet and as she was the most popular lass in the crowd this put a damper on the project until a voice spoke up and offered to swap footwear until the dance was over. We gaped at each other then, for the speaker was the preacher's wife, ten years younger than himself and loved by all.

The swap was made immediately and Jimmy began playing. There was no more than a round or so when the tragedy happened. The leading girl trod heavily on cheap oilcloth covering a large stovepipe hole, punctured the material like paper, and thudded heavily to the floor with a long leg protruding below. It so happened that the room was directly over the dining-room where the preacher sat at the table with many of his congregation. The oilcloth had let the sound of the music and dancing descend clearly and the diners were wondering what would be said when the leg came down and dangled before them. Everyone rose hastily but had time to notice a very well shaped leg with a vaccination mark above the knee. A newspaper was placed on the table and the good man of the house assisted those above by lifting on the leg which was slowly and painfully withdrawn.

Then the preacher finished his dinner as quickly as possible, saying little and evidently boiling with anger. The apprehensive ones followed him into the hall where he shouted for his wife. "Get your things on," he ordered. "We're going home."

His wife pushed through the crowd to confront him. "I know what you are thinking," she said, "but you are wrong. I was not dancing. You probably saw one of my shoes but I loaned them to the girl as hers hurt her feet."

"And am I to believe as well that you loaned her your vaccination mark?" thundered the preacher.

There was a prolonged hush. The preacher's wife was nonplussed, and no one else dare speak. Then the girl who had used the shoes stepped forward.

"It was me went through the pipe hole," she stated, "and your wife has told you the truth. I was wearing her shoes and look." Quickly she hoisted her skirt to above her knee and revealed the telltale vaccination mark. "If you still doubt me I'll show you the marks the stove pipe made!" she added.

Bravely the preacher met the situation. "There is no need, my dear," he answered. "May God forgive me for ever doubting my wife. I apologize to her and ask her forgiveness, and I congratulate you on showing such courage. Furthermore, I feel I have been wrong about Dan Tucker and I hope that after this you'll enjoy the game below stairs where all of us can see."

We had a grand view across a wide expanse of marsh and then were alongside the plant of a comparatively new salt enterprise that affords work for many families residing in Amherst. Water is pumped down into areas of solid salt some hundred feet below the surface and then the brine is pumped up, and the resultant product is in great demand throughout Canada. Soon we turned left on another road and crossed the Nappan river near the railway, reached paved highway and were in the heart of the community, spread near a Dominion Experimental Farm of large acreage. Here the first Acadians had holdings, and the name is said to come from an Indian word meaning "a good place in which to get wigwam poles."

The extensive marshes in this region were flooded deeply by the great Saxby tide of 1869 when barns and stacks were floated away, sheep and cattle drowned in numbers. The tide carried the hay stacks into the many small "coves" formed by the upland and owners found it difficult to identify their own. Many tales survive of strange means of proof but the best account of the unusual concerns the elderly maiden sister of a carpenter who made all the coffins for the settlement. She had such a dread of having any connection with the grim items that she forbade her bachelor brother to dare store a coffin in the adjoining woodshed. At the time of the big tide the brother was absent and the waters swirled in before his sister was aware of what was happening. The tide poured into the house and she was frantic as she saw no way to escape to the upland. But her brother had just finished a coffin in his workshop at the rear and now it floated beside the window of her bedroom. She reached out and grasped it, managed to get into it as she held to the window frame and, using a bed slat as an oar, paddled her way to safety.

We followed the paved road into Maccan, once quite a thriving coal-mining village, and talked with Vaughan Hoeg, proprietor of the principal store. He was active as a star ball-player back in 1921 when Maccan had the Intermediate Baseball championship. Across the river is the old home that was more or less of a museum during the life of its owner, Herbert Harrison. His collection of coins was shown up and down the country and now rests in the military museum at Fort Beauséjour. The doors of the house are single boards, and there are many of such width in the panelled walls of his living-room. He had items from all over the world, ancient weapons and Micmac arrow heads and trophies from the tropics. The Baptist church is 110 years old and has an old-time gallery.

The paved road ran on to River Hebert, another place practically a ghost town, once proud of its coal-mining industry. It is a quiet village with some fine views over the river, and comfortable-looking homes. Leaving the hard surface we turned right and drove out on a road skirting Cumberland Basin, narrow but in good condition. This was going back into yesterday for we were on ground cleared by the Acadians who established quite a village and were prosperous until in 1755 the soldiers came and put the homes and barns to the torch. It had been a happy settlement, with virgin forest at the back of the fertile fields and waters in front teeming with fat shad which were salted by the barrel for winter.

For more than 150 years the crops of Minudie were blessed by an annual rite, but the wide-spread destruction wrought by the New Englanders routed the first inhabitants and they never returned. The district was granted to J. F. W. Des Barres in 1765 and during the years that followed Acadians from the Chignecto area drifted in and began farming in a small way. These were settled in various holdings by a land agent of Des Barres and one of them, Victor Brine, was a most remarkable man. He could not read or write but he did all the surveying for the people with a ten-foot pole, could tell correctly the changes of the moon and was an authentic almanac for the settlement. Des Barres became entangled in the meshes of an adventuress named Polly Cannon, and she rented the estate to the Acadians at a rental of one hundred pounds a year. This placed the farmers on an independent footing, frame houses with wide-mouthed chimneys and low sloping roofs were erected, and over three thousand acres of marsh land was well dyked.

Amos "King" Seaman was born near Sackville, New Brunswick, January 14, 1788, but left home as a boy and landed at Minudie from a birch bark canoe, was received kindly by the people and taken to the log church on Sunday. He reached manhood in River Hebert and then moved to Minudie and began to quarry grindstones which he shipped to Boston. Soon he acquired enough capital to bring back supplies in trade and he opened a store at Minudie. Everything he touched seemed to turn to money. He acquired a coal mine at River Hebert, purchased the Des Barres holding, and rented all the farms, built schooners and traded with the West Indies. His holdings were nine miles in extent and his sole education was that given him by his wife, Jane Metcalf, whom he married May 14, 1814. She taught him to read and write and to appreciate the better things in life. He became well informed, could recite large portions of the Scriptures and wrote a good hand. He bought land at Amherst, acquired quarries at Wallace River, made enormous profits with his West Indian trade from Boston. He prepared a genealogical table of the Seaman family, had artists do paintings of his parents, and kept a diary which was written in rhyme.

There had to be regular instructions given to his tenants and rents collected so he erected a great wooden post at the crossroads which held a message box. There he left messages for his forty-nine tenants and he knew the family history and the welfare of each individual. By 1843 he saw the need of something better than water power and installed steam power, a combination saw and flour mill at a cost of fifteen thousand pounds, the first steam sawmill in Nova Scotia. The opening of the mill brought hundreds to view proceedings.

Everyone now knew the man as "King" Seaman and he began travelling extensively in the United States and visited Britain where he was presented at court. On his return he felt he must have a home in keeping with his wealth so built a main house with four rooms on the ground floor, each twenty feet square. The big hall was flagged with carved stone from his quarries, and he had sliding doors to the rooms. There were five large bedrooms upstairs, and eight ornamented fireplaces heated the home. He had an elaborate wine cellar which was kept well stocked. The kitchen ell measured sixty by forty feet, and was divided into two huge kitchens. Above were sleeping quarters for the servants, and below was the vegetable cellar. A man named Doncaster kept himself and his yoke of oxen busy the year around supplying wood for the kitchen and the eight fireplaces. Scotch elms were planted around the house and a horse chestnut grew in front.

Remembering the kindness of the priest when he arrived

at Minudie as a boy, Seaman built a church. He also built a church for the Protestants, and an up-to-date school. He had one hundred head of cattle in his great barns and his store was the biggest in the whole Chignecto area, carrying extensive stocks of silk and satin for the ladies. Next he induced a man to build a hotel in Minudie as many came to the place to get grist ground or to buy sawn lumber. But when the hotel began operating Seaman thought it hard that folks had to go where they would pay for their meals, so he invited any he knew to his house, finally putting the poor hotelman out of business. "King" Seaman had seven sons and four daughters, and he saw to it that all of them received adequate education. But they drifted from home, wanting to know of other realms than that of "Grindstone Castle," and after his death there were many legal battles. It was Seaman's desire that his family share the estate equally but jealousy developed and the litigation in connection with the probate of his will is not yet forgotten, and the story of the "red book" and the "black book" in which he set forth how his property was to be divided is still a subject for discussion by law students.

We sat by the front of the ruin of the old house, its great doors gaping wide to all weather, its tiled hall swept by rain and wind, its windows gone, and visualized the splendour of those long-gone days when a dozen thoroughbred horses would be tethered at the hitching rail, and more than twenty guests often seated at the great dining-table. Then we drove along the road and looked for the big post with the message box that had been a landmark. It is gone. Gulls hovered low and gave plaintive calls and the wind was fretful. We saw traces of the old wharf, and where the store had been. The only thing remaining from the "King's" time is the shad fishing, and if motor visitors would take this byroad they, if hardy enough, would see something that belongs to a Ripley "Believe it or not."

Today just one group engages in this fishery but in bygone years several families of Minudie caught fat silver-blue shad in the muddy waters of Cumberland Basin. The shad average two and one-half pounds in weight and have firm white flesh which is delicious when either fried or baked, and is so fat that the frying pan needs no additional grease. The season lasts from mid-May until September—a time of hard, unremitting toil, of little sleep, of ever-present danger. The nets are cleared twice a day, at low tide, regardless of whether it be noon or night, and the men work on the hour as the tide comes in swiftly, rising twenty-eight feet or more in six hours. The fishermen go out in rain and in fog, in bitter winds and in blazing sun.

They use their own time table and start with a hearty meal in Edmund Brine's house—cold pork and boiled potatoes and plenty of strong tea and cookies. Then the two horses are hitched to a box wagon containing stakes, mallets, guy ropes and nets, and off they go on a six-mile drive that takes them to their "camp," weather-beaten shacks huddled behind a dike which keeps the Basin water from the marsh. There the horses are turned loose to graze while the men splice new guy ropes to replace the frayed ones and another snack is had before the horses are hitched again and a ladder added to the waggon's gear. Then over the dike they go and meet the wind bringing in mist or heat and no time is lost as they drive over the red mud flats using a curving line of stakes which mark the three-mile route from shore. The first distance is sticky mud that clings to boots and hoofs like glue but further on there is hard bottom usually covered with an inch of water. The stakes, two feet high and about fifteen feet apart are followed easily no matter the fog or mist that may roll in.

Soon the long line of nets is seen, the nets bellied out in the breeze, with gulls screaming around them, trying to tear at the trapped fish with their beaks. Often, too, there are crows trying to rob the fisherman. Then it can be seen that the silvery specks in the nets are shad, caught fast by their gills. Birch posts that hold the nets are twelve feet high and so the ladder must be used to reach the top fish. The nets are twenty-three yards in length and often the wind has some down in a tangle so that the men must work fast to make repairs. When a new post is set there is no digging. It is set upright and rocked back and forth so that it settles quickly into the sand and is supported by guy ropes. The shad that are badly torn are tossed to the gulls, but there are usually one hundred and fifty undamaged fish. The round trips make thirty-six miles a day and when the men get home they have to split and salt the fish and pack them into puncheons which hold about four hundred fish, worth around one hundred dollars. At night the men use an electric light from a dismantled car, taking two batteries along in case of trouble. Tourists display a broad grin when told that men go fishing shad with a waggon and ladder but a trip on the Minudie sands will cure any disbelief and is an experience not forgotten.

We drove along to Lower Cove and only a great depression remains of the old grindstone quarry, its edges rimmed by small bushes. The sheds are gone but the great chimney stands there in majestic solitude, and few who pass that way the first time will guess why it was built. Soon we were in a wooded area and a hen partridge with a dozen small ones boldly crossed our way so that we had to stop. Then we were at Joggins, where some coal is still being mined. There are records of its coal being sold in Boston as early as 1720 and different New England companies tried to operate there before the Expulsion. We went to a high bridge crossing a stream and gazed at the rugged shoreline, famous for its rock formation and large beds of fossils, samples of which are on exhibition in museums throughout the world.

H. A. Brown, E.E., of New York City, visited the Joggins area in 1950 and was greatly interested in the fossil forests of Chignecto Bay, but the best descriptions are in a book written by Sir Charles Lyell, F.R.S. He states:

The beds through which erect trees or rather the trunks of trees, placed at right angles to the planes of stratification, are traceable, have a thickness of about two thousand five hundred feet; and no deception can arise from the repetition of the same beds owing to shifts or faults, the section being unbroken, and the rocks, with the exception of their dip, being quite undisturbed ... No part of the original tree is preserved except the bark which forms a tube of pure bituminous coal, filled with sand, clay and other deposits, now forming a solid internal cylinder without traces of organic structure. The diameter of the first tree was fourteen inches at the top and sixteen inches at the bottom. The bark is a quarter of an inch thick. The second trunk was about nine feet in length. The cliff was too precipitous to allow me to discover any commencement of roots, but the bottom of the trunks seemed to touch the subjacent coal. I observed in all at least seventeen of these upright trunks, but in no instance did I see any one of them intersecting a layer of coal however thin, nor did I find any of them terminating downwards in sandstone but always in coal or shale. The usual height was from six to eight feet but one which was more than a hundred feet above the beach and which I could not approach to measure, seemed to be twenty-five feet high and four feet in diameter.

He states that the action of Fundy tides continues to undermine and sweep away the face of the cliff so that a new crop of fossils is laid open to view every three or four years, and every summer a new class of students come to investigate the entire area.

Then we entered what seemed primeval forest, a narrow winding road that goes miles through a district deserted by all save wild life, passing through what was once Sand River and Shulee. This is a drive those who love nature will enjoy to the full. A doe with a fawn leisurely sauntered in a glade and eyed us with mild interest. A complaining porcupine shifted position in a low-branched hemlock and let us know visitors were unwelcome. Miles later, near Sand River, a red fox bounded ahead of our car for a hundred yards or more, and a great white owl sailed across the road in silent flight.

We reached Apple River and were sorry to have left the woods but here was the sea again, and farms, and small orchards, and wonderful views. A man in tired-looking overalls came from some garden chore, rested on the fence and chatted. Deer hunt? Well, hardly ever, as any man could get a deer for meat most any morning, and why waste a day hunting? He grinned when we mentioned game laws and allowed they were meant for other places. Soon he was telling us about Henry, an honest fellow who married a comely girl and when an agent came along supplying crayon enlargements Henry got one of Sarah and had it framed. But Sarah died of lung complaint and her last request was that Henry leave her picture on the wall whether he married again or not.

Henry waited four years and then married Roxana who was middle-aged and quite content to have the picture on the wall providing he had one of her photos fixed up by the crayon people. Henry owned that was fair enough and put both in one frame of walnut that cost him twelve fifty. Some sudden ailment removed Roxana but she had time to extract a promise from Henry to keep the pictures on the wall.

Number three was Emily, a sharp-featured lady who had a mind of her own but nothing she could say changed Henry's mind about the pictures. They stayed in place and then came the spring of the flu and it was Henry who was going. He had wit enough to get Emily to promise to leave the pictures up as long as she lived in the house, and she kept her word faithfully. She lived alone for fourteen years and the picture hung to the same hook—turned to the wall with a pretty calendar painting in front.

We went on to Advocate and visited Captain Collins ninety-odd years young. He had sailed the world as a young man and could talk about any foreign land, had relics that would please any collector, such as pitchers and coins and needles that were more than a thousand years old and had come from the Balearic Islands in the Mediterranean Sea. I asked him what there was around Advocate that might be different from the next community, and he grinned and reckoned no other place had a "bear tree" beside the road. Then he pointed out the huge spruce not too far from the houses and told the story of a big bear coming across the field and meeting with a farmer. The farmer called his big dog and the bear went up the tree. Another man happened along and he had to run a mile to get a rifle but the farmer and his dog kept Bruin aloft and finally the runner was back with a trusty weapon and a well-aimed shot brought the large animal crashing down. Needless to say, all traffic along the road was held up while the excitement ruled.

From Advocate to Parrsboro the road is newly paved and one of the best in Nova Scotia. We lingered a time, however, for there is much to talk about at Advocate. The rock formation known as "The Three Sisters" looks much like three giant ladies and legend has it they displeased Glooscap, the Micmac god, and were turned to stone. Nine miles off the coast, and looking less than a third of that distance, is Isle Haute, where the Indians went to hold their feasts of dog meat previous to engaging another tribe in battle. Two or three gorgings of dog meat was supposed to give the brave the courage of a superman. It is lonely out at Isle Haute after the winter storms arrive and weeks on end the boat cannot get to or from the land.

At the store in Advocate a man told me of a keeper going to the shore for supplies and leaving his hired man and wife to look after the chores. But a strong gale brought in drifting ice and no boat could live among it so the keeper could not get to the island until six days had passed. And the first night just before dark the hired man died from a heart attack as he was carrying wood for the kitchen stove.

The terrified keeper's wife managed to get him on a sofa with casters and she pushed the sofa and burden through the living-room and to the tower stairway where she left him. She attended the light and each time she made a visit to it she had to pass the corpse. The wind raged and the ice cakes imprisoned the island. The poor woman kept the light burning but her nerves got worse and worse so that when the husband returned, with three in a big boat to help him get through the ice, he found her reading one of Scott's Waverley novels to the dead man. "It was on his bureau where he had the page marked," she said, "and I thought he'd like to know how the story ended."

It was a short and very scenic drive to Spencer's Island, which is the name of a shore village. We descended from the top of a high hill and as the day was warm drove down to the wharf to get a breath of cool air. We never go there but we think of the time nearly thirty years ago when we did the same thing and heard a tapping noise as we sat in the car. We looked and saw an old man overhead in a boathouse, beckoning to us. So we went up the stair to his place and found he was making chairs. He was, however, much more interested in visitors and showed us a large stone rigged on legs and with a supporting back. This was the original Glooscap's "throne," he said, and whoever sat on it and made a solemn wish would have that wish fulfilled. Then he dramatically pulled back a curtain over a corner shelf and revealed a small god with bright red eyes. He had stolen it from a temple in India when he was a young man, he said, and though there had been a search of every vessel in port they had not found his treasure. It was more than five hundred years old and those who attended it daily never suffered ill-health. He stated he was over seventy and had not known a sick day from the time he got the idol. So I wrote his story for a national magazine and more than two hundred cars found his little boathouse and the climax was an American from Ohio offering five hundred dollars for the idol.

When you talk with others at Spencer's Island it won't be long until they ask if you have heard of their most famous vessel, and no ship has taken a tighter hold on the imagination than the *Mary Celeste,* made of birch, beech and maple to the waterline, and spruce to her scuppers. She was built at Spencer's Island and launched in May of 1861, a hundred-foot brigantine for coastal trade, and then christened the *Amazon.* She ran into trouble and was damaged, had to be repaired and, under new ownership, was re-named the *Mary Celeste.* Eleven years from the time she slid down the Spencer's Island ways Captain Ben Briggs purchased a one-third interest in the craft and sailed for Genoa with one thousand, seven hundred barrels of alcohol as cargo, taking his wife and two-year-old daughter along as company. They boarded the *Mary Celeste* at Pier 50 on the East River, New York, October 27, and, with the first and second mate, cook and four seamen, made a total of ten persons on the brigantine.

They sailed on November 5th and the ship and cargo was insured for $17,400. The weather was bad as they started so they anchored off Staten Island until the next day and then headed into the Atlantic.

Twenty-seven days later the sailing ship, *Dei Gratia,* headed for Gibraltar from New York, sighted a sail five miles off the port bow. When it was nearer they saw the vessel was under very short sail and there was no answer to any of the signals they made. So a boat was lowered and Mate Deveau with two seamen rowed to the stranger and climbed on board.

They found no one. The single life boat was gone. The hatches were open and about three and one half feet of water sloshed around in the hold. The skylight in the captain's quarters was open and the bedding cold and damp. The child's toys were strewed on the deck and the rosewood melodeon belonging to the captain's wife stood in a corner as if it had just been played. The log was in the mate's cabin, but the navigation instruments were gone, the compass knocked out of place and ruined. The oilskins and pipes of the crew were still in the forecastle but there was no cooked food in the galley. Two sails had been blown away but the ship was seaworthy and was soon pumped dry. The log slate had hourly entries, neat and precise, until eight a.m. on November 25th. None of the casks had been touched, no alcohol taken. The weather had not been bad. No one ever learned, nor will, it seems, why the ten persons took to the life boat and left the *Mary Celeste* with an unlashed helm. No trace of any of those persons or the boat was ever found.

Port Greville is a pretty little village on the shore and children were flocking to an ice cream parlour during the afternoon. Until 1865 the place was known as Ratchford River.

Much lumber has been shipped from Port Greville, a man by the store told us, and in the old days it was a thriving settlement furnishing plenty of business for three stores. We walked along the road and admired flowers in several gardens, then heard an organ being played and voices singing. We remembered the music as we went on to Diligent River and found several summer cottages, the beginning of a summer colony. It was evening and we had lunch from our basket beside the beach and enjoyed the view as a big red moon appeared above the horizon.

We walked back to the car and stopped to chat with an old man who said he did not like seeing a "blood moon," and likely there would be a fight at the dance on Saturday night. Then his better half came along, heard our discussion and said it was a "war moon," and she could remember one just like it back in June, 1944. Their son came for them in a small truck and laughed and said it was a "drought moon," and meant a week of dry hot weather. He had a couple of teenagers in the back on crates for seats and they giggled and called it a "love moon." So we swore they were right and all the rest wrong, and drove to Parrsboro.

Luck took us to Riverview Cottages situated off the road and beside a small lake. It was clean and quiet and cool after the hot day and not only were boats free for rowing but a honeymoon couple were out there fishing and, amazingly, despite the hot weather, got a few nice trout. Mrs. Antrim, the proprietor, took us under her wing the next morning, insisted on driving her own car and away we whisked on back roads past the golf course and on a few miles along very narrow road that dipped deeply into ravines and climbed to cliff banks from where we could see right across Minas Channel. Soon we were at Two Islands, as remote from the outer world as if we were one hundred miles away. The views were magnificent, and we were not surprised to learn that many lots have been purchased and summer homes are going up in that area. We saw the ruin of what had been a grand old home, with the walls insulated with birch bark. The once-proud settlement now consists of only three homes. At one a farmer came out to watch as Mrs. Antrim managed her car with the utmost skill in turning. He pointed to a dark opening scarcely one hundred yards from his barn and told us it was the home of a pair of foxes with three cubs. He wished we knew some one who wanted to buy a live fox, he said. I asked how he would get one. "Easily," he said. "I've a roll of six-foot wire ready to use. I'll stand it around the mouth of the den and dig them out with a shovel and put them in salt sacks."

"Did you ever dig any others out?" I asked.

"No," he said, "but I've got it planned exactly what to do."

The beach is far, far down. We walked over to the edge of the cliff and saw places where one might descend and then noticed many sun bathers on the sand. When the tide was low, Mrs. Antrim said, they walked out to a big island in front of where we stood and gathered dulse. This they dried and many considered it a great treat. I well remember being forced to eat it for worms when a youngster, a spring idea as regular as ministrations from the old blue china cup—sulphur and molasses. Not a youngster in our neighbourhood had worms, but all were treated for them.

We drove thirteen miles from Parrsboro to Five Islands on Highway 2 and then turned left and went up-grade for three or four miles on a gravel road that wound around curves in careless abandon, and had woods on both sides. We disturbed a flock of ruffed grouse that did not take to wing but hid in fern clusters scant yards from the roadway. At last we came to Lynn, a scattering of houses along a cleared stretch with several farms abandoned. A deer leaped a fence and darted across a field, stopped suddenly, turned and stared at us, then we were in woods again. Lumber is hauled by trucks to Five Islands from the area and so the road has been widened and is in fair condition. Years ago the trees almost met overhead and after a heavy rain it would take a week for the road to dry out. Away back in the old days there were many tales of a woods devil lurking in the area and there were those who swore by all that was good and great they had followed the creature's tracks after a snowfall and the distance between the fore-paw tracks was about eight inches, that they went both sides of a tree!

About 1897 a hired man working in Mapleton, five miles along and the other side of the Lynn woods, purchased the first bicycle ever rode in the region. It was a wondrous affair and had a horn on the handlebar, a thing that made an unearthly wail when pressed slowly. A farmer at Lynn took his grist to the mill at Southampton, eight miles down, and was much worried as night came on before he reached the woods. He had a long buckboard loaded with bags of mashed grain and flour, and soon he whipped his nag to a fast trot. The buckboard bounced in and out of ruts and a bag fell off at the rear, but was not noticed. Meanwhile the hired man had wanted to visit Lynn after work but was rather timid of the woods and when he saw the farmer with the grist hurriedly had his supper and started on his bicycle, hoping to catch up and ride through the woods in company.

He came upon the bag of mashed grain and immediately put on speed to overtake the farmer and make him aware of his loss. He pedalled desperately and at last heard sounds of the buckboard going at good speed, so pressed his horn as a signal to stop. The fearful farmer, watching as best he could for the woods devil, heard the terrible wail behind him and knew he was being pursued. It was a desperate situation and he never hesitated but threw off every sack he could snatch hurriedly and lashed his poor horse into a gallop. The wail sounded louder than ever as the excited hired man found more sacks in the road and did his best with the bike. Finally they emerged from the woods with the horse in a lather, the farmer exhausted, and the hired man wringing with perspiration. He told his story and pressed the horn to explain, then had to exert himself to the utmost to escape the farmer's rage.

We came to the County Line between Colchester and Cumberland, and I stopped the car and began exploring. Bush has almost smothered apple trees and garden of a farm that was once quite a stopping place for Lynn folk. The house had fallen and there was little trace of the barn. Some old iron kettles and the debris of an ancient cart were in a clump of raspberry bushes gone wild. I tried to raise a portion of wall to get a look into what had been the kitchen but could not. Old Nancy used to live there in the long ago, a woman who could do her part indoors and out, could rake hay or dig potatoes or use a bucksaw. She had one failing and it was whispered about the length of Mapleton—she smoked a pipe. As her husband smoked, it was easy for her to get tobacco and she smoked Index, a plug that had a tin heart impressed on it. Each noon when she finished eating, or at supper, she sat in her rocker and enjoyed a pipe before going on with the chores. But whispers reached her and she knew folk were curious. No one could get near the house without being seen and a big apron pocket concealed plug and pipe, but there were the whispers so one day Nancy casually pressed one of the tin hearts into the wood panel beside her rocking place. Then another was pressed in, and another, until there came a time when letters four inches high ran across the wall, the warning MIND YOUR OWN BUSINESS. Once on a hunting expedition I went to the old house and looked in. The window was gone and the floor has rotted but the letters were still there, black with rust.

We drove down through East Mapleton, all down grade, where sugar maples dominated, and old dam sites can be traced along the two brooks meandering toward Maccan River. The old schoolhouse of split slab seats and home-made desks had vanished. Stone walls, the pioneer's signature on his land, are still there, his indelible mark, the boundary passed on to his heirs. Lilac bushes guarded an old cellar and fine maple trees sighed in the afternoon breeze, whispering they were planted on a "Victoria Day" many long years ago.

At the foot of the hills we came to an old wooden bridge and two boys were there with fishing poles lying beside them as they sprawled flat on the planking to peer under the bridge. It is about eight feet above the water and the long brook pool seemed four or five feet deep. I stopped and went to see what the boys were watching. "Look," said one. "That old brute of an eel. He took our hooks and we couldn't even budge him. He just breaks a line like it's twine string."

It was an enormous eel, thick as a man's arm and about a yard long. It had a dark retreat under the ancient log abutments and the boys said it had lived there for years and it ate small trout that seemed fairly numerous.

We drove onto the pavement of Highway 2 at the Mapleton church, turned sharp right and drove to Leamington where, near the school, we swung right again and went down into a ravine and then wound up a long dirt road into Rodney, a straggling settlement with houses perched on hills, cats sleeping in the sun and an atmosphere of peace and quiet once associated with Sunday morning. Then there was Windham and more hills, a sawmill at the foot of a slope, black and white cattle in the pastures, a flock of crows chasing an owl, and a brown rabbit sitting at the edge of a garden patch. We had our picnic lunch in the shade of some tall trees near a farm house, and again heard a house organ being played softly. Then a woman came out and shyly asked if we would like a cup of tea. We accepted as we wanted to see the organ, and found she was alone, her husband and son being in town.

In these days a man can watch television and see lady wrestlers pull hair and kick and scratch until he has no qualms about the pioneering qualities of modern womanhood. The parlour organ belongs to a quieter more flavourful era of our history. When a family could afford the instrument it was a big event and satisfied one of mother's long-cherished ambitions. It was a handsome affair, elaborately carved, with bevelled mirror and several fancy little shelves to hold dust-collecting bric-a-brac. There were five octaves and four sets of reeds. On a cold, starlit winter evening it was heart-warming as friends and family gathered around the organ and mother played old familiar home songs and cherished hymns. Voices were not trained but were rich and true, and people sang because they loved to sing, "Annie Laurie" and "Old Black Joe" and "Flow Gently, Sweet Afton." At nine-thirty yawns were near so the last piece was always "God Be with You till We Meet Again." Then the boy took his lamp and climbed the stairs and all the world was safe and happy.

"I play the organ when the men folks are away," smiled the woman. "It keeps me from getting lonesome."

The house was quite some distance from the nearest neighbour and when we remarked about it she smiled again. "It was very funny last year when we got a sudden call to go to Parrsboro. In the hurry I forgot to fasten the back woodshed door and we had to go to Springhill. There I met my brother who was on his way to visit us and I told him to catch a ride and go in by the woodshed door, and we would be back the next noon. When we were on the road again my husband said he had met his brother on his way to our place and had told him to go in by the cellar door which he had forgotten to fasten. His brother had a bicycle and knew the neighbours. Well, my brother got a ride and arrived about dark, got in the woodshed door all right but couldn't find the matches and so didn't have any light. However he got upstairs and went to bed. My husband's brother rode to a neighbour's and stayed there the evening. After ten he came to the house, found the cellar door and used all his matches getting up the stairs to the kitchen. It was pitch dark and he couldn't find anything. My husband had told him no one was there so his hair almost stood on end as he heard a floor board creak under a step upstairs. My brother had wakened and he heard someone cautiously moving in the kitchen. He had a dread of burglars and so quickly donned his trousers and coat, picked up his shoes and resolved to make a desperate dash for the woodshed and escape. My husband's brother is a young fellow and he was petrified as he heard the movements upstairs. He thought first of trying to get out the front door but by the time he had got his bearings the intruder was coming down the stairs. So he stood perfectly still, hoping the man would go. Down came the careful tread, down to the hall. He stood quietly but when the steps headed toward him he hastily backed to get out of the way and tripped over a stool. My brother, shoes in hand, heard what he thought was a charge at him and, yelling wildly, drove toward where he thought the door to the wood-shed was. The two collided heavily and crashed down. My brother was half under the kitchen table and as he struggled up he upset it and the knife drawer emptied to the floor. My husband's brother jumped up, pawing frantically to find a door, and found the switch instead. The light came on and the two stared at each other—then grinned in enormous relief. They still laugh about it."

We could visualize the happening as she told her story and we drove down to River Philip chuckling over the fun. Soon the road ran along the river and elms added their beauty to the scene. A man was repairing the gate to his driveway and and we stopped to chat, asked him where the old Pugnose Inn had been situated. He told us and added that the road was changed considerably from coaching days and that while part-ridge hunting in the woods he had found tombstones in thick growth with names and dates still decipherable. Old cellars were near the spot but no one then living knew anything about that isolated corner of the settlement.

Collingwood Corner was next and a few cars were parked by the store. We chatted with men who stood in a group discussing lumber and soon were being told of roads through the woods by which one could cut off ninety miles on the way to Halifax. Cars with low undergear could not go but in the old days the Fords could ride through in safety. We declined to explore but heard many accounts of moose being observed by motorists, and were told of one oldtimer who had shot more than forty fine bulls, in and out of season.

"There weren't another could follow a moose like him," declared a lanky fellow who chewed tobacco. "He'd pick a rainy day and he knowed right where to go to find moose lying down. Then he'd work to windward and creep up on them. He knew just how a bull would act once he'd smelled man, how the bull would circle to make sure, and he'd move accordingly and soon be with the scent coming from the bull. So they'd tack back and forth through the wet bush till the bull got careless and that was the finish. One time, though, there was an old bull six feet high in the shoulder who knowed all them tricks and he just lit out for other territory. However Joe was smart enough to know moose like to keep to thick woods when they're nervous so he cut right across country through clearings and hardwood and by dark was near where he figured the bull would arrive. So he just stood quiet by a big hemlock and waited and darned if the bull didn't come right long and never stopped till he was so close Joe had to step back to get room to raise his rifle. Yes, sir, Joe was the best of them all."

We went into the store and asked about the first settlers and a man brought us a paper, the 50th Anniversary Edition of the *Oxford Journal,* and answered every question readily. One William Donkin and twenty-one others were granted a tract of eleven thousand acres along the River Philip on July 5, 1785, the land known afterward as the Yorkshire Grant, and the beginning of Collingwood. Many of these firstcomers sold their grants and so had little to do with the history of the place. In a field is a headstone to Henry Atkinson, a native of England who died in 1840. The legend is that Henry was an infidel and when he was dying he told his wife that if he had been wrong in his refusal to accept Christianity his hair would turn black. He was seventy-two and his hair snow-white as he passed away. At midnight his wife went into the room and fearfully raised the sheet—to see his hair black as when he had been a boy. The Atkinsons had a grandfather clock with the works made of Corinthian brass and it went year in and year out without stopping, has been in many homes. There are several relics of the 18th century around the area.

In January, 1839, a strange woman called at the home of a settler and had a cup of tea and some food. The settler's wife asked where she had come from and where she was going but the questions were not answered. Then the settler's wife gave the woman a portion of a loaf as she was leaving, but became busy and did not notice the direction in which she travelled. A week later a young man of the place was three miles above Collingwood on the north slope of Cobequid Mountain hunting caribou when he found a track in the snow which he took to be that of a boy about fifteen years of age. He returned and found at his home people talking about the disappearance of the strange woman. A search party was organized at once and the next day the woman was found huddled under a large tree with hanging branches. She merely said "You have been a long time coming." It was thirteen days after she had called at the home and had a cup of tea.

The search party made a litter of poles and branches and carried the woman on the improvised stretcher through the woods to Economy five miles distant. A doctor was summoned and he found that both of the woman's feet and legs were frozen. A second doctor was consulted and it was agreed that both legs should be amputated at the knee. The woman stood the operation well and was taken to the poorhouse at Halifax where she lived for twenty years but never would reveal her name. She was a skilled needlewoman, of fine appearance and well educated. We were told much of working bees, barn raisings, the making of maple sugar, the use of wool in the household, all the work that belongs to the early days. An old man came into the store and was queried about his memories. He said the thing that stuck in his mind was seeing a circus arrive in his childhood, the elephants and camels walking the old coach road and the wild animal cages and equipment being drawn by horses.

On we went to Williamsdale and there was little traffic other than an occasional truck and the road was surprisingly good. Then a fish hatchery took our attention, and a car with a Massachusetts licence was there. The children were watching the fingerlings with avid interest and a woman was taking pictures. The man, in a bright blue shirt, just strolled around and grinned from ear to ear.

"I was in Springhill," he told us, "and when I was getting

gas I asked the fellow if I could get somewhere off the pavement without getting stuck, and find some place to let the youngsters out. He told me how to get here and boy! Say, I never saw a fish hatchery before. And we saw a rabbit on the road. And we're going to picnic somewhere on a logging road in here. These country roads are wonderful!"

Williamsdale was first called East Branch and dates back to 1820, and legend has it that the wife of one first settler rode all the way from New Brunswick carrying an old-fashioned clock in her arms. Another settler brought a number of cherry stones and started the many cherry orchards that are in the vicinity. First roads were only blazed trails and an Englishman who bought the first four-wheeled waggon got it caught in stumps on the highway until he had to abandon it and return the next day with his axe and hew and chop enough stumps from the way to give him a clear passage. No doctor was around for years and one Aunt Sally Taylor looked after the sick, using remedies made from peppermint and balm and wormwood, burdock, tansy, life-of-man and many others.

We drove along a road through half farmland and half woods and in ten miles met just two cars and four trucks. On our left we saw a vacant house in a field and below it a small cemetery. We had been told about it as it is the house where John J. Stewart was born, one of the founders of the *Halifax Herald* and its first editor, he being in the chair from 1876 to 1907, when he met death through an accident with an oil stove. It was a shock to the people of Cumberland who were proud of his career and there was much condemnation of the new-fangled oil stoves. Then we reached a crossroads. A man told us the road on the left led to Thompson Station and part of Millvale, and he announced that we were in Millvale's other part. The road on the right went to Sugar Loaf, the highest point in Cumberland County where there is a fire tower. The man said this was the road we could take to Economy but he was not going to recommend it.

Next we reached Rose and at the schoolhouse the road divided, the left going to Westchester, which we decided to leave for later on. Nine miles on we came to Sutherland's Lake, named for two Sutherland brothers who lived beside it and rented their boats to fishermen. One, Lorenzo, was a copious water drinker, never seeming to satisfy his thirst and legend has it that when younger he had been playing in the yard of his grandfather when an old crone came along the road and demanded that he get her a drink of water. He had not seen her before, was frightened of her and ran back of the house and hid, whereupon she raised a hand and wished that the remainder of his life thirst would torment him. And it was said that when he went to bed at night a pail of fresh water was always beside him. It was also said that he was an expert angler and got to know the exact spots in the lake where trout could be taken, but would only act as guide for those whom he liked.

One mile further we reached what used to be Buckwheat Bridge but now it is a culvert and on the right before it is the old Downing Clear where the Downings lived at the turn of the century. There were four girls and a boy. The latter was sickly and did not live long, while three of the girls did not have ample mental equipment. The oldest married and went to live at Bangor. The other three picked berries as long as any were in season and carried them to various customers, walking in single file wherever they went and all three talking to themselves. One year berry prices were exceptionally good and one of the trio picked buckets and buckets from dawn to dark, kept all the cash returns, slipped away from the family and bought a ticket to Bangor. She did not know where her sister lived but got from the train at Bangor in her usual attire and walked the streets, talking to herself and asking for Laura. The police questioned her, finally located Laura. But Laura was not having her and so she was put on the train and sent home and the cost charged to the community.

Three miles more and Cumberland Bridge. Everything

along the way was peaceful. Crows sat on a fence and watched us go by. A woodchuck popped out of his burrow in a clover patch and sat up to eye us. The usual white horses were in the fields, and seventy-five per cent of the horses we had seen anywhere were old white fellows, finishing out their time while tractors spun around the farm and did the chores. We saw oldsters puttering around vegetable gardens, pushing wheelbarrows or plain sitting in the shade, and we stopped occasionally to chat with them. Twice we had some luck. An old man with veins ridged sharply on the backs of his hands told us he had been a mail driver before coming to live with his daughter, and had had many queer experiences. Once he had found an alarm clock in a mail box and a note: "Please wind clock and set it right as we have had no time in two days." Another day he found a bake pan containing a mustard plaster awaiting him, and the attached note said it was for a neighbour three miles on who had an ailing back. "Maggie's all thumbs," the note said, "so please take time to help her put it on and be sure to have the corners tight." One hard-fisted old fellow had surprised the mail driver by sending a parcel the size of a shoe box to town, then getting it back the next day with the wrapping reversed. This continued some days and the driver noticed the parcel went each time to a widowed sister of the old fellow, so he asked the sender what he was doing. "Fooling the gov'ment," said the old man. "When my wife died she had a big supply of stamps on hand and I hear they're getting out new ones. So I'm using mine up while they're good and I'm fooling them post office fellows. There's only an old scrub brush wrapped in that box."

Here and there we saw sugar maples and we saw marks where someone had tapped them, making us think of verses in the town paper on "Sugar Makin' ":

It's April and again I turn a page in memory's book,
And walk again the mapled hills and hear a noisy brook;
In Cumberland the miracle of spring is more sublime
Than anywhere in other lands—it's sugar makin' time!

Fondly I eye the amber gleam of candy on the snow,
No mortal mind can e'er concoct or man's wisdom bestow
A gift so rare to palate's bliss—God holds the recipe;
He wrote it just inside the bark of each tall maple tree.

A man beside the road was changing tires on an old truck and we talked with him about the way we had come. We mentioned that Sutherland's Lake looked a good place for fishing and that it should be fed from the fish hatchery. He grinned. "They tried that. They fetched up tanks of trout and put them in the lake but they'd been so tame they'd almost eat out of your hand and some Springhill fellows came with crackers and teased them to water's edge with crumbs, then baited hooks and hauled them in. In a week they had got every last one and all there is now are the big fellows that stay deep and know the tricks. There have always been some real big trout in the lake."

We drove on and reached Acadia Mines, questioned someone and were told that Lloyd K. Smith of Londonderry knew the history of every road and man and woman and child, so we hunted him up as a guide and started at Londonderry Station. Another road from Great Village on the paved highway joins the road at Londonderry, and for years the Station settlement was known as "The Curve." The reason, Mr. Smith explained, was that the heads of the Iron Works at Acadia Mines prevailed on the Federal Government to bring the railroad close to the works. Sir Sandford Fleming had another survey which he favoured but he received orders from Ottawa to build the Grecian bend and to place the station at the top of the bend.

One mile from the Station we crossed Salt Springs Brook, the first bridge in a town of many bridges. On the right was Purdy Inn. Farther on was a small brook and wooden bridge where back in 1897 the present editor of the *Truro News*, A. R. Coffin, missed his way on a dark night and ran his bicycle into the water and got drenched. We crossed the Fleming Bridge and one hundred yards on was a crossroads and the Chapel Bridge which leads to Docherty Bridge. We

turned left at the crossroads to the Londonderry School, a
modern bungalow type, built in 1920 after a big fire had
wiped out most of the place including four churches and a
hall. The churches all burned at the same time and so great
was the fury of the flames that debris was carried high and
pages from burning hymn books were picked up in Great
Village five miles away.

Farther up from Chapel Bridge we saw the Manager's
Bridge on the road leading to a mountain area where the
mine managers lived. It was on this old bridge that lovers
met in the old days and the story is that many plighted their
troth as they stood on the old planks. However there must
have been additional thrills for a man was murdered at the
spot when the bridge was built and it was said that his ghost
walked around on moonlight nights and called for help. Up
beyond the school was Scollay Bridge not used now because
that road has been closed. It was named for an Edward
Scollay who lived near it. Scollay had been a hammer operator
and forger at the mills but was retired and he worked daily
in his home with the blinds drawn, toiling in secret over an
invention which, he let it be known, would startle the world.
From time to time he had been seen salvaging metal wheels
from the scrap pile beside the Pipe Shop. Finally there came
a great day when Scollay announced he had completed a
"Perpetual Motion" machine and he invited in only the
priest and banker to inspect it. He had the machine going
as they entered, allowed them to inspect it for a short period,
then invited them outside. It was not known whether or
not he received the priest's blessing or the banker's money to
assist him but not long after he died and the contraption of
gear wheels was returned to the scrap heap from whence it
came.

On March 6, 1775, the Government of Nova Scotia issued
a writ of partition to James Fulton of Bass River to survey
and lay off the township of Londonderry. In doing this he
ran several base lines a mile apart. The north base line fell
near the foot of the Cobequid Mountains and crossed several

ravines and streams. In 1812 the Government appropriated money enough to cut and clear a wide road on this north base line in order to attract settlers to the area. The road became a path for trappers and hunters and loggers but some settled along it on Folly Mountain including a family of Crows who were the most easterly on the location, and the most westerly was a family named Cook. Today it is part of the highway from Folly to Bass River. In 1908 an article in the *Colchester Sun* stated:

The only track between the Cooks and Crows in 1820 was the old one cut in 1812. The hills were so steep a horse could not get up or down and in places the land was swampy. "The forest primeval, the murmuring pines and hemlocks" were there in natural shape and beauty, and had great attraction for ship and bridge builders. The bear and moose dwelt there almost unmolested where the iron works and the beautiful village of Londonderry now stands. What had already been done enlisted the curiosity of the late George Duncan in 1848 to search in this northern range for mineral property. He would stay at the late Wm. Morrisons overnight and travel on foot in daylight over hills and mountains searching for specimens of different ores. When he had finished these researches he was satisfied that iron was plentiful and brought it to the attention of the late Charles Dickson Archibald then of England but a native of Colchester County. Mr. Archibald formed a small company and began work in 1849. During the period from 1847 to 1903 the Iron Company was re-incorporated eleven times. While in early years good pig iron was produced and supplied as far as Germany, it is apparent that the Company was always having difficulties in producing iron and enough money to keep the plant running. Most of the shareholders were in England where they could not enquire too closely into their investment. While the plant was running it was a good thing for Acadia Mines but the ultimate end was never in doubt. The whole thing folded in 1913 and the Blast Furnaces and Steel Plant were sold for scrap.

The original company working the ores from the Devonian rocks of the area was known as the Acadia Charcoal Company. About 1870 the plant consisted of a blast furnace thirty feet high with a heated blast, a blowing engine with cylinder of

eight-foot stroke and four-foot bore driven by a water wheel.
There were five puddling furnaces and a small steam forge.
The annual product was one thousand, five hundred to
two thousand, five hundred tons. In 1874 the Steel Company
of Canada was formed with Sir Wm. Siemens as chairman.
He had invented the process of making open hearth
steel by the ore process. This company located on a different
site and built two blast coke furnaces, a puddling furnace
and a bank of sixty-seven beehive coke ovens. It is recorded
that merchant iron of good quality was produced and
that Londonderry Pig Iron was well and favourably known.
The Company discontinued operations in 1897 and in 1900
the Rolling Mills was destroyed by a fire set by four boys.

The Montreal Pipe Company was a separate concern and
carried on a profitable business in cast iron pipe until 1913.
It depended to some extent on a supply of iron from the blast
furnace, but was able to carry on without it and brought in
scrap iron and pig iron from other sources. This company
moved to Three Rivers and became the Canadian Iron and
Pipe Company. Charlie Jobb, a native, rose from office boy
to President and General Manager, and his feat was duplicated
by another native, William Perrot, who retired in 1955.

In 1902 The Londonderry Iron & Mining Company Ltd.
bought the assets of the old company and started operations
at the Blast Furnaces and ore mountain. This company was
headed by the Drummonds of Montreal and continued in
full operation until 1911. In 1909 a new steel plant was built
but proved unprofitable. Then came 1913 and John Simon
of Halifax bought the plant as scrap. Up to 1896 the Federal
Government paid a bonus of one dollar per ton on the
product but that year there was an election and the promise
of free trade with the U.S.A., which ended the bonus.

Mr. Smith told us about a character who ran a small
tobacco shop and dubbed his neighbours with titles they did
not favour. One was Squire Morrison whom he called
"Teebow." A new teacher looking for a place to board was
sent to "Mr. Teebow's" by him, and the poor girl did not
know why the door was slammed in her face. In his time
this man had a nickname for everyone in Londonderry. Then
there was Jonah Esau of Acadia Mines who was a great singer
and director and in constant demand. But he never forgot

his interest and would stop utter strangers on the street and ask them to say "Ah," then give them a short singing lesson. At the Coke Ovens there worked John McSween and his mare, Old Jane. The mare pulled the coal cars and used to get her white face covered with coal dust so each night John washed her before retiring. One night he forgot and old Jane would not work until he had washed her long visage as usual. We thanked Mr. Smith for his guidance and extensive information and drove on, noticing the high bridge on our left built in 1872, the piers of stone brought from Wallace by ox and horse cart. In 1925 they were replaced by steel and were only removed last year when they appeared as strong as before. This high bridge has no railings but the sleepers are closer together than on the road bed. A horse attempted to cross but was met halfway by a train and jumped to its death. But Dr. Crowe of Debert was making a call in Debert when his horse became impatient, tore himself loose and had different luck. He got on the railroad and dragged the sleigh along it, over the high bridge and all, arrived home safely in Debert by the shortest possible route. A man who was painting the bridge stepped on a loose plank and fell to the ground below, almost a hundred feet. He was badly hurt but recovered and seemed none the worse for his tremendous fall.

We drove on and crossed the railway and through East Mines Station and soon saw the rifle range of Debert on our left. An elderly man was seated by the open door of a barn with three cats sitting around as if milk rations were due. We stopped to chat with him and he said the pussies were his pals as he stayed around the barn most of the day where it was nice and quiet. That made us curious and soon he tugged a folded and worn paper from a pocket. "Read that," he said gently, "and you'll know what I mean."

The caption was "Cold As a Barn." Then we read:

On a winter day a tight, big-beamed barn can be a mighty snug spot to come in to and get the burlap-edged door closed and hooked. It can seem to a man about as cosy as a farm living-room is to a quilting party sitting around the parlour stove and taking the basting threads out of last week's village happenings. There are concrete-floored, fancy-ventilated new-style barns which can really be kind of cold-footed and over-airy in a cold snap. Such barns seem meant more for a silo and a milking machine than for a barn cat and a man sitting on a tin-patched feed box figuring how many calves there are going to be in the barn come March. A barn in winter is a lot different from a barn in summer. A winter barn is an inhabited and friendly place where a man, tired of splitting wood, comes in out of a snow squall. There is always a cow that will say something. A horse will paw at a hemlock plank and speak a word, too. Even the cat is extra lively after having a noon nap on a streak of sunlight and a forkful of hay. No barn cat is ever around in a season of stone walls and chipmunk afternoons. No heifer stretches out her head to be rubbed when there is summer pasture and an empty barn right up to milking time. But now a winter barn is filled with sights, scents and sounds which make it seem mighty homelike and companionable. It would be a poor place, of course, for a sewing circle to meet and talk shop. But it is a warm and happy refuge for a man when the snow blows and the house is full of women. A winter's barn, a man thinks, is something like an ark stranded on the mountainside with a bunch of assorted animals. There is even a flighty, nest-stealing Leghorn up on the old cross-beams acting as a stand-in for the unreturning dove.

In wartime Debert was a huge military camp, mushroomed overnight, and a military hospital was operated there. From a sleepy little centre with a car or so meeting the trains, it jumped overnight into a military town of several thousand with an airport and movie theatres. But now it is fast reverting to a peaceful existence and no more than a few dogs romped around to greet us as we visited where the military quarters had been. A man came out and called angrily at the dogs, declared that some day he would get a gun and shoot the lot.

"If a body wants a dog," he said, "why don't they look after it?"

We talked to him about wartime Debert and the big gravel depot there, and he said that the place had another distinction. It was one of the coldest spots in the province, and as he talked of winters when he was a boy we could almost hear the moan and wail of an icy wind sweeping down the railway, the hiss of the driven snow over the hard-packed banks left by the snowplow. "Indoors," he said, "you could hear the humming of the wires but there was the singing of the teakettle to drown the discord, and never was there a tonic as good as a cold snap to give edge to an appetite. We'd get in from doing the chores," he said, "and mother would have a pan deep in fried potatoes but we'd clean up the lot and look for more and she'd declare we were clean hollow inside. Then we'd take off our larrigans and sit back to read and the cat would purr back of the stove and every once in a while mother would look up from her knitting and say: 'An awful night to be out on the road.' Often our breath would freeze to our scarves and mittens as we held them in front of our face on the way to school. We'd even have frost on our eyelashes, and if anybody thought they had a touch of frost bite we'd rub snow on the place. Worst thing was getting a hot hand stuck to an axe blade or door latch full of frost. I can remember waking in the morning and seeing frost on the nailheads in the woodwork of my room, and nights like that I slept in my underwear. Then father would yell up to us to get stirring and out we'd go with our breath a cloud around us, fur-lined ear lugs down on our caps and thick mittens on our hands. Dried beech made a quick hot fire for mother to cook the porridge, and a whiff of breakfast set our stomachs rolling as we headed for the barn. There was a comfortable tangy odour as we went in and though the barn latches were frosted white it was not too cold inside, and father would be milking and the horses stamping a demand for their oats. I mind more than once going out to find fox tracks around the hen-pen, and even rabbit tracks in our orchard. Animals seemed to come nearer the farm in a cold winter. We had snow in those winters, too. Back in 1905 it was so deep that we just made a tunnel through a big drift between the house and barn and I remember it stayed a week or more."

We drove along through Lower Belmont, and into Belmont, where lumber is king, and the main street a part of the old Indian trail to Tatamagouche, over the Ingonish River and to Upper Belmont, through it and Higgins Mills to Onslow. To us it is a reminder of "The Cake Box," in Halifax, operated by Mrs. McCurdy Lindsay who came from the village to establish and maintain a bakery with a reputation second to none. We saw several persons and enjoyed our talks. A lady possessed of some charm was anxious to flirt after she became a widow and aroused the ire of a spinster making desperate efforts to land a widower. They battled in the open about it but the spinster always lisped when she was angry and everyone laughed afterward. Then the winsome one's teeth decayed and she went on a visit to New Glasgow, had both uppers and lowers installed, and returned to flaunt her charms. A radio contest was on and questions were to be asked that evening, Christmas week, but wire troubles prevented and it was announced that the queries would begin as soon as possible. It was a very cold night and the lady slept late, heard the phone and rushed down in dressing-gown, answered, and was asked the money question. She had the correct answer but the questioner was suspicious and asked who was speaking. Two listeners cut in and said it was the spinster, as the lisp was pronounced. So the man said the cheque would go to her and the poor lady lisped worse than ever, but could not tell the truth—that both her upper and lower teeth were frozen fast in a pitcher where she had left them overnight. We still laughed as we reached Truro.

2

Off-trail in Hants County

WE started from Shubenacadie on Highway 2 in the morning, swinging to the right in the village, and were on a dirt road where hurry is forgotten, a winding road that was narrow in places but gave us an enjoyable sense of adventure as we rolled up hill and down dale and across small bridges until finally we found ourselves in South Maitland, once a famous ship building centre but now as quiet and steady as an old man living on his pension. There was a "For Sale" sign on a store and we went in to talk with the proprietor, an elderly man who had enjoyed the days of prosperity and was now impatient with the present generation.

"Dances and good times is all they have in their minds," he said. "They don't do as much work in a week as we would do in a day. Look at the young fellow going for the mail on a tractor. In my day we'd think nothing of running over to the post office, and I'll wager there are sixteen tractors around here and not one of them paid for."

The evidence everywhere of the good old days that were made us understand his ill-temper and then he told us about a cave to be found by following a side road to the railway and then walking a distance and crossing a stream. Away we went down a steep grade and over a small bridge and to a deserted farm. We saw signs of others who had picnicked in the place and as we enjoyed our lunch a chipmunk came within feet of

35

us and begged crumbs. An anxious robin chirped loudly and
we soon spotted her nest in a maple close by. There were
gravel heaps and truck tracks beyond and a deer leisurely
climbed over them, stopped to eye us, circled and stamped and
investigated for ten minutes before sailing into the undergrowth with its flag high.

We locked the car and went through long grass and weeds,
crossed the shallow stream and kept on skirting a slope
streaked with gypsum until we seemed to have walked miles.
The cave mouth was smaller than we had expected. It was
almost hidden by bushes and inside the walls were damp and
dripping and there was no more than ledges beside a long pool
of water that sounded very deep when we threw a stone into it.
I've no idea how far the cave extended and I soon lost any
intention of finding out for it was a fearsome spot if ever I
saw one. We strolled back in long grass and saw a deer bound
away with white flag high as we got back to our picnic spot
near the abandoned buildings. There was not a sound from
the outside world, no train whistle or rumble of traffic, just
bird song and the droll chipmunk and a high-sailing hawk
overhead. Crickets added their harmony and the still heat
made one want to rest there all the afternoon.

But we climbed the hill and got back to the road and drove
on to Maitland, a bigger village than South Maitland with
some very nice homes, a general store packed to the door,
shelves and floor, with anything a man could want. A man was
working in a garden near the road so we stopped to chat. He
was seventy-nine, he said, and looked twenty years younger,
had served as postmaster fifty-three years, had spent forty
years back of the counter in a store nearby, and had known
the village in its heyday. One of the men who had built many
ships was Alex Macdougall. One after another, year by year, he
had built twenty-six barques to sell to the firm of Brown and
Watson in Scotland. Macdougall was a man of his word and he
expected everyone else to be honest. He never made a bargain
about any vessel that came from his yard but when it was
finished he sailed it to Scotland and on arrival the firm would

invite him to a dinner that had all the trimmings and when the glow produced by a bottle of Scottish dew was at its best the subject of price was discussed. Each time the buyers finally agreed, after much groaning and objecting, to Macdougall's price, and the next day he would be paid and then take passage back to Nova Scotia.

At last he thought he saw a fortune smiling at him from the gypsum hills back of the village. Water transport would be cheapest so he constructed a railway to carry his product to the wharf, and began operations. The market for raw gypsum, however, was not as good as he had thought, and operating a private freight line became an expensive proposition. So the project failed and the rails rusted and today one has to study the distant slope to distinguish old marks of the working.

Maitland was named in 1828 in honour of Sir Peregrine Maitland and it, like so many other Nova Scotia communities, prospered during the era of wooden ships and iron men. One of the many fine homes belonging to the last century is that built by W. D. Lawrence, a stately old home with magnificent trees at the front, with unusual winding steps to the front entrance. A descendant of the famous shipbuilder lives in the historic home. It was W. D. Lawrence who made Maitland known as the home of the "big ship," and the vessel was given his name. He decided to outdo other builders, to have a ship that could carry as much freight as two ordinary vessels, and the keel was laid in 1872. Seventy-two men were employed in the construction, and from keel to rail the great ship measured fifty-five feet, and the breadth of beam was eighty feet. Records say that each of the three decks was nine feet high, that tons of iron bolts were used, that one hundred and sixty iron knees reinforced the beams of the lower deck. The ship was two hundred and forty-four feet long and the bowsprit reached across the road to the wharf. A master carver was engaged to shape an appropriate figurehead, eight thousand yards of canvas was purchased for sails, and the mainmast from keelson to truck measured over two hundred feet. It took eighteen months to build the giant and the launching was held October 27, 1874. In eight years of operation the giant netted more than $140,000, a fortune in those days.

We saw a big stone house with a brass knocker and a man at the store told us the farm was a mile in length and that part of it used to be the ancient drill ground of the Hants County militia. One colonel had a frosty eye and a deep bellow that made men shiver. They were afraid of him and one summer they were to have a final parade just as a heavy rain set in. The men were assembled in the drill shed and it was feared the colonel would carry on despite the weather so the sergeant forced a luckless character to go to the house where the colonel lodged during training and beg him to be merciful. The poor lad went in trembling but returned capering with joy.

"There'll be no parade," he called. "We're to stay under cover and we'll be paid this evening."

"What happened?" asked a doubter. "Did he tell you that?"

"Not him," snorted the one who had dreaded. "He didn't say anything. His wife heard me and she give the orders, and when he started to butt in she told him to shut up. And she said we could go home in the morning. She's only half as big as him but is he scared of her!"

There is an airfield at Maitland, a fine one, and the drive along the shore is all a tourist can wish. Those who dare the dirt roads are well rewarded for their venture but it is a pity the highway is not paved so that thousands can drive there each summer and savour one of the best sections of Nova Scotia. Not till we were in the next village did I learn that the friendly gardener who gave us much information was C. S. Waugh, that he had been an outstanding tenor for years, singing in choirs and with concerts, and blessed with a voice that would have brought him fame in larger centres.

Stirling Brook was only a few houses but there were feathers on the road and in the fields and soon we saw chicken pens and hen houses galore, a great poultry plant that keeps trucks busy carrying the products to market. The scenery was beautiful, with the Basin sparkling in sunshine, tall elms like sentinels, gorgeous flowers in almost every houseyard. The road would dip into hollows where there was always a bridge, then rise abruptly to a new and more spectacular view. Scarcely a car was on the road and we saw only one foreign licence in the whole area. A man chased a calf back into a pasture and came to close the gate as we stopped.

"The young fellow feels frisky," I said.

"It's them danged deer," puffed the farmer. "One was in the field and he near set that calf crazy chasing around him and butting him."

"This must be quite a place for wild life, then," I suggested.

"All kinds," grunted the farmer. "There's a dance every once in a while, and the young fry meet at the ice cream parlours, but the other kind is worse. Down the road a piece there's a woman who's alone most of the time. A bit ago she was sitting quiet after supper when she heard steps at the back of the house. She went to the kitchen and got the gun, then bolted the door. The steps came nearer and nearer, not heavy at all, just sneaking in, and they come right to where a pen for hen and chickens is under her kitchen window. Then she hears nothing and waits, gets nervous and goes to look out. Just the other side of the glass, looking in, is a big raccoon. She was so glad she took something and went to the door and fed the animal, and it's been back every evening since, fetching a small one with it."

It seemed the kind of a day to test the patience for we were not a mile along before we saw another farmer chasing a black pig and shouting threats. We stopped the car and the porker tried to get by so we headed over at an angle that prevented and jumped out to aid the perspiring runner. In five minutes we had conquered and assisted getting the unruly one into a long yard ringed with thistles and tall weeds.

"One month more and that one will be pork pies," said the farmer. "He can dig under a gate good as a woodchuck, and he's scared of nothing. There's been generations of him raised on this farm, and I've heard my grandfather tell of a fall when he was a boy and they let six pigs loose to feed on the beech-nuts that were very plentiful. There was a large grove of beechnut trees just over the rise and a neighbour had his pigs there as well when a bear came from the woods. The pigs made such a din that grandfather got his gun and ran but when he reached the back field the bear had taken refuge on a stump and the pigs were milling around it and squealing savagely. Suddenly the biggest pig charged at the stump and knocked the bear to the ground. In a moment there was such murderous noise from the pigs and wild roars from the bear, that grandfather could only stand and stare at the melee. In less than three minutes the bear was nearly torn to bits. Yes, sir, they're a great breed of pigs."

Signs by a crossroad near a store said we were in Noel and we took plenty of time to look around for Noel has the highest tides in the world. At Burntcoat Head, a local point, they rise to from forty-six to fifty-two feet above low water, and on August 5, 1869, the Saxby Tide rolled in to the depth of one hundred and three feet. Legend has it that a pirate, often named as Captain Kidd, brought his vessel in to Sloop Rock to get a new mast. As he had a threatening crew the local residents provided the required timber and helped place it. The pirate then offered payment but the good folk of Noel regarded such ill-gotten gains as tainted and refused the money at which the pirate threw a number of bars of silver on the beach and sailed away. The bars could be seen for years afterward but no one would touch them and at last sand washed over them. Another generation was not so afraid of tainted coin and tried to locate the bars but to date they have not been successful.

The Acadians had early settlers at Noel and the story is that they named the place as they did because they arrived on Christmas Day. But New England soldiers arrived during the Expulsion and put the torch to every home. Only the cellars remain to show the old village location. We met Chester Hennigar in his workshop on his farm that was once the holding of Nicholas Densmore, a first settler who had the land granted to him by George IV. He has many old documents that were in old chests for a long period. A prescription made out to his great-great-grandfather, John Densmore, reads:

Take one of the small powders every six hours and tomorrow evening put the plaster on the place where I showed you. Be sparing of your diet and drink as little as possible. You can drink some of the tea of juniper berries two or three times a day. If you find a copping taste in your mouth or your gums become tender you had better leave off for a day or two.

Mr. Hennigar showed us a grant issued in 1825, the sixth year of the reign of George IV, giving permission for John Densmore, Sr., and his four sons to settle in the area of Douglas township or Hants County with one thousand, three hundred and twenty acres of land. And papers Mr. Hennigar has show that in those days men were named according to the area in which they settled, such as John-at-the-mill, Sam-on-the-hill, and Jimmy-Shad Creek.

A legal document yellowed with age was drawn up between the father and the four sons regarding provision for his care and keep in old age, for which the sons received "land, all the horses except a mare, a colt and two cows" in return. Their agreement was:

One horse to be kept in summer and winter and in proper manner, also a comfortable room and bedroom with a good bed and bedding, also wood to be provided and fire kept suitable for the room and victuals to be cooked in a suitable manner and suitable attendance to be provided in every respect suitable to the age and circumstances, also all medical attendance necessary. Shoes to be delivered and the following articles half-yearly — three pounds Souchong Tea, twenty pounds brown sugar, twenty-five pounds butter and two hundred weight flour, one hundred weight of meat of such quality as may be required, fifteen pounds of cheese, five pounds tobacco, four pounds candles, ten pounds dried apples and ten bushels potatoes and $8 for pocket money and a riding sleigh at his pleasure. All provisions, comforts and profits to continue during his natural life.

Papers dated 1856 show recordings of money subscribed by residents of the area to defray expenses of sending Hon.

Joseph Howe to England to deal with some provincial matters. The famous Howe was beloved by all and nearly every citizen in the settlement gave a few dollars to the cause. The receipts were tied in bundles with linen thread that had been spun by ladies of early Noel. Other papers proved that the ladies had their own societies back in those good old days, a sewing society and a knitting circle. They held regular meetings and an old minute book of the "Ladies Society at Noel. 1858" shows that they did not want to be bothered with male folk in their midst as Article Seven of the Constitution read: "Resolved that no male member be allowed to attend the meeting more than once before paying entry fee."

A highway contract of July, 1816, shows that three men were hired to build five miles of road between Noel and Kennetcook for the sum of $155.24. The same contract today would have called for $100,000. An old Bible that must have been in the possession of the Densmores for many years is quite a relic and Mr. Hennigar would like to know its age. He told us about the first settlers and showed us where the fathers erected a whipping post. As there were no jails and a magistrate must mete out some punishment to a wrongdoer, a number of lashes on the bare back was supposed to be the equivalent of the same number of days in a jail. Nearby the site is the home of Silas McLellan, a farmer who liked to run. He entered many races in the neighbouring towns and in Halifax and has a table decked with trophies of his prowess.

In 1771 a Timothy O'Brien, newly arrived from Northern Ireland, with his wife, five sons and two daughters, chose Noel as the site for his home. Only cleared fields remained to tell of the Acadian occupation as New England soldiers had burned all the buildings and killed the cattle. Creeping grass had all but covered the ashes and rotting timbers. Descendants of Timothy O'Brien still live in Noel and Miss Pearl O'Brien of the fifth generation supplied us with the most of our material regarding the place. For many years shipbuilding was the leading industry, and Noel barques and brigs and schooners sailed the Seven Seas. The first schooner, fittingly named the *O'Brien,* was built in 1843.

Noel also produced plaster and wood pulp for a long time but now most attention is given to farming and the shipment of Christmas trees. More and more visitors are reaching Noel in the summer and they are intrigued by the tide, barely three hundred yards from the highway at full, and two miles away at low tide. One visitor from inland U.S.A. spent the day picnicking in a spot by the shore and then sent a batch of postcards back to friends at home saying he had found the place where Moses led the children of Israel to the Promised Land. Although there are only two hundred people in Noel, seventeen young men enlisted for active service during World War II. Those who remained on the home front knew something of war, too. Not too far away was an American Naval Air Training Base which used Cobequid Bay for bombing practice. The residents of Noel were requested to keep electric lights burning outside their homes at night to guide the planes along the shore. "Many a night," said Miss O'Brien, "we thought the war had finally reached our village."

Fifty years ago Noel was stirred by trouble between two pack-pedlars. One had served the community for a year or two before the rival appeared. There were arguments but the newcomer persisted in making the rounds and one day vanished mysteriously as the older man was in the vicinity. There was considerable apprehension and then searchers found the body of the missing man hidden in some bushes. He had been murdered by the other pedlar. But there has been little crime along Noel Shore and even the small troubles that arise often end in a laugh. Rumour has it that a lady claimed ownership to a neighbour's heifer that was in a local pasture with some of her own cattle, a white heifer that was quite a prize animal. So one night two men gave the heifer a fine coat of deep blue paint. Settlement of all animals in the pasture was to be made the next day and the lady, quite near-sighted, pointed out those that belonged to her. "What about the blue cow?" someone asked. "It doesn't belong to me," declared the lady, and all laughed as the rightful owner went home with the heifer that eventually became white again.

In 1812 the flour mill at Noel became useless and next year "Miller John" Densmore arranged to build a new one and engaged a man at Mount Denson to cut new stones for him, there being no stones of the right grit any nearer to Noel, and the man was to deliver the stones at Mitchener's Point at the mouth of the Avon River, a little below high water so they could easily be loaded into a boat. The man put the stones at the place designated and left them standing on edge with a pole running through the eye. Before Densmore could get around with his boat winter set in and froze inches of ice around the Point. The cold weather continued and made more and more ice. Then came a great storm in March that broke the ice into huge cakes and drove them into Minas Basin. One great floe carried the mill stones, still upright with the pole in position. Then wind and tide shifted and the floe was driven into Noel Bay and high on the bank of the mouth of the Noel River. April sun thawed the stones free and an astounded passer-by saw them and reported to Densmore who only had to move them one and a half mile to his mill. He soon had them there, fitted them in place and had his mill going by the time the road permitted the farmers to take in their grist. The new stones worked perfectly and the women of Noel declared that the good Lord had known their wants and had the wind bring the stones around by way of the Basin.

There was a deaf preacher in the area in the good old days before a regular preaching appointment had been established. This man would ride around on horseback to marry and bury and baptize when needed and in the summer held some meetings at various points. He was to baptize several children at a date agreed on and when he had a baby put in his arms asked the name of the child. "Wilmot Albert" shouted the father with heavy accent on each syllable.

The good man smiled and nodded, and baptized the lad "William Otto Alton Burton," and the parents were too timid to protest. They still called the boy "Wilmot" but all others called him William.

Beyond Noel we dipped sharply to a bridge where the sea almost reaches the highway at Tennycape. A mill site is near the bridge and we talked with a man there who told us that some years ago when the tide was high a boy had been swimming just the other side of the bridge. Finally he tired and crawled out to sit on a log that was stranded on the sand at water's edge. A mill hand happened to look that way and saw something large and dark in the water. It kept coming in closer and closer to the boy who was watching with wonder. The mill hand seized an axe and ran across the road just as a shark drove full at the lad but misjudged the depth and was hurled out on the gravel. The man struck hard and fast with the axe and killed the big fish which measured more than eight feet in length while the lad, who had been frozen with fear, found use of his legs and darted over the hill as if on wings. But bathers use the place regularly and no one has ever seen another shark.

Moose Brook extends three miles east from Tennycape River, which forms its western boundary and runs inland two miles. An old man told us the place got its name from the fact that moose would go to the brook daily for water long after the first settlers arrived. He pointed out an old cellar on a small rising and said it was called Nigger Hill because a coloured man once lived there, the only one along the shore. First settlers were Scottish and Irish, according to our informant. William Ferguson was one of them and lived in a log house until 1855, then built a home of sawed lumber that stands as staunch and sturdy today as it did in that long ago. Mr. Ferguson started a tree nursery from seeds and scions procured from Scotland and many orchards of Hants County had their origin in this nursery stock. He was the first resident of Moose Brook to own a horse-drawn buggy, the first to own a mowing machine.

Another pioneer named Faulkner arrived on "Cold Friday," February, 1858, on foot, was not daunted by the cold reception and was soon joined by his wife who became the midwife of the area and seemed always in demand as the nearest doctor lived at Maitland. Her fee for a confinement case was two dollars, and very often she did not receive that in cash. There was no road at that early time but all travelled by way of the beach and our historian told us that one settler's wife, riding on horse back, was overtaken by the high tide and drowned, though her horse managed to swim ashore. A post office was opened in Moose Brook in May of 1863 and the mail carrier rode the route twice a week while the worthy postmaster received the grand salary of twelve dollars per year. There have been but two postmasters in the ninety-two years of the little office.

A school was erected and parents had to pay for each child they sent to class. The teacher was a Noel lady who obtained a licence by going to the Court House on Gore Hill, then called "Judgment Hill," and taking an oral examination. From 1860 to 1925 the Tennycape River was crossed by a wooden bridge. In 1925, said our man, it was replaced by a bridge consisting of a central steel span with a wooden span on each end, this because the provincial government changed during its construction and the Conservative engineer disagreed with what the Liberal fellow had done.

Walton was next, a hustling bustling place with many new cars around the village and a general atmosphere of prosperity. It will be one hundred years old this year and was first called Petite Rainy Cove. There was a road to the government wharf and the Gypsum Shipping Wharf, and a truck driver told us that a three-million-ton deposit of barytes was discovered in the area in 1941. The ground product is shipped away for chemical manufacture, and for heavy fluid for oil well drilling in South America. The gypsum is shipped in raw state to New York.

An oldster was going along the road so we offered him a lift which he accepted gratefully. He said he was headed for Cheverie, the next "town" and told us there were two gypsum quarries there and that the product was shipped to New

Haven, Connecticut. He said he had been born at Walton and had watched general developments with great interest as in his boyhood the only incomes were derived from either fishing or logging. He said he was going to visit his cousin who was a slow-witted fellow but had got along fairly well after marrying.

"It took Jed a day to get something through his head," cackled our passenger, "and sometimes longer'n that. He never got on good in any courting either so he was middle-aged before an old maid helped him out. She's a real sensible sort and not too hard on the eyes, either. So the boys used to tease Jed that another man was calling on her, this when Jed was nightwatchman down at the plant. So he goes home one morning and sees man tracks in his front yard. His wife told him the fish pedlar had called but Jed decided it was time he did something so that night, after pretending to go on his job, he sneaked back and got on his shed roof with his shotgun. He stayed there all night, having arranged with a man to spell him on his job, and it was a drizzly night. In the morning he was wet and cold and cranky. He went in and had the first row with his wife because he had had his long watch for nothing."

We let our friend out in Cheverie and drove on slowly for the whole drive from Maitland on had been a delight to the eyes. Any visitor who leaves the paved way in Nova Scotia in dry weather is well rewarded for the scenery is wonderful in the majority of localities and there is little traffic, while the people are the friendliest on earth and possessed of a dry humour that is a tonic for any ailment.

Kempt Shore was brought to our minds by three youngsters walking in the middle of the road and completely indifferent to cars. Then a lady came from a house and scolded them gently, taking time to remark that she was glad to notice we were not "crazy drivers." So it was easy to get into conversation and learn that all Kempt and Walton townships were once known as "man-o'-war's-land." This was because an over-whelming number of grants in the area had been given to officers retired from the Royal Navy. Our informant said it was also a hiding place for a few privateers during the war of 1812 when they crept up the Bay after dark and hid in river mouths while the crews foraged around the country. She said she had been born "inland" but loved salt water, and would not want to go back as the rivers were slowly drying up and everything was different. No one would believe today, she said, that the river thirty miles from where we were would be a raging torrent fall and spring, and often the only way across when the freshet was on was by an ancient dory handled by Cap'n Henry. Once his passenger was a lady from Halifax who was very nervous as she hung to the dory sides and observed the swirling white water and many rocks. "Do you ever lose any passengers here?" she quavered. "Nary a one," comforted Cap'n Henry. "We always find 'em the next day." There were also springs when the water receded far quicker than expected and one such time Cap'n Henry was trying to run a number of logs down to the mill. But summer-like heat and lack of rain played hob with his efforts and as he struggled to keep his timber from snagging in every shallow he saw a woman from a house getting a pail of water. "Put that back!" roared the Cap'n. "Can't you see the trouble I'm havin'?"

We drove into Summerville and stopped at a quiet country store where a pleasant lady proprietor assured us that nothing ever happened in Summerville worth writing about. We admired the finest peonies we had seen anywhere and questioned carefully but she declared there had never been any romance or crime or hunting episodes, and that there was nothing outstanding in the place. Sighing, we left her and strolled toward a trail to the beach, were amazed to come across anglers with much equipment and a car with an American licence. We timidly asked what the tackle was for.

"Striped bass!" said the man heartily. "I've never had better fishing anywhere. I've been after striped bass in many places up and down the coast of America but this is the best of them all. I've been three days and I've caught nineteen fish. And I'm a camera fan and yesterday got along the beach to a spot where deer came and got a dandy shot of one standing on a boulder with its hooves close together. I just discovered this place by chance last year and say, if they had a topnotch hotel here it would be filled all summer. They've got everything."

It was dark and now and then the odd drop of rain fell, more of a threat than the real thing, but an old chap came along wearing a straw hat and minus a coat. He had an easy grin and when I had talked with him he said there was a chance, once, for some romance in the place. Elsie was a school teacher who seemed anchored to the chore while she wanted very much to get married. The difficulty was to find a right man, and then to have him propose. So she was delighted one summer when a fellow from town came for a vacation and proved easy to meet. Elsie could row a dory or walk the legs off a man and when she found that the visitor liked to explore she rowed him down shore to an isolated spot and spread a rug in a likely glade. Everything seemed right until the man suddenly discovered he was covered with sand fleas, and the haste to escape the place rubbed away all hope of romance. But Elsie kept up her hope and was delighted to see her lad in church on Sunday evening. It was easy to get him to go for a stroll and presently they were arm in arm and the moon was full and the wind from the west warm and alluring. Just when things seemed sure for the girl a black-and-white-striped pussy emerged from a hedge beside them and the man fled at top speed. She learned later he had a perfect dread of skunks. But there was one more chance as he was not going home until Tuesday so Monday afternoon she took him walking to a pretty spot among white birches where the air was still and birds sang in harmony at sight of them. Elsie did her best and managed to get him on the moss with his head on her lap as she tenderly stroked his brow. He seemed to get sleepy and she had to urge him several times to get any response and time passed swiftly. At last, in desperation, she asked softly, "Are you thinking of me, Jimmy?" He stirred and sat up. "I am," he confessed. "I know by the way that your stomach rumbles you are hungry, and it's supper time. Let's hurry back."

We went out on the beach with the oldtimer and as he talked of the sailing ships built along the shore we could see that the furious tides of Fundy are tearing away the seaweed-ensnared piling of old wharves and slips and soon there will be only memories in the Minas Basin coastal area, almost forgotten cradle of seafaring Nova Scotia's Golden Age. The people now are farmers and truckers and lumbermen. But along the shore snug homes often atop red-clay cliffs look over the racing high tides which bore the wooden ships to Boston and the West Indies and all over the Seven Seas. At one spot a garden path meanders under a white Gothic arch made of a whale's jawbone. Over old fireplaces along the shore are carved boxes from China, brass from the bazaars of Benares, sculptured gourds from Antigua and tea chests from Ceylon; thousands of knick-knacks from markets of the world's seaports brought home by fathers and husbands and brothers to excited and waiting families. Many of the fine sturdy, weather-tight old houses, the descendants of those old sailormen live in, were built by money gained in the West Indies trade. Oil paintings and curios are in the parlours to entertain the occasional stranger but in a few more years there will be none left to tell great stories of storms and perils and transatlantic races and adventure on the high seas. The old shipyards are crumbling and forgotten, the tides eat away the piers, and the old men with memories deep in their eyes smile sadly as they talk with you, for they know that they'll never see again the tall, proud giants with billowing white sails standing out to sea.

We came to the Burlingtons, Lower and Centre and Upper, with neat farms and flower gardens and quietness that had its own appeal as did the sight of a small boy playing with a pet calf and a woodchuck eyeing us with mild interest from a clover patch. We drove slowly and chatted with various folk who were puttering around the buildings or using a hoe in the garden but they seemed guarded in their answers until we came to a short little man with wrinkles at the corners of his eyes as if he had been smiling the most of his life. He told us about oldtimers who had the history of the communities in their minds but now had departed this vale of tears and reckoned we were thirty years too late with our mission. He told of a man mowing in a distant field when a bear appeared and chased him to a tree. The man climbed high and stayed there and the bear stayed below until it was dinner time and the irate wife came in search of her laggard husband. She shrilled her anger as she spied him, then saw the bear, picked up a stick and drove the shaggy one into the bush. The husband, awed speechless by what he had witnessed, descended and bore without resentment the tongue lashing he received for allowing a mere "critter" to keep him from his work. " 'Course, that were Aunt Jennie, and she feared nothin' on legs," chuckled the wrinkled one.

We inquired if there were any others like her in the communities and he chuckled and said we should meet Aunt Maggie. "She's always nagging Sam to take off the storm windows, whitewash the fence, mow the lawn, spray the roses, do this, do that, until orders is waiting him at home natural as if he was in the army. The only thing around the house that got much attention in the way of loving was a big black tomcat she called Winsome. Sam hated the cat but never let on, and he hated to be first in the place to get the screens on. Last spring just as the outdoor chores set in a skunk made its appearance in the backyards and everybody was near scared to go outside. So Sam had a week's grace. Then Aunt Maggie said he just had to clean the cellar and as Saturday was a warm day everyone along the road was busy, putting up screens, white-washing, rolling lawns, washing windows and cleaning cellars.

Late afternoon Aunt Maggie sent Sam to the store for something she needed for supper and while he was gone word spread that the skunk was around. Aunt Maggie took a quick look around her yard, then peered in the cellar and saw shiny eyes and black and white stripes. She tore into action. Went across a field like a ten-year-old and fetched a neighbour with a ten-bore shot gun. She told him not to miss as she didn't want her cellar smelled up so he poked the gun in the cellar window and took good aim. There was no smell. The animal hardly kicked and then the neighbour went down with a fork and fetched it out — poor Winsome, dead as a doornail, with white stripes along him where he'd squeezed through a newly-whitewashed fence. Sam never stopped working till dark, he felt so good."

I told our friend I knew many places of interest and beauty were hidden away behind and beyond well-known communities, vistas of scenic charm that the average motorist never discovers. He said I was right. He said secondary roads were often narrow and winding, climbing hills and dropping into little valleys but most of them were rewarding. He said he could go along with me and show me a dozen paths to good hunting and fishing leading from a back road, places where he could find nests of blue heron. If I wanted he would show me a place that was once a hustling village but now was forgotten. So we took several turns before reaching the pavement and went into Avondale, no more than ten miles from Highway 1 but as remote from motor visitors as if it were ten times that distance. It was once a living link with the world's ports, where ships were built and Avondale sailormen brought home strange souvenirs from foreign cities. Three shipyards operated on the banks of the Avon River, and the workmen built staunch homes for themselves and their wives made neat gardens. Today you cannot find the name of the place in a postal guide, and the residents are part-time farmers whose official address is now Newport Landing.

On the top of a hill is a great rambling old house a century and a half old. The big colonnades and cornices that grace the imposing front are weather-beaten but their dignity is unimpaired, reminders of a day when gay parties from the garrisons at Windsor and Halifax were entertained. The sweep of land included in the original grant of this holding now makes up nine farms, and in the cellar of the old place leather buckets to be used in case of fire still hang on iron hooks. The doors still swing true and the windows close tightly proving the workmanship of early days.

In the heart of Avondale is the home of Edgar Cecil Hamilton who could use his hands far better than the average craftsman. He improved his home with fine ceilings, added deep French windows with long panes, panelled walls in spruce and pine, made beautiful mantelpieces fretted with carvings, fashioned fine tables of walnut. In the dining-room a patina of age has given the wood a deep rich color which harmonizes with the soft dull green walls. The design is fashioned in squares and is composed of between five hundred and six hundred pieces of wood in a quiet design carried out with strips of spruce in varying length. The squares are separated by strips of walnut with an embossed whirl at the intersections, and the difficult pattern embraces the broad deep window. Mr. Hamilton did the work in his spare time as he earned his daily bread in Windsor, travelling fifteen miles each night and morning. Now he has retired and the house is in a setting of green lawn and fine shade trees. All the houses are neat and trim and there are no roadside canteens or eyesores of any nature. Stacks of neatly piled wood show the fuel that is used for heating and cooking, and the only landmark is the square tower of the light which guides ships up the Avon to Windsor.

On we went to Brooklyn, after leaving our friend, and found it a busy little centre, granted in 1761 to sixty-six persons from New England. We talked with people who were shopping and were told that many descendants of the early New Englanders still lived around the region and that it was one of the best church-going communities in Hants County. It has a co-operative store that is a pride and joy and everyone points out the paved road leading to the main highway. One oldster I talked with had been viewing television and he was steamed with praise of the advantages of today's generation. Another old chap standing by listened in silence until his patience was spent and then made blistering remarks about the "rat race you call living."

"Forty or fifty years ago," he argued, "people boiled coffee and settled it with an egg and had a drink worth while. Now they boil water in a fancy 'lectric contraption and pour it over powder in a cup. It takes about a minute or so to do, and ain't worth that much time. Has no taste or body or anything. Television! Humph! Just like the radio and the papers. Eternally howling about the Reds. I'm sick of that word. All the reds we had in the good old days was red flannels."

"Sure," blurted the television man, "and you had outdoor plumbing and women scrubbed their knuckles to the bone on washboards, and you had a horse and buggy to get around in which took half a day here to Windsor, and the papers you had only come once a week. Who wants to go back to that?"

"Only papers any good are the weeklies," came the retort. "The others, them city ones, are all ads and funnies and a sport page."

"Them days a boy didn't have to have a high-powered car to pursue happiness," serenely continued the debater. "And ladies rode sidesaddle, didn't smoke cigarettes or wear slacks or almost nothing at all, and people went to church and when the preacher spoke a truth they said 'Amen.' And a candidate had to be economy-minded to get elected, parents were baby-sitters and when a man dressed for the evening he put on his nightshirt."

"Yeah, and you got mail twice a week if you were lucky and wages was a dollar and a half a day and each man had to do roadwork."

"That never hurt none," came the rejoinder. "When neighbours asked about your family they meant it, and they saw to it you got fresh liver at pig-killing time. Nobody was arrested for speeding and a man made the same wife do a lifetime."

"And the roads were bog mires spring and fall and men wore whiskers and women had skirts trailing the mud. You can have them days and I'll take . . ."

We took ourselves carefully and quietly to the car, looked back and saw they were at the finger wagging stage and hoped it would go no further. The turning confused us and first we knew we were in Mosherville and not on the road we had intended but it led back toward Kennetcook and we wanted to see one of the two remaining covered bridges in Nova Scotia so we kept on, saw three deer in one field and scared a partridge from a fence, reached Kennetcook and took a snap of the bridge. A woman and two children had pails and had been picking berries. We were invited to stop and have a dish of them with cream, and who could resist. So we chatted and heard once more a story we treasure of a man we can call Lem who disregarded the truth to such extent that no one trusted him. His neighbour was a staunch Presbyterian who held the truth sacred and worried much about Lem's failing. Getting married didn't help Lem and as the years passed his reputation grew until there came a Baptist preacher to hold revival meetings. The good folk flocked to hear him and by the week-end sixteen had agreed to be baptized in the river on Sunday morning. The weather was cool for summer, however, and Saturday was cloudy. On Sunday morning the Presbyterian could not refrain from going to witness the immersions and when he saw Lem among the converts he was delighted beyond measure. He made opportunity to congratulate the preacher and said his trip was surely worth while if Lem had been the sole person to respond. Then the service commenced and when Lem's turn came the good Presbyterian went near to be first to shake his hand. He saw another participant shaking with chill and tested the water with his fingers. It was icy cold. Then came Lem and the Presbyterian kindly said: "How's the water, Lem?" "Warm as anything," quavered

Lem through chattering teeth. His neighbour heard the answer with amazement, then gripped the shivering man, whirled him about and propelled him to the preacher. "Put him under again," he thundered. "He's not cured yet."

We made sure of right turnings after a drive around Kennetcook, a delightful little community, and at last reached a high hill and knew we were at the Gore. A man leading a cow stopped long enough to tell us the ancient court house on the hill had seen "more law in its day than two others they got now." To him it was an almost sacred edifice and he could not understand a government letting such a landmark go to ruin. The view from the hill was magnificent and it also took in a paved road that we discovered led to Milford on Highway 2. So night found us in cabins and planning next day's adventure.

3

Off-trail along the Fundy

W E drove along Highway 1 until we reached Greenwich where we turned right and went down a slope, across a railway track and turned left to Port Williams.

Near Port Williams is the site of the French settlement "Boudro Point." On June 6, 1760, twenty-two vessels conveying seven thousand settlers from New London, Lebanon, Colchester, Lynne, Norwich, Hillingsworth, Hebron, Saybrook, Stonington, Windham and Windsor, in eastern Connecticut, made a landing at Port Williams. The village was then named Terry's Creek. The name was changed in honour of Captain Fenwick Williams, a native of Annapolis Royal, Nova Scotia, who had distinguished himself in the British Expeditionary Forces in Turkey. He later won additional fame as the defender of Kars in the Crimean War and at the close of the campaign was created General Sir William Fenwick Williams of Kars.

A few miles along a pleasant hard-surfaced road took us to great buildings bearing legends of Manning Ells & Son Poultry Farm. Never in our lives had we seen as many hens at one time. They were in ultra-modern quarters circular in shape and each holding ten thousand plump biddies scratching for exercise, eating from feed belts that run continuously, laying eggs or just gossiping. The din was terrific. The huge establishment has more than sixty thousand hens besides the chickens and everything is on a grand scale. We saw the way in which the debris and hen manure is taken away and spread on the fields, making such rich fertilizer that Mr. Ells has a fine herd of thoroughbred cattle to eat the grass and grain that grows so freely. In one building we saw gigantic incubators. In another crews were grading eggs so swiftly and efficiently that one had to see to believe. Only long experience could win a stand on the line as the eggs roll along an endless belt and there must be no mistakes.

We had a fine visit around the farm and then asked about "Bird axes" once made in that part of Kings County and were told to go to Canning, not much farther along and on the way to the Look-Off. But on the way we talked with a man beside the road and he headed us to Starr's Point, jutting out in Minas Basin, one of the richest parts of the Cornwallis dikelands. And there we saw the Prescott estate, a three-storied colonial-style whitewashed brick mansion among century-old trees and three acres of rolling lawns and flower gardens. The house was built by the Hon. Charles Ramage Prescott, a wealthy Halifax merchant and member of the Legislative Council, who retired in 1799 to live in the country. It took ten years to build the house as the bricks were made from clay taken from the banks of the Cornwallis River. A huge fireplace was constructed in each of the eight large rooms on the first and second floors, rooms that are elaborate with decorations. There are another four rooms on the third floor. The Prescotts lived in the home for two generations and lived in luxury for the family carried on extensive farming operations that paid handsome dividends. Then came the time when no one of the family wanted to stay and the place was sold. The property passed through different hands and about thirty years ago the house was simply used as quarters for hired help and the lawns became cow pasture. Then Miss Mary Allison Prescott, a great-granddaughter of the original owner, who had been a registered nurse in Montreal, returned to the old home and purchased it together with the three acres of land. She at once began to restore the fine old house to its original glory and, one at a time, she located and bought back much of the original furniture, chairs and china and tables. She spent four years restoring the house and then two sisters came to live with her and soon the gardens were restored to old-time beauty and once more Prescott House was a showplace of the countryside. A large painting of the original owner hangs in the drawing-room and nearby are two of the original chairs.

It was pleasant to stand and gaze at the house and flowers and visualize the old-time grandeur of fair ladies in hoop skirts descending from coaches to attend some stately function, and gentlemen resplendent in top hats and tails acting as escorts. But we had to go on and view the Wellington dike we had heard much about from a man at a filling station. The great dike was built over one hundred and thirty years ago by early settlers from New England and protects about two thousand four hundred acres of rich marshland from Fundy's rampant tides. Many dikes have been built in the area with the utmost care but tremendous storms have driven violent tides that washed them out and caused losses running to millions of dollars. Yet the Wellington Dike has survived all those storms, its mile-long ridge bucking everything that has come along. Men laboured incessantly with ox carts and spades and axes and logs to construct the dike and legend has it that rum was their greatest inspiration yet they builded a sentinel that has stood guard faithfully over the decades and surely has earned the distinction given with the name of a great British general. It was built in layers of brushwood and mud, each layer being well staked, and the material hauled in by cattle or trundled by wheelbarrow. It took three years to complete the project but was the pride of the countryside when finished.

Some years ago it became apparent that the sluice was worn past usefulness and the Federal Government assisted the Provincial with the installation of a new sluice costing $120,000. The highways was interested because the main way linking Lower Canard with Church Street goes over the dike. When the workmen dug down to make room for the new sluice it was found that the birch and spruce boughs used in construction so long ago were as sound as the day they were placed there, the spruce having the needles still attached.

We stopped in the centre of Canning and saw it as a delightful little village in the very heart of the fruit belt, and wondered anew that motor visitors do not get off the main trails to discover such spots. A monument nearby caught our attention and we discovered it was erected in honour of a young man of the place who had given his all in the Boer War. An old-looking man came along with a small girl, and both of them were eating ice cream with relish. So we asked about Canning and soon learned it was first called "Apple Tree Landing" and, like so many other places along our shores and rivers, famous for its wooden ships. Here schooners loaded with apples for the English market in the old days and many a citizen, said our friend, had a cheap trip to Britain and back. But it was the potato that gave the place its first touch of prosperity, he said, and that was away back in the forties when the New England farms were hard hit by potato blight. The average price had been forty cents a bushel and now the farmers around Canning were offered three times that price at the wharf. Every man and his son began digging and soon schooners were crowded in the river a dozen at a time while ox carts stood in a line for hundreds of yards waiting chances to unload. Cash was paid and Canning had more money that winter than the most optimistic had thought possible.

"Yes," said the old man, "we've had our ups and our downs. But there's been more of the first and I wish I had a small percentage of the money brought for apples shipped from here. Then we had a bad fire one time, in the night, and plenty of folks lost all they had as no one carried insurance. The country was dry for days before and everything burned like tinder so some had no more than their night clothes. Them nearest the river got on board a small schooner with all the belongings they could carry and they were the luckiest ones."

We asked him about the axes. "Yep, they were mighty

good axes, too, made by Blenkhorns. Don't know how they happened to get called 'Bird' axes. But they have to take a back seat, like so many things. Today they've got power saws you lug around in the woods and cut trees down so fast the squirrels can hardly get out of the way. And saws cut up the firewood. Only thing they need an axe for is to cut off a chicken's head, and soon they'll have another way of doing that."

"Any good stories around here?" we asked. "Family happenings, runaways, elopements, robberies?"

"Not that I know of," he grinned. "I've only been here a few years. I'm from over the mountain and just come to live with my daughter. If my father-in-law were alive he'd give you a few but he's gone, may the Lord rest him for his wife never did. Even when he had a heavy cold and it caught in his lungs she had a go at him with one of her eternal mustard plasters. He had that on his chest and hot flatirons at his feet and sweating like a bull. Now my woman, that's her daughter, was maid with a Kentville doctor before she married me, and thought she knowed a lot about doctoring. She'd had a look at them diagrams or whatever they have in a doctor's office and said the lungs were tight against the spine and easier reached from the back. But mother said that was nonsense and my wife had to wait until supper time before she had a chance to slap a big plaster of her own on her dad's back. He was like the ham in a sandwich, with the heat on front and rear, when they asked me to sit up with him the first part of the night. I hadn't dare offer a word to either side but when I saw how the poor man was suffering I went to the pantry in my sock feet and got down a bottle of brandy they always kept on the top shelf for an emergency. I give my father-in-law a sip or so to help dull the pain, and then I found the room so warm that I just fell asleep in my chair. When I woke I found the bottle empty and the poor man dead to the world. He was sweating enough to raise steam and I filled the flask with cold tea and put it back on the shelf quick as I could. The plasters had lost their bite by then and he slept till daylight and woke with the congestion cleared. All he had was a headache and both my wife and her mother thought they'd caused the cure. I never said anything but the old man always give me credit for having the right medicine."

He was still chuckling when we left him and went to read the inscription on the monument:

To commemorate the patriotism and Courage of Lieut. Harold Lothrop Borden, who was killed at Witpoort, South Africa, July 16, 1900, while leading his men to victory (Erected by friends in Kings County and Elsewhere). The only son of the Hon. Sir Frederic W. Borden, Minister of Militia and Defense, and Julia M., his wife, daughter of the late John H. Clarke, esq. He was born at Canning, May 23, 1876, graduate in Arts of Mt.A. University, 1897. Entered his third year in medicine at McGill University.

Before we were back in the car a man in shirt sleeves stepped up and asked if there were anything in particular we were looking for, and I said I wanted to get to the Blomidon Look-off. "Go right along that way," he pointed, "but I want to tell you something. Along the road there is a better 'magnetic hill' than they have up at Moncton, and not a soul knows about it except a few around here."

He told us what to watch for and when we arrived at the spot he described we stopped and shifted to "neutral." The car started backward immediately and we rolled back "up hill" for more than one hundred yards. It is one of those things you have to see to believe and as we've been several times to the hill at Moncton we were amazed that the same phenomena would be found in the Blomidon area. So few drive over the road that it has never been advertised and yet I am sure the average visitor would get a great kick out of letting the family car roll backward up hill.

The drive up to Blomidon Look-Off will not make anyone nervous for the height is not as great as imagined when the bold headland is seen in the distance. The view is wonderful and well worth the venture. We gazed around the vast marshes and over apple orchards, the great country reclaimed from the sea by the Acadians and later settled by thousands of New England Planters. Old Fundy surges back and forth and is ever battling the beaches but Blomidon stands a solid bulwark against wave and tide, and one wonders why the area is not converted into a scenic Park. I mentioned such an idea when back on the main highway and was shown a letter in the Wolfville paper, *The Acadian*. It was sent to the editor by Laurie Davidson Cox, Emeritus Professor of Landscape Engineering, New York State College of Forestry. He wrote:

As a Landscape Architect who has surveyed areas for proposed National and State parks in this country and planned and supervised the development of large Naturalistic parks in widely differing sections of the U.S. I read with interest the report concerning the Blomidon area in a recent issue of the *Acadian*. I was especially interested in the criticism of the Blomidon area since I visited last summer the existing National Parks in Cape Breton, Prince Edward Island and New Brunswick, and examined each from the viewpoint of the professional park planner. The points taken up in the report on Blomidon are logical and similar to those considered in selecting parks in this country. The size of the Blomidon area certainly compares favourably with the areas of the national parks in Cape Breton and P.E. Island. Again, the finest of the Maritime national parks that of Fundy Park in New Brunswick has nothing on the Blomidon area in the way of natural facilities for recreation. Its only such facility is fishing. The swimming there has to be provided by an artificial formal pool and the other main recreation feature, the Golf Course, is man made, and could be readily duplicated at Blomidon. The swimming beach with the very high tide at Blomidon is comparable in everything but size with the beaches at P.E. Island and Cape Breton and is large enough for any possible number of bathers who would ever visit the area if it were a park. The views and nature study facilities at Blomidon are far superior to those at either the P.E. Island or New Brunswick parks and are not greatly inferior to those of the Highlands in Cape Breton. Why not lead a movement to secure an area of from two thousand, five hundred to three thousand acres at Blomidon and develop there a Nova Scotia park similar to state parks in the U.S.A. Such a park would be developed with such recreational facilities as Beach development, Foot and Bridle trails, Cabin colonies and Camping areas. Nature study trails and museum, extensive Picnic facilities, etc.

After wandering around the area an hour we were in full agreement with all that Prof. Cox has written and reluctantly made our way back by way of Sheffield Mills and Upper Dike Village to Kentville on Highway 1.

As we looked around a little man trimly clad asked if we had seen any spot prettier than the Cornwallis Valley. We countered by inquiring if he came from there, and he admitted he had known it in boyhood. He talked about the famous people who had gone from Valley schools and asked if we had seen a grave in Camp Hill Cemetery at Halifax erected by Imperial Oil to Abraham Gesner. Not only had we seen it but I had a copy of the inscription:

Abraham Gesner, M.D., F.G.S., Geologist, born at Cornwallis, N.S., May 2nd, 1797. Died at Halifax April 29th, 1864. His treatise on The Geology and Mineralogy of Nova Scotia, 1836, was one of the earliest works dealing with those subjects in this Province, and about 1852 he was the American inventor of the process of kerosene oil.

Our friend told us Gesner was a tall man with thoughtful eyes, a dreamer, showman, scientist and adventurer who wrote books, played a flute and took his small black bag with him when he travelled so he could help any sufferer he might encounter. He charted the minerals of Nova Scotia and New Brunswick. He started Canada's first museum. He gave an Atlantic coast lighthouse a brighter light than it had previously shown. He lost a chance to become a millionaire as mine owner and then made a fortune from his kerosene patent. He had eleven brothers and sisters but spent his boyhood collecting insects and wildflowers and rock specimens. At fifteen he shipped before the mast on a ship going to the West Indies but when he was home again father told him he must be something better than a deckhand and so off Abraham went to a medical school in England. He returned with his degree, having been a brilliant student, said nothing about having taken geology as a side line, hung up his shingle and married the daughter of a Kentville doctor. Soon he was off to Blomidon chipping rock samples and gathering specimens, and then he closed office and went to explore New Brunswick. He located such an assortment that he was hired as a provincial geologist, then fired in 1842 whereupon he arranged his specimens in glass cases, rented space and set up a museum. Wanting more items of interest he inserted an advertisement in the Saint John paper asking for:

Specimens belonging to the animal, vegetable and mineral kingdoms, fossils, works of art, ancient books and papers, models, inventions, domestic manufactures, and curiosities of all kinds will be thankfully received, and admissions to the museum will be given for them according to their value. Masters and supercargoes of vessels who make donations will be entitled to free admission, and they are respectfully requested to aid in this useful and interesting work.

The request brought results and soon he was chasing after birds and animals of all sorts in the woods. These had to be mounted and he employed a Micmac family of experts and, needing house room for them, put them in the attic of his home. But folks were not much interested in such specimens at a time when every sea village had souvenirs of distant ports loaded on parlour tables and the project failed. Gesner had borrowed funds from two friends and he handed over his museum in payment, went to Halifax and started medical practice. There he met a sailor-scientist, the 10th Earl of Dundonald who had patented a new kind of oil lamp, and soon Gesner was experimenting and by 1846 was distilling kerosene from Nova Scotia coal.

We advised our friend to give lectures on Gesner and he smiled and admitted that he had, many times, and that he had searched Blomidon for thirty years and had found many fine specimens of Nova Scotia amethyst. Every spring, he said, great masses of rock, weakened by the frosts of the preceding winter, make avalanches that cover the narrow beaches at the foot of the cliff with fragments among which are crystals of amethyst, cornelian and moss agates, jasper and hornstone, bloodstone and spar and many others. And each year, he said, eager collectors were there and the first ones got the crop. The only safe way to visit the place was by motor boat, as the tides were treacherous and a man could not carry some large pieces that had to be taken back in order to cut from them the wanted specimens.

We had lunch and heard American guests talking about the amazing store of Palmeter's they had discovered outside the town. We had known of Palmeter's store before and knew that Mr. Palmeter had great knowledge of the byways of Kings County so decided to make a call at his establishment. But first we had a look in Don Chase's store for he stocks everything that interests tourists and has intriguing scarves and large kerchiefs stamped with maps of the original Acadia, old spelling and all, one of the finest things I have seen in that line.

Palmeter has no ordinary store. He purchased a beautiful farmhouse and added to it and uses the entire floor as his china store. The great barn is warehouse and shipping office. There is a miniature lake where the youngsters can paddle a canoe as you wait, gorgeous flowers everywhere, and the peace of the countryside. Harper's Bazaar has named it the finest china shop in North America, and the write-up in the April issue of *Better Homes and Gardens* was very enthusiastic, and stated:

Near Kentville is the Palmeter Country Gift Home, one of the most unusual shopping centres for fine English china in all of Canada. Around it are fifty acres of lawns, driveway and shade trees. Visitors have free use of such recreational attractions as canoeing on the lake, golf and afternoon tea— at four—with the compliments of the proprietor.

Cars from eleven different States were parked under the trees and everyone looked happy. Mr. Palmeter, always gracious, took time out to tell us not to miss Hall Harbour or any of the Fundy villages. "It's not the main highway," he smiled, "but there's no traffic and all you have to do is take it easy. You'll find it very worth while."

He never spoke truer words. We followed his directions faithfully and went up and over the ridge of hills known as North Mountain and suddenly were down the other side and looking at a horseshoe-shaped inlet of wharves and fence and fishing boats. You can drive right around the little harbour and picnic on the beach below the clustered buildings, enjoying the sunshine and surprised to find the sun not a bit too warm. And if you take time to roam around and explore in lazy fashion until a few hours have passed you will hardly believe your eyes when you return to the gravel road around the water. For it is low tide and the place has drained to an oblong pool and trickle. You won't believe it unless you see it, and it should be in Ripley's book.

Those who like table and mantel decorations of distorted wood should find enough along these Fundy villages to do a lifetime for piles of driftwood have been flung up on the rocks in hundreds of places.

Nearly every coastal settlement in Nova Scotia has a legend of some sort and Hall's Harbour is no exception. The story goes that back in the early days a pirate ship commanded by Captain Hall had twice visited the harbour and taken the hard-won supplies of the small settlement. This was too much and the settlers armed themselves and made fierce resolve to fight the next time the raiders appeared. Captain Hall tested his luck again the night of May 30, 1813, but an Indian had seen the ship and had run down the hills to warn the settlers. Every man rushed out with his musket ready and lay in hiding until Hall and his men had started toward their homes. Then they rushed in between the pirates and their ship in an effort to account for every raider. But a fog was closing in and as the first shots were fired Hall and his men fled into the murk. One pirate had stayed on

the vessel as guard and he had with him his Indian sweet-
heart. The settlers boarded the ship and vengefully shot
both the pirate and girl. Then they found a chest of gold
and jewels in Hall's cabin and took it ashore where they
hastily buried it for safekeeping before resuming the search
for the rest of the pirate gang. The chase led up the slope
but the settlers were too intent on getting Hall to organize
properly and the wily rogue doubled back to the ship with
his men and got away. The settlers had to be satisfied with
firing at the pirate's deck as he edged away and whether or
not they killed anyone the ship never returned. Then came
the matter of dividing the spoil but one man after another
said he wanted no part of such ill-gotten treasure, and those
who had buried it began to feel the same. So they did not
go near it and the years passed and the men died and when
a later generation decided that gold was gold no matter how
it came there and tried to locate the chest they failed. There
were a dozen different locations suggested by the stories of
oldtimers and no one alive had actually seen the spot. From
time to time others have dug but all in vain and somewhere
along the shore of Hall's Harbour a chest, probably rotted,
contains more wealth than possessed by the present residents
of the port.

We went up the long slope again and through Centreville
on the down grade to Upper Dike Village, former home of
Alfred Fuller, founder of the Fuller Brush Company. It
was a pleasant drive for us but if you are the impatient or
nervous type stay away. You cannot hurry over these hill or
shore roads and, anyhow, if you are in a hurry you won't see
what an easy-going couple will find, rare bits of seascape and
queer corners and friendly folk who have lived much fuller
lives than you think. I'll not forget the look on the face of a
gentleman from New Jersey who was in one of the tiny ports
and felt he had reached the end of the world. He was talking
with a leathery-looking Nova Scotian who had pulled in his
boat, asking him what it was like in winter, what they did
when they wanted a doctor, if the road to "civilization" was

kept open. He received calm answers, and evidently thought
he had awed his man. "I don't suppose," he said pityingly,
"you've even seen New York or Boston?"

"Once or twice," smiled the man in overalls. "We called
at New York on a trip I had to India, and I remember being
there on my way home from Egypt, but we often went to
Boston on our way to the West Indies when I was a young
fellow."

Don't try to talk down to someone you meet in those places
no matter if they look like rubes for ten to one they've seen
more of the world than you have. And they've braved old
Fundy's wrath in dories until danger has become a common
thing. And if you are nervous don't go along shore but
return to the main road and go over the mountain again
farther on, as the mountain roads are not alarming. We went
over the hills to Canada Creek and down shore to Harbour-
ville to see what the driving was like and there wasn't a thing
to worry about. Drive along at twenty-five miles an hour
and you can miss the bumps and ruts and there is no one
ahead of you to raise dust. But when you drive along the
shore you'll find narrow sections where passing places would
have to be picked and now and then you'll dip down a ravine-
like hollow and turn a jack-knife curve over a wooden bridge
and up another steep climb. Don't worry. Anyone you
meet will know that road, will hear you coming and pull off.
They want you to see their country and to like it. And now
and then we startled grouse or pheasants from the roadside
and deer peered at us from glades. Twice we had to slow
down to let a grumbling porcupine cross over.

We turned again at Auburn to return to the Fundy side,
and stopped to have a look at the old church there, built in
1790, its walls plastered with powdered mussel shells that the
French fugitives left in heaps at Morden. The wood frames
and windows of the church were brought from Halifax on
horses, and the hand-made nails were carried in fifteen-pound
packages by soldiers who walked the entire distance. There
are three large gilt balls on the church spire and one fell to

the ground about fifty years ago and was found to contain a record of all details relating to the building of the church, from the names of those employed to the number of nails used. The record was copied, then replaced in the ball and the ball returned to its place on the spire.

Looking back as we climbed the first slopes we had a grand view of the Valley and as we got higher and higher and saw the Fundy at last we wished that motor visitors had a paved highway on the shore side as they are missing one-half of the province, and the scenic half at that. We stopped at a small store in Morden and talked with some veterans of the coast who were taking life easy.

It was a beautiful morning and no one was in a hurry. We were told of the first settlers and about old families in the area, with special mention of such names as Orpin and Dugan and Finley. We were told where to see the stone work of the first Dugan cellar, and that the old Orpin house was still standing. Then we heard about the famous John Orpin, a most unusual man in every respect. He was born in 1804 and in early years showed he possessed tremendous strength. He stood six feet one and three-quarter inches in his sock feet and weighed two hundred and ten pounds, all bone and muscle. He had large shoulders, arms and neck, but was slim waisted, remarkably agile and quick as the proverbial cat. He had a double row of teeth both upper and lower, and was double-jointed in both wrists and hands.

On reaching manhood he became more fully aware of his amazing strength and it made him all the more careful to be friendly with his fellow men. He had no quarrels and dealt justly with all, read his Bible daily and was an honest, kindly and upright citizen. In those days the mail was carried along the Valley on what is now Highway 1. It was then called "the Post Road," and all the villages along the Fundy shore had to have mail carriers go out to the Post Road for the mail. There were some bothersome Indians about, and white renegades who several times had robbed or molested mail carriers, so John Orpin was asked to carry the mail. He rode on horseback and in 1838 was returning with the mail when a fallen tree blocked his way on the mountain. He dismounted and went ahead to drag the tree from the road when he was fired on by men in hiding. The bullet caught the fleshy part of his shoulder. Orpin had a flintlock musket and he fired as he caught sight of a fellow, and wounded him in the leg. He had aimed at the legs as he did not want to kill, but to defend His Majesty's mail. Then three men sprang from hiding, swinging clubs, and attacked John. He had no time to reload and dropped his musket. Then he moved so quickly that he grasped the club of the leader, wrenched it from him and seized him before the second man had a clear swing. John grabbed his club as well, tore it from his grasp, seized the fellow and then bumped the heads of his prisoners together with force enough to stun them. As they lay in the snow he tried to catch the fourth fellow, but that lad had seen what befell his mates and he was running for his life. John had to return without him. Then he reloaded his weapon, took the musket of the wounded man, untied his horse, put the wounded man on it, and went on to Morden, walking the two unwounded prisoners ahead of him.

The residents of Morden were greatly enraged when they heard what had happened and a party of eight vigilantes was organized. These set off at daybreak and ran down the fourth man and brought him to Morden. Then there was a wait of ten days before the wounded man was fit for travel. When he was recovered the party set off for Windsor where the trial would be held. They covered half the distance the first day and that night as one vigilante stood guard he was suddenly attacked and two of the prisoners escaped during the fracas. The guard was clubbed viciously and the vigilantes were more furious than ever. They chased the escaped pair and caught them, took them back and hanged all four at the nearest tree, then returned to Morden. Word of what happened filtered to Halifax and an official visited Morden. He was given the facts of the case and agreed that the four had received their just deserts, as they had robbed other postmen, but gave warning that in the future all culprits must be dealt with in due course at a proper court.

During the potato famine in Ireland many Irish had come to Nova Scotia. Some of these had moved first to Lunenburg county, then had moved across to the Valley and finally many located along the Fundy shore so that a stretch of it was called "Irish Mountain." Some of these were far from desirable citizens and it was their creed that might was right. The law of their community was that laid down by the biggest bullies. Two of these were continually defying each other as to leadership and it so happened that both of them attended an Anglican church gathering at Morden. The two met and one word led to another and soon the astounded churchmen saw the Irishmen fighting savagely. John Orpin waited not a minute. He strode over and grasped a fighter in each hand, held them firmly despite all their struggling, then began bumping their heads together gently. "Stop your fighting," he ordered, emphasizing his speech with bumps, "or next I'll spank the pair of you in turn."

There was no need of spankings. When he released the two who had been furiously trying to maim each other, they were so awed by the man who had handled them like children that they slunk away, their differences forgotten.

John Orpin was of a retiring nature. He had many friends but lived largely to himself, and preferred to work alone. He was a master hand with tools and his strength and agility were such that he could do as much in a day as two ordinary men. There was a great demand for shingles and there were many trees then of old growth having large boles of straight grain. The tree was cut down and the boles sawed into shingle lengths. These were then split for shingles, placed in wooden clamps operated by foot pressure, and shaved to smoothness. Orpin used an Indian knife with a thumb rest at the handle for this work. The splitters were made by the local blacksmith, were like a wide-bladed chisel with thick back. A wooden mallet was used as a striker to prevent "brooming up" of the back of the splitter. The shaver was also made by the blacksmith and was a thin-bladed knife with a handle on either side.

At a barn raising an accident occurred while the rafters were being hoisted and a workman was trapped by dislodged sections on a crossbeam. Orpin did not wait for a ladder but quickly climbed to the pinned man, raised the weight of two sections of rafters and freed him, put him under one arm and carried him back to safety as a mother would carry a child.

In 1858 John Orpin went to Saint John on a trip and was recognized in that city. Tales of his superman strength had gone far and wide and a trio of sea captains at once arranged for a weight lifting contest. They had noticed the feats of a two hundred and thirty pound Irishman on the docks, and there was a Swedish vessel in port that had, in the crew, a giant Swede, standing six foot four inches and weighing two hundred and fifty pounds. Both the Irishman and Swede were young men at their best while Orpin was then fifty-four years old. An anchor was chosen for the test and the Irishman had first lift. He raised the anchor about two inches from the dock. Then the big Swede took hold and lifted it more than two feet above the dock floor. It was John's turn and he lifted the anchor with ease, let it down, held it with the shank upright and asked the Irishman and Swede to stand on either side on the grappling hooks. They did so and John lifted the anchor with its load.

Men crowded around the dock simply gasped in wonder. There were twenty reliable eye witnesses of the feat and it matters not that there is no exact record of the weight of the anchor. Some say it weighed 450 pounds and others say it weighed six hundred. At any rate it was so heavy that the big Irishman could barely raise it from the floor, and the Swede had all he could do to raise it above his knees. Yet John, almost twice their age, lifted it with them standing on it.

A few years later John Orpin became Collector of Customs for Morden and in 1870 the *Trader* put in with some cargo from a foreign port. Orpin told the captain the duty must be paid and the captain objected, argued and would not begin unloading. Finally, at high tide, he upped anchor and sailed down the Bay. John was suspicious at once, and went along to Port George by land. Sure enough, in came the *Trader* with the foreign goods. The captain had feared that Orpin would guess his intentions and he had on board as cook an enormous native from the British West Indies. So he told this man to keep Orpin away and he would be well rewarded. As Orpin came on the dock the hired giant walked up to him and told him to be gone. It must be remembered that Orpin was then sixty-six years of age. He gave the fellow a good-natured answer but received a blow in the face. He tried to make the man understand that he was an official carrying out his duties but the giant took the explanations as a sign of fear and struck twice more, rocking Orpin back on his heels and daring him to fight. Once more Orpin tried to explain and then the huge cook yelled "Coward!" and spat full in John's face. No man had ever done such a thing, and John's fist flashed and landed. The big black seemed almost to rise in the air, then landed with a terrific jolt on the planking. When he remained there, inert, the watching captain of the *Trader* ran to him, knelt and discovered the cook was dead. He was shocked with the discovery and fearful of consequences as there had been witnesses to his hiring the man to attack John. So he gave out that his man had fallen from the deck to the dock and died from injuries received, and there was no inquiry. The full duty was promptly paid, but John Orpin always regretted that he had struck a man in anger, though he had been foully insulted.

After hearing of Orpin we were greatly interested to know that a man was still living in Morden at the age of one hundred and four, and that he had followed the sea for years. Orpin had lived to be ninety-two, and there were others around in their nineties. Furthermore, this oldster had been quite a teller of tales in his prime during the period when tale-telling won prizes in Morden. He was born at Victoria Harbour, two and one-half miles from Morden, and had been a very shy man in his youth. Legend had it he had walked over seven times with a girl who worked at the Harbour and in all that time had spoken just once, to remark: "I bet there is gum up in that tree." However he got over the shyness and after years at sea became an amusing entertainer. There were many others at Morden and these men had had so many amazing experiences that it was decided a gathering would be held when the majority were ashore and those telling the best account would receive an award. Arch Minnis was a sea captain, and one of the winners. He told of sailing into Constantinople with a cargo and going ashore in the evening to explore the Turkish city. Arrived at a fine park he was admiring the scenery and listening to Turkish music when a beautiful woman appeared beside him and began talking in broken English. After much conversation she told him she was lonely and unhappy. She looked a lady in every respect and was well dressed but insisted that her life was not worth living, words that disturbed the Nova Scotian so that he tried to comfort her. It ended in a long and serious talk and as he left her they embraced and he kissed her.

As they finished unloading the ship the next day the British ambassador came on board and acted as if he were greatly disturbed. He questioned Minnis about his being ashore and Minnis told him about his evening at the Park.

"You have been an awful fool," he said. "That woman was from the Sultan's harem, she had slipped out of a window, and she was seen with you, and it was reported to the Sultan you had kissed her. So I have received a challenge from him to you. This is most serious because you were on Turkish soil and broke a Turkish law."

Just then two Turkish warships drew alongside the Nova Scotian ship and moored there, and Minnis began to realize he was in deep trouble. He saw two British warships steam into port and anchor nearby but was still very troubled.

"You have the right to choose weapons," said the ambassador, "and that is all."

Minnis was a big man and very quick with his hands. He had boxed in various ports so he said "boxing gloves."

The ambassador was surprised at the choice but went ashore, then sent word back that no boxing gloves were available in Turkey and there would be a delay of two weeks while some were being imported from Gibraltar. This was a good time to get in some training so Minnis wrapped his hands in burlap and sparred morning and afternoon with the second-mate who was an experienced ring man. When the gloves arrived an armed guard came to the dock to escort Minnis to the arena. The guard was composed of British marines from the warships and a brass band led the way. When they arrived at the arena Minnis was amazed to see all the ambassadors from various countries of the world in attendance, as well as many high ranking army and navy officers. Then an official stood and announced it was against custom for the Sultan to strike anyone with his hand and so a member of the Sultan's household would act as his substitute. Then there strode into the arena a huge eunuch almost seven feet tall, and the official stated that the loser would die, and explained why the challenge had been issued. At this the British ambassador stood and said that the British people had only one wife and she received careful protection and attention, also that Englishmen the world over were always ready to help a female in distress, that Minnis had not known the woman was married, and had but tried to cheer her. However he was not begging release for his man. A challenge had been given and accepted. Let the fight begin.

The eunuch made a wild rush but he was awkward and Minnis knocked him down five or six times until he had the right chance and then put him down to stay. A servant at once ran out to Minnis and handed him a large sword before applying something that restored the eunuch, who bowed and asked Allah to receive him, then waited the stroke of the sword. But Minnis said he had no quarrel with the man or anyone else. All he wanted was to sail his ship from the port and never would he return. At that moment in came a

sedan chair borne by four big men. It halted and out stepped
the woman Minnis had kissed, while the official announced
that the Sultan was presenting her to Minnis as he did not
want her longer. Minnis started to refuse but the ambassador
warned him it would be regarded as an insult, so the lady
was taken on board the ship and there flung her arms about
his neck and poured out ardent love in Turkish. Minnis put
her away from him almost by force and placed her in his
cabin. He gave all attention to getting from port and decided
to face his problem the next day. A lively wind sprang up
and soon there were wails from the cabin. The beautiful
Turk had not been to sea before and she was terribly sea-sick.
She implored Minnis to put her on land and he was glad the
wind stayed with them. He sailed near Crete and put the
anguished woman ashore at Candia, giving her fifty dollars.
He had known a Turkish colony was there and she was so
thankful to reach land that she did not so much as say good-
bye. When Minnis reached home six months later he was
amazed to find a cheque for five hundred dollars awaiting
him. The battle in the arena had roused the sporting blood
of the Turks and they had sent in huge orders for boxing
gloves. The factory had shipped everything in stock and
worked the clock around for months. The cheque was in
appreciation of the business he had initiated.

William Finley won second prize. He was out fishing one
day and getting such a catch he wanted to stay in the area but
the wind kept shifting him out so he dropped anchor. Too
late, he saw with horror a great bank-like darkness below and
realized a whale was under the boat. He was further horrified
to see the anchor plunge downward into the blow-hole of
the monster. The next instant he was flat on his back among
his catch and the boat was being whipped down the Bay at
terrific speed. He struggled to get a grasp of a seat as the
speed was so great many items were taken as with a great
wind. He knew that the whale might dive at any time and
that would be his finish so got out his knife and sawed
desperately at the anchor rope. They were going so fast that

the shore was but a blur yet he knew they must be near Grand Manan island and the rope parted just as the monster dove. There was nothing Finley could do except hang on for dear life as the boat was literally on top of the water and going at such speed that everything happened in the twinkling of an eye. The tide was in full and so the boat zipped in on the sloping beach without slowing the slightest. It went through two fences with hardly a jar and then seemed to thud against something yielding but kept on into dense brush where it finally stopped, a complete wreck. The shock of stopping almost wrenched Finley's arms from their sockets and what helped was his catch of fish which was buried about him.

He was so stunned that he lay where he was for some time and when he did climb from the debris he was still dazed. He staggered about, noticed that the boat had sheared off a sizable tree before stopping, that the mast was gone, and all his equipment. He stumbled around until he was able to get his bearings and wondered how he would get passage home. He could not think clearly and found himself wandering over a field some time later and then a man came up to him and asked who he was. Finley explained as best he could, and the man said, "Come here." He led the way to a pasture and three cows were lying there, dead. They had been struck by the boat and would be the thuds he had felt. Beyond there were two wide gaps in fences and rails were scattered like match sticks.

"Now come with me," said the man. "You'll have to pay for this damage."

"But I have no money," said Finley. "I was just out fishing. I'll have to send it from home."

"Oh, no you don't," snarled the man. "I happen to be the sheriff and I've had dealings with your kind. You'll stay in the jail overnight and then the judge will see you."

Finley was not in condition to argue and was placed in jail and given some supper. When they got him for the court at ten the next morning, however, his mind had cleared, and he quickly explained to the judge exactly what had happened.

"A fine story," snapped the judge. "But who pays for my cows?"

It was then that Finley realized the judge owned the cows that were killed. And soon sentence was pronounced. He was to work for one year, being placed in the jail each night, to earn enough to pay for the damage done by his boat.

Then the judge laughed, and so did everyone in the court room. Finley asked mildly why they laughed, and the judge said. "Everyone said it was a comet that had hit the island, and if you hadn't walked around until the sheriff found you we would not have known the difference. It's a big joke—on you."

There was nothing to do but accept the conditions and a month or so later while Finley was hoeing the judge's turnips he was surprised to see a very noble-looking gentleman, dressed in the best, picking his way across the turnip rows. While at some distance, near the road, stood a number of gentlemen, waiting.

The gentleman walked up to Finley and asked his name. Then stated his case.

"I was to a function a short time ago," he said, "where the judge from here told a remarkable story of a boat killing his cows, and he having a man work a year for nothing. Please tell me the entire story."

So Finley rested his hoe and himself and gave the full account, and back by the road the group fidgeted about and watched.

"Thank you," said the gentleman. "Now, Finley, throw away that hoe. Here's some money." He handed over fifty dollars. "Get yourself good clothes and shoes, shirt and all, and then come to my boat. It's at the wharf now, the only one there."

Finley had noticed that the judge was in the party that kept at a distance, but he took the money, thanked the man, went to the store and bought the finery suggested, shaved and cleaned himself, dressed in the new togs and went down to the wharf. The only boat there was a grand yacht but he went on board and soon was ushered into a dining cabin and seated beside the gentleman who had interviewed him. There was rich steak and all the trimmings and when they had had a great pudding with fine sauce, the gentleman began talking.

"When you were thrown up on this island," he said, "your status quo was that of a mariner in distress. Canadian law states that such persons shall be cared for by the proper officials in the port. Instead of that, we find a judge and sheriff guilty of the gravest violations of that law, and you their victim. I'll arrange your passage home and this island will provide you with a new boat as good as the one you lost plus all equipment needed. And you will also be paid fullest going wages for the time you worked for this judge."

"Thank you, sir, most kindly," said Finley. "Is it permitted for me to ask who you are?"

"Of course," came the answer. "I happen to be Lord Dufferin, Governor-General of Canada, and I was visiting in Saint John when I heard of your plight."

Finley thanked him as best he could, and soon was on his way home in his fine clothes and with his wages in his pocket. Shortly after he received a fine boat in the best of shape, fully supplied with the best fishing gear, but the biggest surprise of all came after his story had been published in the Ottawa papers. A boat from Maine put in and delivered to him the anchor he had lost. The captain explained that the State of Maine had paid him for his errand, that the whale had driven ashore near Machias at such speed that its huge carcase was found half a mile inland, lodged against a stone wall, the anchor still in its blow hole.

We could see that more tales were forthcoming and hastily said we must be on our way. Our friends told us we should call on Finley and we promised to return and have a talk with the grand old man. Had we known he was to pass away within a comparatively short time we certainly would have seen him, but we had been a long time by the store and we wanted to see the spot where the Acadians had stayed that winter of 1755, grouped in hollows to avoid onshore winds, in ragged dress, gaunt with hunger, trying to snare rabbits, eternally tearing mussels from the rocks and hoping the Indians would continue to bring them fresh meat. Then the snow came and the ice and frost and they hacked deadfalls into fuel for fires they dare not let go out, day or night, and tried to exist on one meal per day. Old ones and sick ones died, the heaps of mussel shells grew larger, and hope faded. When spring came an old one and a youngster crossed by boat to where other fugitives were hiding from the New England soldiers, and soon boats came to carry survivors to rest and succour. We stood and inspected the spot, and the large cross of stone that bears the inscription:

On this site the Acadians from Belle Isle wintered in 1755 to 1756. In the spring of 1756 Pierre Melanson with an Indian boy crossed the Bay for aid. On the return trip he died. The original cross was erected by the Acadians.

We walked on the shore and saw a boy and girl by the rocks where the Acadians had searched for mussels. It is a rugged coastline and we saw many summer cottages tucked here and there, were surprised to learn there were twenty-seven, that some were rented each season by Americans who had "discovered" Morden. An oldtimer told us the area had one peculiarity. No bears. After the Dominion Atlantic Railway was constructed along the foot of the mountain not a bear had crossed it.

There were four thrilling descents into gorges and climbs to higher ground and after twelve miles of woods and wild life that was most enjoyable we arrived at Margaretsville, and found it quite a large place, practically a young town. We drove down carefully and parked near the lighthouse, saw three places where ice cream was sold, a shed with the sign "Fresh Fish," and gulls by the hundred along a pier. We walked to one shop and were welcomed by the lady in charge and shown a small booklet entitled "Margaretsville—Where the Busy Breezes Blow." Then we ambled around with the camera and loved the balmy sea air, the freedom from mosquitoes, saw youngsters playing on the beach and visitors in slacks and shorts. Eleven different cars bore American licence and proved that some left the paved roads to explore.

It was easy to get into conversation with men working near a road and the place has many tales of the days of wooden ships, of pirates and ghosts and wreckers. The tide was low and dulsers were out picking dulse from the rocks. They took it to shore in bags, spread it to dry on the grass and thought it a treat. Margaretsville was one of the best spots we had found along Fundy, with neat homes and many roads entering the place, kind folk and good accommodation. They told us that when a storm rises many go to watch the waves roll in with teriffic force as though everything in the path would be destroyed. They beat against the pier and end in clouds of flying spray and foam that is awe-inspiring.

Over a sunporch of one home was a sign: "Aunt Hepsy's Curiosity Shop." Joe "Dody" Cleveland a lifelong resident of the place was a collector for years of anything that caught his eye. He owned and sailed schooners in his younger days, was keeper of the light, shipping master of the port, a justice of peace and customs officer, a distant relation of a president of the United States, and of a man who once preached in old St. Matthew's at Halifax. He collected over 1000 old books, many over one hundred years old, compasses, name boards, whale bones, the sword of a swordfish, one of General Wolfe's swords, tomahawks, arrowheads and many many strange items. He also collected stamps and had a large collection.

We soon discovered that Margaretsville was once called Peter's Point, and were given various versions of what happened the original founder of the village. At that time a feature was a jagged ridge of black rocks extending three hundred yards into the sea and known as Black Ledge. In

1780 Peter Barnes, an Irishman, was the only inhabitant of the place and he lived in a cabin constructed from timbers salvaged from the sea. Peter grew vegetables in his clearing and fished for a living, but in 1793 an early frost ruined his garden and fish failed to make their annual run along the coast so Peter faced famine. Christmas Eve came and with it a wild storm of wind and snow, and the provisions Peter had put in for the winter were nearly exhausted. At evening Peter saw a sail out at sea and he at once lighted his lantern and placed it in a tree at the top of the cliff so that it might appear to be a lighthouse. Miles up the coast was a port that vessels used to shelter in during a storm and a light shone at the entrance. Soon Peter and his housekeeper heard a crash on the rocks and the cries of the crew of the foundered vessel. But Peter and the housekeeper stayed in their cabin until morning. When they went out they found the bodies of six men encased in ice at the foot of the cliff and produce and provisions had been washed up on the beach. Peter gathered these and took them to his cabin and lived on them until spring. Fishermen saw the wreckage and recognized the *Saucy Nancy* but could only be suspicious of Peter. Twenty years later, on another Christmas Eve, Peter was out to a tavern in Middleton. Returning late in a snowstorm he lost his way and looked for a light in his window, not knowing that one of the villagers, out on an errand of mercy, had placed a lantern in the recess of a cliff to guide his return journey. It was exactly the same spot where Peter had placed his light years before and Peter went over the bank. They found him on jagged rocks encased in ice and on her death-bed the old housekeeper told of Peter's awful crime.

The booklet loaned us showed that nine roads led to Margaretsville. It could be reached directly from Middleton, a road that may be paved; via Delusion, along the top of the Mountain; via McGill Road, via Prince Albert, via the Dodge Road, from Kingston-Melvern Square via the Ben Phinney Road, via the Vault Road and from Brickton via Mount Hanley and Port George. This latter sounded interesting and proved a most beautiful drive providing shore, valley, mountain and woods scenery. The view from Mount Hanley was thrilling as Blomidon, and the trip through Cottage Cove to Port George was an experience to remember. If the visitor were staying a few days at Margaretsville he would be well repaid if he sampled each of the nine routes to the port.

Port George was first known as Gates Breakwater and was an important shipping point fifty years ago but the tides have taken the wharf and breakwater and no move is being made to replace them. This shows the change in attitude during the march of time for when the first breakwater went out in 1845 a new pier was soon constructed, the cost being borne by shipping interests plus a grant from the provincial government. Two first stores supplied the settlement and the son of one merchant became a customs officer, the son of the other a leading merchant in Middleton. Twenty vessels were built at Port George and it was a thriving place until most of the business section was destroyed by fire. Buildings were replaced however and the fishing industry flourished with one firm exporting seven thousand barrels of herring in one year besides shipments of codfish and hake. Then ship building waned and the railway took much of the shipping and fish prices fell. Soon Port George became better known as it is to-day as a summer resort, and the top of the mountain affords a wonderful view, there is fishing and boating and the entire neighbourhood is a delightful vacation spot.

We talked with an elderly man whose nose had peeled with sunburn. "Always does," he said ruefully. "No, I don't belong here, but I have a business in the Valley and fine days in summer the wife and I drive in here and picnic. You see, this is where I met her, on a little vacation, and we come back a dozen times each summer."

I asked him if he knew of any special romance around Port George. "No," he grinned, "but down where I live Aunt Sabine had five daughters she had to marry off and she was determined every one should be a fine honest Baptist with decent ideas about hours and drink and so forth. They had horsehair furniture to sit on in the parlour and stereoscope views of Niagara Falls and the like. Each time a chap came courting he had the girl in that parlour and mother sat there to see there was no nonsense, and she kept busy with needlework. At ten o'clock she held it up before the young man, and it was a motto reading 'There Is No Place Like Home.' I've heard she used it through the courting of all five girls. The only boy was the youngest of the family and I reckon it was tough enough with all them girls. And Sadie, she's third in the lot, had a young fellow coming to see her who was a great talker about himself. Jimmy, the boy, couldn't stand him, and one Sunday night this calling chap boasted about being to Boston twice, to Halifax and to Saint John. Jimmy had to sit and take it but never joined in with any of the 'ohs' and 'ahs' of the girls. So the young man looked at him. 'What's the matter?' he asked. 'Don't you think I've been around a lot?' 'Yes,' grunted Jimmy, 'and so has the button on our backhouse door.' He was never allowed to sit in the parlour again while the girls had callers, and I doubt he felt that was punishment.

All we had heard had made us eager to travel more of the unknown roads so we listened to directions back in Margaretsville and went over Stronach Mountain, taking a turn first at Evergreen Church. There were sharp turns and a drive through Forest Glade and a right turn on a Phinney Road and next we knew we were in Melvern Square and not far from the paved highway. We stopped to chat with a man by the road and asked if there was something we should see.

"Come tomorrow and see Dan Outhit," he said. "Too bad he's away just now. He's ninety-two and he's been on the King's County Municipal Council since 1898. You know anyone else who has a record like that? And he's been County Treasurer for forty-one years. He's seen the county business jump up about fifteen hundred per cent, so he tells me, and he's mighty active for his age. He's got a three-hundred-acre farm and his house is one hundred and thirty years

old and good as the day it was built. Great view of North
Mountain, as you can see from here, and of Greenwood
Airport. His great-great-grandfather got the land he's on in
a grant in 1785, and the first log cabin was right where his
house stands. All around here has a history, and you should
go up the Ruggles Road. Wilmot, over there where I'm
pointing, was named after a governor—Lemuel Allen Wilmot
and in the old days there was the Gibbons Hotel which was
a coach inn, and had the post office, and a general store, and
it was headquarters during an election. All gone now and
hardly a soul knows they ever were there. And right over
there" our friend pivoted and pointed to all parts of the
compass, it seemed, "close by where you come from Margaretsville, is the Phinney's Mountain where Brigadier Timothy
Ruggles had a grant of five thousand acres. He built a big
house and planted an orchard in a ravine that was wind-
sheltered and grew peaches and quince and apples, and he
had a lot of black walnut trees. Two men, Stronach and
Fales, worked for him, and after three years good service
he give each of them one hundred acres. Stronach Mountain
is named after one of them. My grandmother used to tell
me about a school teacher that taught over near Spa Springs
or maybe it was nearer Middleton. Anyhow the school was a
log building with slab seats, and school only run from first
of May till October. Well, this young woman teacher was
going good with her youngsters when Indians come for spring
salmon fishing and camping not too far away. The next
week a wigwam caught fire and was burned and when the
teacher come in the morning here was the chief and his squaw
with two young ones, camped in her schoolhouse. She tried
to argue with them but they wouldn't move and the chief
said he liked hearing the classes recite. That night she
went to the trustees but they were scared of the Indians
and told her not to make any trouble. So the chief and his wife
stayed on and fished in the evening, and the youngsters had
their attention so taken by their company that the teacher
was near crazy. She tried the trustees again but they were

same as before. Then came some hot days and the Indians smelled to high heaven. So the teacher arrived one morning with a big boy carrying a tub for her and another carrying an iron kettle. When school ended for the day she heated water in the kettle and filled the tub and told the squaw she must have a bath. The Indian woman refused, saying water was weakening but the teacher had strong notions and a bar of soft soap and the chief so enjoyed the situation that he willingly gave a hand and they stood the red-skinned lady in the tub and the teacher scrubbed her thoroughly, taking off so many layers the water got thick and she had no more to heat. The chief chuckled all the time, till the teacher was leaving. Then she said 'Tomorrow, we wash you.' When she arrived the next morning the chief and his family had vanished and they didn't show up there again."

"What happened to the orchard you talked about, up in the ravine?" we asked.

"Oh, different folks owned the property and let it run down and the trees died, most of them, but one man went there to cut his firewood and found a dark tree and it was so hard he showed it to neighbours who recognized black walnut and the local carpenter bought the trees, had them sawed to size at the local mill, and made furniture. There are several pieces of it around the valley yet."

We left the main highway again at Bridgetown and yet stayed on paved road until we struck off to the right over the mountain to Parker Cove and came along to Delap Cove and back to where the paved road ended at Port Royal. This is the oldest permanent white settlement north of the Gulf of Mexico and those who do not leave the main highway —seven miles distant—to see it are missing much. There is an exact replica of the Champlain Habitation built in 1605. It occupies the exact site of the original building and is the same in every detail, having colombage walls with small logs filled in between, the racks caulked with clay. Outside, the walls are covered with lapped boarding which looks as if it were sawn by the old whip saw. The chimneys are made of field stone mortared with a mixture like clay, and the bricks used in the fireplace and bake oven are made of clay dug at the site. Throughout the building all timber framing has been mortised and tenoned and pinned together in the old manner, no spikes or nails being used. The hinges and fastenings of the one hundred and twenty doors, windows and shutters of the Habitation make an interesting display of handwrought iron of early seventeenth century design. The well shelter and pigeon cote are covered with oak shingles of the size used three hundred years ago. Antique glass and parchment is in the windows. The first social club in North America, the famous Order of the Good Time, was installed by Champlain, and tens of thousands of summer visitors to Nova Scotia have qualified for membership and possess beautifully coloured Certificates of Membership.

The first cereal crops in Canada were grown at Port Royal, the first water power grist mill was constructed, the first drama was written and staged, the first bricks made, the first highway, the first conversions to Christianity. It was at Port Royal that Samuel de Champlain had his garden and his "promenade." There is a replica of an ancient French arbour, a cairn with a tablet commemorates the work of America's first playwright, Marc L'Escarbot, who wrote "The Theatre of Neptune," America's first play, and produced it there on November 14, 1607.

In 1621 all Acadia was granted to Sir William Alexander by King James the First and the country renamed Nova Scotia, the Royal Province. One hundred and twenty-two Baronets of Nova Scotia were created in the castle grounds at Edinburgh and each was granted land in the province in a Scottish attempt at colonization. Sir William's son led an expedition to Port Royal and a fort of stone was built and occupied but the project failed when the land was handed back to France.

We drove on a gravel road to Victoria Beach and at trail's end climbed a hill and found ourselves on a ledge above the water with homes and a store and little church along the way. There was a hotel on the left and several cottages in the rear. We stopped there to ask questions and were amazed to meet Martha Banning Thomas, the noted poet whose work has appeared in *Saturday Evening Post* and many American and Canadian publications. She had occupied the same cottage there for years and knows the country. It is a delightful spot and we went down a steep drop to wharves where gulls rose in a white cloud at our approach and boats passing made great echoes along the hills.

The tides rise to between twenty-four and twenty-eight feet at Victoria Beach and the village is at Digby Gut, the narrow entrance to Annapolis Basin, so that Fundy forces its way through the Gap with great force and causes whirlpools and eddies and tide rips and currents which only the local fishermen understand. There are many tales told by these men and Helen Creighton has some of them in her *Folklore of Victoria Beach,* such as an account of the Indians shooting porpoise and then rolling their canoes so deftly they could take the fish on board. The Indians liked the place as ash grew to the water's edge and was good to make handles and baskets. Sharks are a nuisance in the area and have been known to attack boats and drive the fishermen ashore. One bit a boat and left several teeth embedded in the hard wood. And there are whales as well. A boat went out to set trawls and as they waited for the tide to slacken ran onto something like a shoal, but the shoal moved and they discovered a whale beneath them. Before they could do anything the whale went down but was back again at once, and though the fishermen pounded on their water barrel and made great noise they could not frighten the big fellow. It went down four times and rose again to catch the boat but the fifth time the men were ready and got away. The best yarn is about a scare the Beach fishermen had back in 1890 when they were coming from Port George. A sea serpent appeared close by the schooner and rolled hoop-like lengths thirty or forty feet beside them. It had a huge head like that of a horse in shape and eyes large as saucers. A gale was blowing and the crew clapped on all sail but the creature kept up with them all the way to Point Prim light. A second vessel sighted it the next day, then a third one, and it has not been seen since that year.

Then there is the Beach story of a Scot coming with an old chart which showed where treasure was buried at Hudson's Point. So the men went out, four of them, at dark, and began digging. The ground was not too hard and they worked with a will but there was no moon and it was misty so they had to be careful. Then one man noticed there were five of them instead of four and as they had agreed not to speak he made signs with his hands, asking about the stranger. Then came a noise like thunder and the ground shook and everyone started to run except the fifth man who just rested on his pick. One fellow turned back to join him and next he knew was in the water to his neck, and didn't know how he got there. But his pals pulled him out and all kept on for home and not one of them set foot on the Point again.

Miss Thomas told us of local superstitions and that ghosts had been seen at many places along the shore but none would appear for us and so we had to have a look at Point Prim light at the entrance to the Gut. The keeper has a wooden covered register that has names of people from all corners of the world, visitors who have found their way to the Point and are proud of it. The keeper is a veteran of World War One and his home is in the base of the light tower. There he lives and enjoys life no end for he likes company and has plenty of it.

We went back to the Beach and paused where a small truck was pulled to one side to change a tire. Two young fellows worked a jack and were doing the labour while a man old enough to be their father casually watched gulls over the water. We spoke about the light at the Gut and the boats making use of it.

"This place was always important," he announced. "Go take a look at the plaque on that boulder to the north side of the road. It tells you that this was the end of the pony express from Halifax away back in 1849. They had the telegraph to Saint John by that time and the New York papers wanted to get the news from overseas fast as they could. So a fellow in Halifax got it from the ship, about three thousand words, and give it to a chap who started from the city with his pony on the dead run. At twelve miles he changed horses and kept going fast as they could make it. At Kentville a second rider took over. The first run was February 21, 1849, and from the time the first man started till the second chap tore in this road to where the steamer was, just over there, was eleven hours and ten minutes. Mister, that's a hoss ride in February. But the old records tell they did it later in just over eight hours. I reckon they had better horses. At Bridgetown the rider left the front road and come along back of the river and they watched for him over at the old fort in Annapolis and when he passed Granville Ferry they fired a cannon. This was to signal the steamer here to get her fires going and steam up so that soon as the man arrived they could head off for Saint John. It cost about a thousand dollars, all told, to run each mail, but they kept going regular till November 15th when they got the telegraph system to Halifax. People were flabbergasted when New York papers published news in the evening that had come by boat to Halifax that morning."

We studied the plaque and tried to visualize the rider dashing up the road on a sweating horse, conscious of the time he had made, of the waiting steamer and the admiring crowd watching his arrival. It must have been an exciting John Gilpin ride and the roads of those days were pretty rough. Legend has it that once the riders came in the night as the ship docked late at Halifax and as the rider tore along above Bridgetown he felt his horse gather itself under him and make a tremendous leap. The jump almost unseated the rider and he kept wondering about it until he rode back by daylight and saw that a small bridge had washed out in a freshet and the horse had jumped the stream.

Our friend was not averse to talking as he watched the boys change the tire and soon he was telling us that he had been born no more than twenty miles from where he stood in a house so poorly built that on windy days the mats would be lifted from the floor by the gusts coming in beneath the door, and to keep him from getting cold his parents had hung his cradle from the ceiling by ropes. But he had got along all right and had learned a lot about life, including the fact that not doing was sometimes strong as doing. To illustrate what he meant, he said he had been very fond of eels but his wife had a horror of them and so during his forty years of married life he had never had a mess. Then she died and at first opportunity he got himself a fine pot of eels, and couldn't eat them.

Back we went by old Port Royal and to Granville Ferry where the old "Entertainment House," now the home of Mr. and Mrs. L. M. W. How, stands among grand old trees back of a spacious lawn, a stately old colonial house built around 1790 and having its restored rooms filled with relics of the early 1800s. It was the first licensed Inn in Nova Scotia and the original sign stands over the dining-room mantel—a slab of slate weighing sixty pounds and inscribed "Entertainment by H. and L. Hall." The old lantern which illuminated the sign at night may still be seen, made of translucent panels of horn, with three ventilators at the top, a welcome light to travellers in the old stage coach as they rattled in from the Post road to the cobblestone court before the Colonial Hostelry. The Hall brothers were the largest liquor merchants in the county, they operated the ferry to Annapolis, operated a large livery stable, and raised great herds of cattle on their large farm. The barroom of the tavern had a large opening on the east side. In the old days an officer rode his horse right into the room, ordered his drink, downed it, flung a gold coin in payment and rode out again. The prints of the horse's hoofs on the floor are still seen.

The old ledger tells the story of early days, and amazing prices. "Lodging and victuals for one night—16 cents." The hearth room is the best restored kitchen in the province, with two flues from throat to top of chimney so that a fire could be made on either side. The tongs, trammels, toasters, skillets, scoops, broilers and bellows are all there, as well as bed warmers, iron griddles, copper kettles, the brick oven, the dutch oven, the swivel pan, a huge iron pot that holds a barrel of water, a frypan with a yard-long handle, peels for taking bread out of the oven, mortar and pestle, brasses and forks for clotted cream. Pewter plates are used daily and on the walls are the works of Currier & Ives while the cupboards are filled with old glass and precious china, one collection having forty moulds for jelly. There is the wine cellar and the brass pump used in the tavern when the gentry flowed in after a horse race. An original Hall desk stands in the living-room. An old clock bears the note: "First cleaned in 1792."

It is all so interesting that one would want to live there a few days to become fully acquainted with the many items but one wonders after hearing about "grandma." She is a dear old lady with a sweet expression and lace cap and ruffles who will drift in at twilight before the lamps are lighted and seat herself in the old "Sleepy Hollow" chair. She may nod to you and give you a smile but that is all and she has never been known to appear unfriendly. But she belongs to the period one hundred and fifty years ago, was a Hall, and cannot stay away. And her presence has unnerved more than one owner to the point of selling and departing, for it troubles some to have a lady appear at your elbow and squeeze by you, leaving a trail of scent in her wake, go straight to the chair you had thought to occupy and there be seated comfortably as she smiles at you. And the dog bolts outside and you cannot speak a word to save your soul. Three different times she has calmy walked in while company was present and each time the wanted chair was most hastily vacated. But the Hows do not mind her in the least as she does not roam around in the night and always makes her appearance at the same time—first dusk.

And as if having such callers were not enough, there is the hidden treasure. Before there were banks the Halls made so much money they had to place it in some safekeeping so a mason was employed to construct a cache of some type and both Halls died without leaving any instructions about the place while the mason was drowned in the Basin. First owners after the Halls removed stones around the huge fireplace, certain the gold was there but they found nothing. A generation of Reeds occupied the home and made casual search but never uncovered the cache, and it may not be found for years to come.

We crossed over the bridge and into Annapolis and went along the main highway a few miles until we saw a sign pointing to Bear River. The off-trail road was also paved and after a delightful drive we were at the picturesque community noted for its cherry trees and Cherry Carnival held each July. The town rises from the shores of Bear River in terraces overlooking the valley and stream, and has earned for itself the title "Little Switzerland." One of Nova Scotia's first Micmac reservations was on Indian Hill at Bear River and the redmen of the place were famed as guides. The surrounding country is a network of lakes and streams, famous for its hunting and fishing, and it is natural that the young men became expert guides and in years past have won all honours at the annual Sportsmen's Shows held in New York and Boston and Hartford. Bear River became known as the home of champion log-rollers and Eber Peck, a native, was world's champion for years. He and his brother, Watson Peck, scored many victories in canoeing and tilting and other games. Henry Peters is another son of Bear River who has won fame in the Shows, and Miss Viola Paul of Bear River, is the champion woman log-roller and probably the only woman in the world making a living at log-rolling.

It was a lovely day and we loitered around the stores that stand on posts above the river and heard some wondrous tales of hunters, and of big fish taken at the Faith, Hope and Charity lakes. Old Judson was a tough guide who liked staying in the woods and as he and his wife did not agree on any more than two per cent of the topics they tackled he resolved to construct a simple habitation and stay from her company as much as possible. He selected a site in the heart of the wilderness and took in hammer and saw and axe and nails, cooking utensils and a blanket or so. In fair weather he did not want a roof over his head but could bunk down, I was told, under an alder clump with a windfall for a pillow. He also took in a crowbar to make holes for the corner posts of his cabin which he proposed driving down below frost ravage.

All went well with the building. Judson cut down trees and used them with care, got the frame up and a roof of poles. Then he had an urge to go fishing and luck went along with him. He landed more lake beauties than he could eat that day and hung the rest up in the space under his roof. It looked like showers that night so he moved under cover with his blanket and was in the land of dreams when a nudge wakened him. His nose told him that some animal of considerable bulk and careless toilet was not far off and his eyes finally made out a huge bear poised on a stringer and reaching for his string of trout. Such brazen entrance and attempt at theft was more than Judson could endure. He rose without thinking and ordered the intruder outside.

The bear dropped from the peeled lumber and made angry noises during the descent. Judson reached for his axe and did not locate it but his hands closed on the cold length of the hefty crowbar. The bear wheeled about, slightly tangled in Judson's blankets, and half-reared to attack. Judson made a mighty lunge with his weapon and chance found him a target —the bear's gullet. My informant said stories varied as to how far the bar entered the bear but most agreed it was a couple of feet for the bear had its mouth wide open, the bar was heavy and Judson was a strong man.

At any rate Judson could not withdraw the bar nor find the axe so he mounted the timbers set for a loft floor and hoped for the best. The bear was in pain and very angry. It tried desperately to dislodge the bar but could not, and the cumbersome length caught against this and that and prevented it going aloft after Judson. Time and again it tried a different route upward but the heavy bar sagged and snagged and the situation was not changed when daylight arrived. Then Judson dropped down outside and tried to leave the scene unnoticed. The bear, however, was quite alert and the chase was on. It was only a matter of yards to Judson's boat, though, and Judson won the heat, managed to push off and rowed across the lake to the home trail. He was well along the route when to his amazement he heard the persistent brute behind him. It had, somehow, been able to swim across the lake and was still full of vengeance. However the effort had been unusual even for a huge bear and by the time it had overtaken Judson the will was still strong but the flesh was weak, a fact the guide comprehended at once. So he seized the long end of the bar and after a short struggle proved the stronger, and the anguished animal was compelled to go along with him, and yet was unable to reach him. The good folk of Bear River were more than astounded to see Judson emerge from the woods leading a bear which, said the relater, was the biggest specimen of its kind ever seen in Nova Scotia. People gathered to behold the spectacle and the bear, completely exhausted, lay on its side until the preacher arrived. Judson had sent for the good man as he wanted a reliable witness if ever his feat should be questioned. Then there was debate about what should be done with the sufferer, and it was pointed out that it could not be fed while the bar remained in position. So Judson reluctantly killed the animal and it took four good men to withdraw the heavy iron.

At this point Mrs. Judson began to give her views on the matter and Judson paused, did some heavy thinking and took up the bar with an intent not difficult to discern. Mrs. Judson fled to the house and Judson followed. Just what was said will never be known but he did not return to his skeleton cabin, the crowbar always stood in a corner of the kitchen, and sweet peace reigned thereafter.

At this point I took leave of my friend and wandered into a small shop and talked with the proprietor, Mr. L. V. Harris. He told me that years ago a road to Lake Jolly was much travelled as an enterprising citizen had established a wood-works there manufacturing sashes and doors and such items as clothespins. It was nine miles into the interior and for a time knew prosperity. Then the plant was wiped out by fire and never rebuilt. I asked him how the place got its name and he brought me a small book of forty pages giving the story of the village. It was written some years ago by Lennie D. Wade, is well illustrated but now out of print. The account begins as follows:

To get our first glimpse of Bear River we must go back two hundred and ninety-five years to January 13th, 1613, when a small vessel bringing supplies to the French colonies at the head of Annapolis Basin was forced to take shelter from a severe snow storm in the lee of what is now Bear Island. When the storm had ceased the captain, Simon Imbert, discovered near them the mouth of a small river to which he returned after having delivered his cargo. This river he explored as far as the meeting of its two branches, now known as "The Head of the Tide." The first sawmill erected there bore his name, and a road nearby is still called "Imbert's Hill." As his name was pronounced "Imbare" among the Acadians, the river may have been known first as "Imbare" and later as "Bear River."

Or the name may have been from the following Indian legend:

Many years ago when the noble redmen reigned supreme as the lords of the forest three hardy braves, each with his squaw and papoose, started down from the head of the river to its mouth to engage in the catching of porpoise, then their chief means of livelihood. Arriving at a suitable point for a camp, the braves went off to their work leaving their squaws to pitch the tents and prepare the meal against their return. The squaws were busily engaged stirring the food over the fire when they saw coming toward them three big brown bears. Of course their first thought was for the papooses and they must have decided that the only way to save the babies was by giving their own lives.

In those days every Indian woman wore a tall, cone-shaped birch bark cap. So the three squaws each rushed at a big bear and as the bears stood up on their hind legs, mouths wide open, made a grand dive, cap first, down the bears' throats. Whether the bear died from sudden severe indigestion or were choked to death we do not know, but when the braves returned they found only the bodies of the three bears and those of the little papooses which had died from fright or hunger. The latter were quietly buried but the braves dragged the bears to the river and threw them in, grunting: Ugh, mooin siboo."

We drove across the bridge and up a hilly road on the left. Near the crest of the hill our way was blocked by a man on a ladder picking cherries from a tree that overhung the road. We stopped and a woman seated on the porch kindly sold us some delicious cherries and hoped we were not in a hurry. She said everyone was tolerant in Bear River and several had to put up ladders from the road to pick the fruit. There were cherry trees almost everywhere and as we gazed at the laden branches we asked if there were no losses to fruit-hungry ones strolling around in the evening. No one ever touched a cherry, she declared proudly. Finally the man came down and said it was lunch time so he shifted the ladder enough for us to get by and we drove along the road looking for a spot where we might have our picnic lunch. At length we saw where someone cutting wood had made a trail into the bush and went there with our camp stools and basket. A brook sang merrily under the trees but it was too warm for bird song. Then, as we were finishing our food, a stick snapped and we looked around to see a deer gazing at us. It tossed its head and stamped a foot as if impatient, then took off. I strolled along the way it had gone and was surprised to find four apple trees in the bush, all loaded with small apples. Then I prowled more and located an old cellar filled with bushes. Someone in the very long ago had lived there and now there was no trace of the ancient highway.

We returned to the village and asked about other roads and were directed to one leading to a small place called Acaciaville, no more than five miles distant, and in a beautiful setting. Some fine homes are there and there is a peacefulness and sense of shelter that makes one want to stay there. We drove slowly and talked with a man picking cherries, and with another who seemed to be counting cattle. They were proud of their settlement but said it had no history worth telling and we were about to leave the place when a woman carrying a basket accepted a lift. She said she was going to Smith's Cove so we took her along and soon she was talking. She was going to visit her sister, she said, who was ailing and not getting much attention as the poor dear's husband spent too much time in a tree with his telescope. We inquired if he were a bird watcher.

"Goodness, no," she exclaimed. "There's summer places at the Cove and a lot of the visitors don't wear much at the beach, and there's them that's forever sun bathing in what they think is secluded spots but my sister's man can see them from his tree and that's his diversion."

Soon she swung to other topics and told us about looking at an old bed spring discarded and thrown back of the barn, and finding a snake skin in it nearly three feet long. She had a horror of snakes, she said, no matter if they were harmless, and so had a hired man take the spring back in the woods. But he carried it to a stony hollow and threw it there and the next time she saw it there were three snake skins in it.

"I was a school teacher," she went on, "and when I started at Deep Brook I found the youngsters playing with snakes at recess, green grass snakes. I tried to get them playing ball and then one morning when I opened my desk to get the register a snake crawled out and dropped in my lap. I dropped in a faint and when I recovered after a pail of water was splashed in my face by the oldest girl a hot argument was going on. Two girls were accusing a boy of placing the snake in my desk and he was denying it. One girl turned to me and declared she had seen him with it before school took in. Whereupon the lad, thoroughly detesting her, reached into a trouser pocket and produced his own snake, his treasured pet, while the one in the desk was still squirming under seats at the back of the room. My nerves were so frayed before snow came and saved me from snakes that I always had a boy open my desk each morning, noon and recess."

We thanked her for the entertainment and drove back to Annapolis Royal to spend the night at the Queen Hotel of high ceilings and big halls, a mansion in the old days with a stuffed moose on the lawn, and now one of the most comfortable places for an overnight stay that we know in the Valley. Mr. and Mrs. Crosby, the proprietors, treat you as one of the family, and the food is wonderful. But write ahead for reservations if you want to stop there as a great many motorists have come to know the hotel and head for there as if it were home.

A couple from Vermont were at our table at dinner and asked what there was to see as they continued on Highway 1. We told them, and then related our finds at Bear River and at Victoria Beach, told them about Port Royal only twenty minutes away by car, talked about the little shore villages along the Fundy shore and the queer little jack-knife turns on the shore roads. Soon they had a map out and were making notes.

"We love the salt water," they said, "and we saw it at Windsor but we're going to find your Noel Shore and watch that tide come in two miles. That's the sort of thing we want, and we can hardly wait till morning to get over to Bear River and have a treat of those cherries. We stopped at Uniacke House on the way, and at Haliburton House at Windsor, and we were to Grand Pre Park, and thought we were seeing everything. It's the out-of-the-way places we want to explore and we're tired of crowds and honking horns and the smell of gas and hot tires. I wonder if we could stay a week at that little hotel at Victoria Beach."

We hope they did and if they did we know they will be back. Three different American couples found it a few summers ago and all three bought lots and now have summer homes at that ledge-like village above the water where the trail ends.

4

"By the Great Long Lake We Found Them"

IN the morning we started from Annapolis Royal on a twisting, up-and-down secondary road that was rough enough in spots and found ourselves entering wooded country with only occasional homes and clearings. A raven gave us discordant greeting and three crows rose from the mangled remains of an aged porcupine that had died in a traffic accident. Blue jays screamed in the bushes and we wondered if they really knew when there was to be an electric storm. The veteran at Bear River had told us we could judge the weather by their clamour. It was nine o'clock but as we came to a clearing we saw a man in overalls and bright-checked shirt milking a cow at a fence corner. A squirrel sat on the fence and made running comment on the proceedings.

We stopped to get a snapshot but the squirrel flicked its tail and leaped into a hemlock. "No use trying to get him," offered the milker. "He comes out here near every morning and when he gets close enough I give him a shot of milk. He's always ready to dodge and it's a kind of game we have."

"That must be a gentle cow to stand without tying while you milk her?" I offered.

"She sure is, mister. I call her 'Elsie' and I think she understands me better'n my wife does. I generally talk to her when I want to get a load off my mind and she just chews her cud and nods." He got up from his stool, hung it on

101

the fence and told Elsie she was free to go where she willed. Then he set the pail down, leaned on the fence and drew a creased and rather soiled clipping from his pocket. "I cut this here from a paper," he said, "and now I can near recite it." He cleared his throat and started and I watched the paper and he did not miss a sentence from start to finish. This is his "piece":

The cow is a female quadruped with an alto voice and a countenance in which there is no guile. She collaborates with the pump in the production of a liquid called milk, provides the filler for hash, and at last is skinned by those she has benefitted, as mortals commonly are. The young cow is called a calf and is used in the manufacture of chicken salad. The cow's tail is hard and has a universal joint. It is used to disturb marauding flies, and the tassel on the end has a unique educational value. Persons who milk cows and encounter the tassel have a vocabulary of peculiar force. The cow has two stomachs. The one on the ground floor is used as a warehouse and has no other function. When the one is filled the cow retires to a quiet place where her ill manners will occasion no comment and devotes herself to belching. The raw material thus conveyed for the second time to the interior of her face is pulverized and delivered to the auxiliary stomach. Then it is converted into cow. The cow has no upper plate. All her front teeth are parked on the lower part of her face. The arrangement was perfected by an efficiency expert to keep her from gumming things up. As a result she bites up and gums down. The male cow is called a bull and is lassoed in Alberta, fought in Mexico and shot in Ottawa. A slice of cow worth eight cents in the cow costs fourteen cents in the hands of the packer and two dollars and forty cents at the nearest restaurant.

Our friend was draped on the fence as if time had lost meaning for him but we gently started our car and left him to his meditations and soon rolled down a grade and found we were at South Milford. A horseshoe approach led to the great wide verandah of Milford House, which has a spacious dining-room, lounge and nine bedrooms, and out along the shores of Home Lake were thirty or more cabins, each with its own canoe dock and large living room with fireplace. We strolled around and liked what we saw. There are no frills. Each guest goes to the Lodge for meals but is on his or her own otherwise. Canoes take them fishing and on camera shooting expeditions. Charles W. Morton, associate editor of *Atlantic Monthly,* stayed at Milford House and afterward mentioned it in his column "Accent on Living." He wrote:

I happened last summer on a totally different kind of resort, a terrific run for the money and at just about negligible prices. It was Nova Scotian, an old-fashioned hotel with cabins on the edge of a wilderness on a chain of lakes. The trout fishing was as good as Florida's game fishing; there was only one tennis court but it was impeccably maintained; and in every respect the Canadian retreat made good on its commitments. I mention all this not because the Canadian place was so inexpensive, but because of the wisdom, the ingenuity, and the common sense which made it that way. It was in the hands of the third generation of its proprietors; and to open up a new place with all these qualities in full force might be impossible . . . There were three reasons for the low rates: no food was wasted, no payroll went for nonessential services, and temptations to "modernize" (and thereby spoil) the property were opposed by guests and management alike.

A guest chatted with us and said he had gone by canoe ten miles from his cabin and had shot a roll of film that he hoped would win him a prize back home. He said a young fellow interested in birds had stayed at the House a few days and had counted more than one hundred specimens such as myrtle warblers, cedar waxwings, alder flycatchers, red-eyed vireos and golden-crowned kinglets.

There was a long stretch of empty road and then we were at Maitland Bridge, a scattered little community where women were working in gardens and few men were in sight. Then we saw a sign pointing to a lesser road on the right leading to Ked-ge. We drove into the forest primeval and wondered what we would do if we met another car, then suddenly were at a clearing where six cars were parked side by side and a lake shimmered into the distance. Not a sign of life was around except a blue jay that inspected us slyly from a spruce top. We got out and saw a wooden box attached to a post. A telephone was inside and printed instructions said to give three twirls of the handle and the Lodge would answer. We tried the trick and were told that a motor launch would be at the Landing in a short time.

When it came we put our bags on the boat and were happy that the man who came for us was a guide. He slowed his speed and we coasted in near a shore where beavers were at work. One big fellow was getting mud with which to patch his dam and he waddled along on his hind feet, holding the mud against his chest, balanced by his tail. He was so droll that we sat and watched for some time and neither he nor his busy wife paid us the slightest attention. The guide said that usually the beavers only worked after dusk but had become indifferent to visitors and, very likely, had established a new forty-four hour week.

We landed at a small wharf and saw paths leading to the main dining-hall and to various cottages. We were soon at home in one and a squirrel promptly appeared on the door-step. "This is his cottage," said the guide. "Each cottage is owned by a squirrel that is on the watch for candy and nuts and if you are kind to them they will eat out of your hand. But you'll hear fighting for they get in a rage if one happens to step over the line into another's territory."

Ked-ge puts a spell over you before the first hour has ended. There is the sheer beauty of the place, the lake like a mirror, the trees, the birds, and the forest stillness. You are away from everything and so cunningly are the cottages situated that each one is quite apart yet within easy reach. Ked-ge is nine miles long and four miles wide, contains more than two hundred islands, has four rivers to maintain its water level, and the actual domain of the Lodge comprises more than three hundred acres of a peninsula thrust into the lake. We went out with our guide after lunch and learned that we were in the very heart of the ancient Micmac country, the most storied region in Nova Scotia, near the scene of the great battle with the Mohawks.

Malti Lou was Micmac chief when there came an exhausted runner to the camp to report that fifty Mohawks were coming by way of Lake Rossignol wearing red and black war paint. The only thing to do, said Malti Lou, was to send the women and children by a back route to a hiding place while the braves led a false trail that would lead to the fort where the soldiers would assist them. The Micmac chief was a great boaster but a coward at heart. Young Jim Charles heard him with scorn and declared he would not run but would go to meet the Mohawks and keep them from sacred Micmac territory. Only eleven of the braves had heart enough to join him in his mad venture and one was Jim's cousin, Steve, a very strong and brave Indian. They started quickly and found the Mohawks at dark on the banks of Eel Weir, in brush camps with no guard set, so great was the Mohawk contempt for the Micmacs. Jim placed nine of his warriors with muskets primed and ready a short distance from the centre of the camps while he and Steve crept in with knives to attack those in the first shelter.

They got in noiselessly and killed several as they slept then Steve stepped on a dry stick and the others awoke. One fired blindly and shot Steve through the heart but Jim brained two with his tomahawk and escaped as the other Micmacs poured musket fire into the Mohawks who jumped from their shelters to learn what was happening. When the muskets were emptied the Micmacs did not reload but unslung their bows and sent volleys of flint-tipped arrows into the enemy, and the Mohawks fearful of unseen numbers, fled across the river. In the morning twenty other Micmacs who had repented their decision joined Jim, and were accompanied by two white trappers who were friends of the Indians. They crossed the river a distance from the camp and got around far enough to attack the Mohawks from the rear, killing more than half of them and completely routing the rest. Jim killed the Mohawk chief and hung his scalp from his wigwam pole. Three days later the tribe made Jim their chief and he married a pretty girl of the camp.

Some time later a white man came to the Micmacs to sell them rum. Jim ordered him away and during the quarrel the white man struck him. That was insult and Jim killed him as he would a wolf, was outlawed and had a price set on his head. Several tried to collect the money and were always outwitted, then one of the white men who had helped against the Mohawks got him pardoned and Jim outlived three wives. In his later days he discovered gold in his hunting area, told no one of the spot and took out a backload in a caribou skin. With the proceeds he purchased a horse and buggy, a silk hat, long coat, three watches, six clocks and all sorts of finery for his wife, Molly, who had been the waif of a logger and still loved and talked too much. Jim loved to smoke his pipe in his house and hear all six clocks striking the hour. A white man visited the spot and was a guest of the chief until it was found that he was making love with the chief's daughter. As a punishment, and to warn any future visitors, the chief had the white man's heel tendons cut and made him virtually a prisoner in a rude camp constructed at Slapfoot Beach. Here the poor fellow spent the rest of his years slapping up and down the beach with his feet out of control, living on fish and scraps the redmen allowed him.

The guide told us that the Slapfoot Trail had been worn so deeply by moccasined feet we would have no trouble following it the four miles along the shore of the lake and through some of the forest. So off we went watching for stakes that mark the route. The first was at Bull Cove, so named because bull moose went there to drink and to battle in the autumn. We found it taken over by a family of beavers who were busy getting a food supply. The next stake was at Honeymoon Cove, a beautiful spot where the Micmacs had a wigwam for honeymooners. A main attraction was a number of sun turtles in many sizes sitting on derelict logs, languid and careless in the warmth. Another stake was at Slapfoot Point where heavy grass and weeds cover the site of the unfortunate white man's lodge. Another stake marked Old Meadow Road, a haunt of deer and bear. Sure enough, as we walked quietly through a tunnel-like passage under the trees we saw a doe and fawn sauntering across a glade as if they had no thought of danger. Stake 7 was beside the river and we saw a grand spot for trout as well as many deer trails showing where the animals came to drink. Then we were at Mother Cary's Orchard Indian Burying Grounds, and we learned later that the district was used as a burying ground for centuries, that the Micmacs told first white settlers fearsome stories of pixies and mysterious beings that ruled the region, so it was named Fairy Lake. The stories were told to keep the white men away. Stake 11 was at the Indians Fern Garden. Ferns stood thickly three feet and more in height in masses and we were told that the redmen used them for many purposes.

We got back to our cottage and had a refreshing bath. It's a sort of Ripley believe-it-or-not to find bathrooms and electricity in that remote forest stillness. Then something tapped at the door. My wife, Ethel, exclaimed in delight and I looked to see a beautiful speckled fawn peering in. It retreated as Ethel went out but she followed it up the path and a cook came from the kitchen and said the animal was probably looking for milk as it had been pampered a few times. So Ethel took a bottle and soon was holding it while the fawn drank earnestly and I got a fine snapshot of the performance. As evening came on the moon was a great yellow lamp among the trees, rising slowly, and then loons began their weird calls. Long after dinner we sat on the cottage verandah listening to the loons and then I heard a faint chanting in odd melody. A woman came along the path from another cottage and I asked her if she heard the music, if someone near us had a radio.

She came up our path. "Don't ask about it," she said quietly. "Some evenings it's so lovely I can hardly bear it, but if you mention it no one will believe you. And no one has a radio on."

She talked long enough for me to realize she thought the music we heard was a ghostly melody, the chantings of some tribe of centuries before, so I said "How long have you been here?" "Since the Lodge opened this spring," she said. "Your first trip?" "I've been coming here seventeen years," she said. "I work the rest of the year so I can vacation here. There's nothing like it anywhere else in this world."

In the morning the guide took us by boat to inspect Indian pictographs on smooth ledges of rock slightly above water level. I was amazed to find they extended over a radius of seven miles, and were from two inches to over two feet in size. First settlers told about the drawings made with sharp pieces of quartz or beaver teeth and many persons came to view them. The October issue of *Dominion Illustrated* of 1888 had an article dealing with them. A party worked five weeks at the Lake and made four copies of each drawing, divided into groups such as religious drawings, hunting, fishing, ships, etc. The Micmac missionary, Rev. Silas Rand, interested the Smithsonian Institute in the field, and many parties have come during the past eighty years to trace and copy the symbolic and ornamental and decorative drawings of ships and canoes and reptiles and birds and animals and humans, in the fabulous, in war scenes and hunting trails. The artistry is now under water to some extent but enough remains to prove the Micmacs had seen Norse ships in the 11th century.

After we had pondered for hours over the drawings the guide took us to a grove where a tall stone shaft stood under the trees and there were innumerable mounds in all directions. The inscription on the stone said: "Respect the Bones of Micmacs Buried Here—Who Knew These Woods and Waters Long Ago." How many graves were there? No one knows, said the guide, hundreds at least, maybe more. Did anyone ever uncover any to find weapons, etc? "A few tried it," said the guide, "but broken legs, unexplained accidents with shovels and boats, soon stopped them. No one ever got below the sod and there hasn't been anyone tried it in thirty years."

We left Ked-ge reluctantly with the fawn watching us wistfully, our squirrel scolding and the beaver working hard as ever by his dam. When we were back in the car on the gravel road and passing through a small settlement, Kempt, we looked at each other and asked if we had been dreaming or had Ked-ge been real. For it is surely something most unusual.

A car roared toward us, braked and came to a halt, a beautiful two-toned affair, bright as a fire truck. The licence was New Jersey.

"Say," asked the driver in silk shirt and distress. "How much further before we get on the road again? Or are we getting lost?"

We explained the situation and mentioned where we had been, the grand food and the quiet. The driver's sparring mate looked away from her lipstick mirror. "Has it got TV?" she whined. "Ain't there any shows anywhere?"

"Just on the road," I said, and drove off.

Then we were driving into Caledonia, and on paved highway. It is a scenic community and we were told it was settled in 1820 by six hardy Scots who built one large log dwelling and shared it the first year. There is hunting and fishing country in any direction, lakes of all sizes, and this small place had a newspaper for years, the *Caledonia Gold Hunter*. We stopped at a store and asked questions.

"Take that road up past the school and see Elton Smith," we were advised. "Or take the road into the Game Sanctuary, Tobeatic Park. You can get a guide easily and travel by canoe and you'll see more wild life than in a night club."

We decided in favour of Smith and found his three hundred-acre farm, an original grant to his great grandfather, Nathanial Smith, and Elton has his family tree beyond the seventeenth century via Massachusetts and a town in Norfolkshire, England. Records in Hingham, Mass., show the Smiths were there in 1633 and that they originated from Hingham, Norfolkshire. A Samuel Smith, one of the ancestors, married the daughter of Giles Hopkins, who came over on the *Mayflower*.

Don't go to visit Elton if you want to admire animals for he hasn't any. The only thing around is a kitten strayed over from a neighbour's. And it is likely that if Elton were younger he would want something from the woods rather than a steer or sheep for he was a registered guide for many years and one of the best. When the Nova Scotia Government had a booth each year at the Sportsmen's Shows in Boston and Hartford and New York, Elton was always engaged to go along and give information to prospective visitors about everything from trout fishing to bear hunting. So it is natural enough that there are deer heads and mounted eagles and owls and other birds among his household treasures of china and antique furniture. There is a sea chest, a sextant, old muzzle-loading weapons and a Spanish cutlass. Also an old pair of ship's handcuffs that are not opened by a key but by a lefthand-threaded bolt that has to be unscrewed, having as a safety feature a plug with a righthand thread that covers the end of the bolt. The original grant which Elton Smith owns records that the mineral rights are reserved but the holders of the property are awarded all fish, game, woods, timber, ponds, lakes, hunting, hawking, fowling and fishing. Only a bevy of lawyers could decide whether or not Smith can fish in his own lake at any time he fancies.

If you like stories of the woods with real flavour visit with Elton for over the years he has seen about everything in wild life, though I had a good yarn from a surveyor whom we met on our journey through the settlements of South Brookfield, North Brookfield, Colpton and Hemford, pleasant small settlements where life is peaceful and everyone is friendly. We had lunch on a school ground from our picnic box and a prompt visit from two lads and a dog. Then the surveyor came along to see that they were not bothering us and we had a fine chat. He was working over in a Digby county area a warm summer and hired a fat youth named Freddy as an assistant. Freddy had not been in the woods very much and he took with him an old army pistol which he carried in a holster like Buffalo Bill. They built a small pole structure for a camp and boiled their kettle over a small stone fireplace. Each meal time Freddy lent no assistance but posed with the revolver, whirling about to make snap shots at imaginary redskins. They finished the job on the third day and as it was very hot Freddy lay on the bunk in the shelter while the surveyor went to a spring for water. While getting it he heard strange noises and then saw a rusty old black bear go crashing through the bush as if blind, grunting and moaning. He tried to get back in time to warn Freddy but the bear blundered directly toward the pole shelter and he heard Freddy shout: "What in blazes are you trying to do? Scare me?"

The bear drove right into the flimsy shelter and Freddy began shooting at sight of his intruder. One bullet smashed the teapot by the fireplace. Another clipped off a branch close to the surveyor's head. A third scattered the cooking fire. The last two shots came as the bear crashed through the poles and the roof fell in. But one lucky bullet penetrated the bear's skull and it sprawled dead with its head just protruding from the wreckage while Freddy, in a dead faint, had only his shoes on the outside. The surveyor rescued him, used the spring water and revived him. "Unfortunately," said our man, "I had drug him so he was just inches from that bear's head as he opened his eyes and he up and went through the bush like a deer. It was near an hour before I could holler him back. And there was a lump bigger'n my fist on that bear's jaw, an abscess or something that had made the brute blind crazy with pain."

We gave the boys a lift up the road in our car and at one farm the mother was looking for them. We explained our errand and she said we should not omit mention of the Brookfield poet, John McPherson, and she brought from the house a *Dalhousie Review* carrying an article about the Nova Scotian. It stated:

John McPherson was born in Liverpool, N.S., on February 4, 1817, and died at Brookfield on July 26, 1845. His whole life, short as it was, was spent in Queen's County, except for a few months in Halifax and a voyage to the West Indies. His education was restricted to the common schools of the day, when, according to a contemporary report, "there was not only a great deficiency of books but those used were nearly as varied as the children's garments," and to private reading of such books as rural Nova Scotia afforded and such newspapers as penetrated into his community.

McPherson taught school a time at Kempt, the article said, and we copied two samples of his work in our note book. One is from "Wild Flowers":

> But one, our Country's Emblem dear,
>   The lovely flower of May,
> Springs in the wild our hearts to cheer
>   While vernal suns delay!
>
> It breathes of some untroubled scene—
>   Some land divinely fair;
> Of skies ineffably serene—
>   Of pure immortal air!

Another is:

> No happy home—no gentle wife—
>   No household band have I;
> The tender ministries of life
>   My cruel stars deny.
> Like some lone bird whose wearied wing
>   Droops o'er a shoreless sea,
> I cannot lift my voice and sing
>   As if my soul were free.

We thanked the lady for her information and drove on into New Germany, named in 1785 by German settlers who had first located at La Have. It is said that one of these carried a bushel and a half of potatoes all the way from Bridgewater and this was all the seed the settlers had the first spring. A delightful village with neat homes and pretty flowers and hairpin turns and vistas of the river that are enchanting. Visitors who miss this area miss the flavour and feel of inland Nova Scotia and the drive from New Germany toward Highway 3 is interesting all the way. A bystander told us about Lake William and the Guides Meet that were a feature there, and pointed out the way via Barss' Corner only three miles distant. A few years ago people went by the hundred to Lake William to watch the annual guide contests. There was log-rolling, a feature at meets in Lunenburg county, wood-chopping contests, canoe-tilting, canoe-racing, with cooking contests and, at night when the camp fires were aglow, the telling of tall tales. At one time, too, the provincial government had a small zoo at the Lake. A sportsman pointed out the features of the lake shore and told us of Sherbrooke Lake not far off, where gray trout, or togue, were taken but we had no desire to go fishing.

There seemed to be excellent fishing waters all along the route as we drove through Pinehurst and Northfield toward Bridgewater on excellent paved highway that had very little traffic. Then an oldtimer sent us over a dirt road toward Molega Lake, which looked ideal for a guides' tournament, and on to Greenfield. This has long been a headquarters for salmon anglers who love the Medway River and there are many fine pools to explore, and capable guides ready to hire with any visitor. A man in a red, yellow and black-checked shirt soon was telling us about Laurie Wamboldt, a native of Greenfield who regularly tours the sportsmen's shows in the United States, has been doing so for twenty years. Laurie, our friend said, tried to take in about twelve meets during the short winter season. Laurie not only is an expert who gets big money from the shows but all his family are tops at log-rolling including Mrs. Laurie, young Billy and his sisters Janet and Elizabeth. Principal competitors who compete against the Nova Scotians come from Maine, Quebec and Wisconsin. Janet is seventeen and Elizabeth eighteen but a year ago they flew to Spokane, Washington to compete in the Rolleo Championship, where Elizabeth placed second in the women's finals and the two sisters placed second, as a team, in the trick and fancy division. This was their first experience with major competition and they were greatly encouraged by their success against veterans of many tournaments. Log-birling or rolling, canoe-tilting, tub-racing, log-sawing and chopping, fly-casting and demonstrations in canoe-handling are features the crowds like to witness at the shows and Laurie is good in any such contest. The water events are staged in tanks ninety feet long and Laurie and his wife have starred in shows at Montreal, Houston, Toronto, Los Angeles, Boston, Cleveland, etc.

"I reckon," said our informant, "that we chaps who live here see better shows when the locals are practising than them crowds do at the cities. There's generally some visitors among the lookers-on and our folks just love to please them." So if luck is with you look around when you visit Greenfield or Molega Lake and perhaps you'll witness something that would be high-class in Hartford or Boston.

We wanted to get back to New Germany and continue northward so an obliging fellow directed us and we were well along a dirt road when the sky fell in. There was a burst of thunder that fairly rattled the steering wheel and down came a deluge on the hard sun-baked earth that simply boiled into small streams and in no time there was a wind that sleeted the rain against the windshield with such force that the wiper could scarcely clear it. We drove blindly, nervous because the road was narrow and in many places we could not have got past another vehicle, and came to a small cross-roads where a man in an old red truck sat waiting. It took us a moment to realize he had known we were coming and had waited there. He lowered a window, had to close it again hastily as rain flooded in, then made signs for us to wait, backed up, came around the other side against the wind, and once more opened the window. He asked where we wanted to go and we told him as thunder crashed and lightning flashed and rain pelted at us in dipperfuls. He roared directions and was gone, his tire ruts small rivers in a twinkling.

Slowly we veered to the right crossroad, and entered a tunnel-like space with trees almost closed overhead and the mud getting slippery. Bigger trees grew close to the road

A few years back Mr. Young felt the public would be interested in viewing the caves and knowing the story so he created the park. Paths lead to the highlights of the place, one of which is Tucker's Tunnel. A stairway of concrete helps the visitor to view the dark chasm. At Indian's Cave a strong platform has been constructed part way down and a wonderful view is obtained. We were thrilled to see a crevice in the far wall almost hidden by the spray in which a seabird was nesting, quite indifferent to the uproar of the Ovens or the presence of the spectators. A path leads to "The Chapel." It is a clearing among the spruce trees and a cross of white birch stands before rows of hand-hewn benches. Seven or eight people were seated there and seemed lost in reverent meditation. As we went back we noticed a large post with small signs and saw that if one stopped and gazed through a small opening a face was outlined on the rocky crags far to our left. Another opening gave a different view to the right and visitors were having a gala time showing others the unique views.

We saw a trailer on the grounds and people were nearby so we went over and found that an artist, L. Scott Croft, had a number of his paintings displayed along the bank. Mr. Croft is a victim of rheumatoid arthritis, but courage and perseverance have enabled him to develop his talent and he makes his home in the trailer during the summer. He had worked in mines and in an aircraft factory before he began to take art seriously after a second trip to Vancouver. He was encouraged to join the Canadian Art Club and so made contact with a Czechoslovakian artist and critic who insisted that if Mr. Croft kept at his work he would become a leading Canadian artist. But the disease began to attack him and New York doctors told him he would never walk again. A long time was spent in hospital and painting had to be abandoned but Mr. Croft did wood carving that brought high praise. However he recovered sufficiently to get back to his beloved brushes and soon was doing marine scenes and landscapes that found ready buyers. He told us his aim was to spend the winter in Florida, and to return to the Ovens with an even better stock of paintings to sell to visitors. We watched him sell four marine scenes to American buyers and as he got around stiffly and carried on cheerful conversation we saw what an excellent example he presents of what courage and determination can accomplish. We hope that many will travel to the Ovens next year and purchase paintings from Mr. Croft. He had sold eighty-six when we saw him.

We went back to the road and soon were in Riverport, pretty with water views and trim homes and flowers. A large wooden building houses F. F. Creaser & Co. who turn out waterproof clothing and overalls and pants and shirts. The windows overlook amazing seascapes and we wandered in on the first floor and said that if one must work in a factory then it is surely a delight to be in one offering such beautiful views from every window. The scenery is helpful, of course, but there is a family spirit as well that makes for good relations. There is no union and no strikes have taken place and everyone is friendly. Sixty per cent of those employed are women and the company has fine apartments for those who do not reside in Riverport.

We rolled on in the sunshine and saw Kraut Point and the fish plant, drove along a road and saw a turn-off to the ferry, went in a small building and pressed a button which blew a loud horn. Soon we saw the ferry casting off from the far shore and a man and boy greeted us pleasantly, took us on board the small craft and wafted us across the La Have River to La Have and a paved road. We drove to the point and knew we were on historic ground for the district about the mouth of the La Have was the first land reached by De Monts in 1604 and was called by him "Cape de la Have." A cairn marks the site of the original village and its tablet bears the following inscription:

LA HAVE. Following the Treaty of St. Germain-en-Laye in 1632, France determined to establish permanent settlements in Acadia. Isaac de Razilly was appointed Lieutenant-General. Here he built a fort and established the capital of the colony.

A landing was made at this point in 1607 by Marc L'Escarbot on his way from Port Royal to Canso, and in 1613 de Saussave planted a cross at La Have bearing the arms of his patroness, the Marquise de Guercheville. This was at the mouth of the river. In 1632 Isaac de Razilly fixed his residence at La Have and built a fort. The Capuchins, a branch of the Franciscan Order, sent six members from Paris with de Razilly to establish a seminary in Acadia. Before the end of the year they had erected two buildings and their records state: "We are inhabiting two houses or hospices." This was the first school founded in Canada, and was afterward moved to Port Royal. By 1634 de Razilly had a settlement of forty families. He died in 1636 and the man who took over uprooted the colony and moved it to Port Royal. But the man eventually was drowned in the Annapolis River and in 1651 La Have was again settled and under the rule of La Tour. Le Borgne, a creditor of the man who died, obtained in 1654 an order from France to take the lands of the deceased and a party of his men on their way from Cape Breton to Port Royal by his direction set fire to all the buildings at La Have including the chapel. The property destroyed was valued at one hundred thousand francs, but the helpless settlers could do nothing about it.

Then the British conquered Port Royal and La Have reverted to them. A son of Le Borgne had come to Nova Scotia with a merchant named Guilbaut and the pair erected a wooden fort at La Have. News of this reached Port Royal and an English force went to dislodge them. Le Borgne fled to the woods but his partner fought bravely for some time before surrendering, and the British officer commanding was killed. In 1657 Le Borgne was appointed Governor of Acadia by the King of France and the next year he was taken prisoner by the British and sent to London. In 1670 M. Perrot was governor of Montreal and got to know about La Have so in 1684 he asked that it be granted to him with all rights of fishing, trading and hunting. He asked for fifty soldiers as a garrison, a corvette of ten guns, a coast pilot and a missionary;

also tools to rebuild the fort, cannon, twelve barrels of tar and three hundred blocks and pulleys. He also asked permission to "collect vagrants and compel them to settle in the country." Nothing came of this request and in 1690 a scoundrel who was ousted from Port Royal came to La Have and vilely treated a settler and his family, and was sent to France for punishment. In 1701 the Governor of Nova Scotia decided a fort should be built at La Have, and though he received no encouragement he made the request a second time, urging "the building of a fort at La Have, for which he was very anxious, as pirates were ruining the people on the coast. He also planned the establishment of a look-out party, to hail passing ships in the spring, and get him news from La Belle, France."

As no move was made about a fort he had to play along with the pirates, then quite numerous on the Atlantic coast, and succeeded in getting them to prey upon New England trading vessels. They made La Have their depot, and the money and merchandise they brought in helped the governor pay the Indians for attacking the English by land. In 1702 a store-ship was taken at La Have, but real trouble came in 1705 when a privateer from Boston "burned the dwellings, and almost the inhabitants, who had begun to settle La Have."

When Subercase became Governor of Acadia he proposed La Have, in 1708, as the chief port and place for building vessels, saying the people were "excellent workmen with axe and adze, and only wanted a few master shipwrights and caulkers" to superintend them. He urged a fort be built and a man-of-war of fifty guns be stationed there to cruise the coast. She would make a million yearly in prizes. He added, in his plea, that the people of Boston had a project to seize La Have and make a station there. After Acadia fell to the British in 1710 the leading French officials who knew the country said it could be taken and held with strong posts at La Have and Chedabucto. In 1720 Paul Mascarene, so long a governor of Nova Scotia, stated that La Have was conveniently situated for the chief seat of the government, and that same year Governor Phillips wrote: "My voyage has fully confirmed me that this

CANNING

KING SEAMAN HOUSE AT MINUDIE

MAITLAND

NEW GERMANY

NEW ROSS

KENNETCOOK

The Look-off, Blomidon

Looking West toward Cape Spencer from near Ward's Brook

Grand Pré Park

PALMETER'S GIFT SHOP, NEAR KENTVILLE

MARGARETSVILLE

Victoria Beach

CANOE TILTING AT BEAR RIVER CHERRY CARNIVAL

KED-GE

Marble Mountain

Sandy Cove

Treasure Pit on Island off Shad Bay

PEGGY'S COVE

TERENCE BAY

HACKETT'S COVE

INDIAN HARBOUR

HACKETT'S COVE

EAGLE HEAD

NORTHWEST COVE

LAKE AINSLIE

CANSO CAUSEWAY—THE ROAD TO THE ISLES

LOUISBOURG

country will never be of consequence in trade until the seat of government be removed to the eastern coast either at Port Roseway or La Have." In 1753 an Indian chief appeared at Halifax to make peace and styled himself the governor of La Have. An account sent to Paris by Charlebois gives an idea of the fertility of the first land cleared. He wrote:

Near the harbour of La Have one single grain of wheat produced one hundred and fifty ears of corn, each of them so loaded with grain that they were forced to enclose all the ears in a ring of iron and support them by a pole; and near the same place there was a field of wheat where every grain of the seed, even the least, put forth eight stalks, every one of which had an ear at least half a foot long.

There were Acadians at La Have many, many years. They endured all sorts of hardships, molested by pirates and raiders, devastated by New Englanders, burned out, driven out, starved out, yet always some of them returned or hung on, hiding in the forest with the Indians until the enemies had gone, returning to rebuild and reseed. There were fish in plenty in the sea and in the streams, the earth was fertile and the land could be fair. They loved and held to it with a passion almost pagan. But in the end the British from New England cleared them out by the roots and took over their holdings, and soon other voices were heard, those of the Hanoverians, as they established homes and held to their possessions.

We drove on to Dublin Shore and saw a miniature corvette and gun on a lawn. West Dublin is very pretty, with the appealing sort of shore beauty that looks so well on a postcard. We remembered that the Rev. James Monro had travelled where we were back in 1795, and looked up what he had to say about the area:

New Dublin is so called from Dublin in Ireland. This township was settled in general by the Irish in about the year 1762, but, these leaving by degrees, it came to be settled by the Germans. There was a town designed and lots laid out on the south side of the river. But as people left these lots the design was dropped. Though there is a good harbour where vessels of considerable burden might lie at anchor with great safety. This township extends from River La Have to Port Medway from north east to south east which is about sixteen miles. The grain seems not to grow so long or high as I have seen it other places and the bread is darker but well tasted. The mildew hurts the wheat but when they sow it with barley it is safe, and so they grind them together for bread. Oats grow well and they have excellent potatoes. Cabbage grows well. The fish are salmon, gaspereaux, cod, mackerel and dogfish. The eels are taken in great plenty on the flats. The dogfish comes about the middle of August and runs about two months and are excellent for oil but the fish is of no use unless for dung to the land or to give to their pigs. It will take about six hundred of them to make a barrel of oil. The inhabitants have got good dwelling houses and those of them that are industrious and saving live comfortably. They have got no glebe, no place of worship, no minister of any religious persuasion nor have they school lot or public burying ground.

We drove around Green Bay, a wide beach popular with summer folk, and saw about sixty cottages along the shore. Then went to Mrs. Arenburg's at Petite Rivière to have lunch. Everyone knows of this good lady and her table and it was doubtful at first that we could get served as many were there before us. However our luck was in and presently we were with the rest. We had a chat with Captain Arenburg who followed the sea for years and thinks the old days of sail were just about right. After lunch we roamed about the village and talked with many around the stores and garage. Soon we were hearing some tall yarns of old days when privateers roamed the coves and raided when they wished. At one point a Boston boat landed at dawn and the men advanced on the nearest farmhouse. The watch dog gave warning but one of the men shot it and then the farmer was told to hand over his money and they took his clock and silver and much of his bedding. All the while the good wife had to work fast as there were eleven men and they wanted a real good breakfast. No porridge or slops, they shouted, but good meat and plenty of it. There was no hope of help so the farmer had to look on helplessly as the invaders took anything they fancied. But at last breakfast was ready and the intruders ate heartily, taking so long over their endless plates of stew that at last a Nova Scotia privateer hove in sight, spied the stranger and sped in, catching him at such disadvantage that the men from Boston had to surrender. The joyful farmer got his possessions back and then his glee knew no end as several of the raiders began to be sick. They thought it was from over-eating, as they had had no supper the previous day, but the farmer shouted otherwise. His smart wife had skinned and cooked and served the dog, "and that old feller was sick all day yesterday with worms."

Then we heard of the sisters along the shore who were careful and thrifty ladies. One married and moved to the States where her husband was successful for some years. The other stayed on the farm. Both were good with the needle, to knit or sew or embroider. Times became tough for the pair in the States and they returned to the community, then moved into Lunenburg. Along came World War II, and everything became hard to get, much food was rationed. Ever anxious to make a spare dollar, the farm sister decided to ravel an old afghan and knit it into socks which she might sell in town, wool being scarce. Then she thought of her sister being rationed and went there to sell a pound or so of butter they could spare. The sister saw the pair of socks that were for sale and immediately bought them, then asked for more. Mystified, the sister promised more and when another pair were ready she brought them along. But the sister was not satisfied. She wanted more so all the afghan was made into socks and when there was an odd one left over it, too, was purchased. Then came Christmas and a large Christmas gift arrived at the farm. "You were so good to us about the butter," said the note, "that when I saw those socks I knew just what I would do for you. I made you a lovely afghan for a Christmas gift and do hope you enjoy it."

At last we had to leave those genial folk and wend our way by Broad Cove, which seemed indifferent. Cherry Hill was pretty and could be reached by three roads and then we were

at Vogler's Cove and at the store talked with some men who
had reached the time to take life easy. One told of sailing a
fine fast boat to the Cove. It was a racing craft that had been
built for some sport at Halifax and was being taken up-shore
for some fitting. Up came a brisk breeze and the lone man on
board found it impossible to handle the sail as quickly as
needed. A great gust caught the boat fairly and over she went.
The water was deep at that spot with a strong tide running,
and the man had barely time to seize a rope and hang on
before he was under water. The current carried the mast back
strongly and its tip just touched bottom, then lurched free and
swung upward and reared high as the great roll finished
with the boat upright again and the half-drowned man
recovered enough to start bailing. "But," my slow-speaking
informant said, "the wind she is so strong and she coom oop
with so a bang that most of the water was flung out. Then Dan
had to be fast as a cat to get sail in afore she run up in that
spruce pasture."

The road took us out to the main highway again but we
swung around at Mill Village and headed back to the sea at
Port Medway. We saw some American visitors roaming around
with busy cameras, talked with an oldster near the store and
heard that the Port had had four churches over seventy years
before, that it had been a battle ground of "hard shell" and
Free Will Baptists for years, that the United Church now used
the building erected by the Free Wills back in 1832, when
pews were three pounds and sixteen shillings. Soon we were
having a look at the building, which is very quaint. The seats
rise in facing tiers from a centre aisle, fifteen on each side, and
our guide said the ones on the aisle used to be the free seats.
Over the entrance is a small box singing gallery directly
opposite the pulpit and reached by a stair. Our guide said that
one preacher was denouncing the ladies who wore excessive
adornments in the House of the Lord when a young lady
seated in the gallery wrenched the large artificial flowers from
her bonnet and hurled them with good aim at the startled man
in the pulpit. There was one Free Willer in the good old days

and all at once a fox appeared, darting this way and that, bedraggled and confused. It leaped convulsively as thunder bellowed and did a small circle as we paused to watch it, then cowered under a windfall like a scared pup. On we went and at last reached the paved road again, turned left and soon were at Cherryfield. There the rain stopped as suddenly as it had begun and the pavement began to steam and the sun emerged and did all it could to prove how sorry it was for what had happened. And we stopped by the post office and got out to see how badly we were splattered with mud.

It was a surprise to see that the violent deluge had washed the car almost clean and as we stood and enjoyed the sun a man came up wearing rubber boots and a straw hat. He saw us glance at his attire and grinned. "I got two errands to do," he said. "If'n I went toward New Germany I'd wear the boots because it's been raining pitchforks down there, but if'n I turned Meisner's I'd wear the straw because they've not had a drop of rain."

This seemed hard to believe but we were soon to see it was true. And while we lingered the rubber boots—straw hat man told us about the Sink Spout Falls in the locality, said they were something to see as the Falls had worn the "bottom clean out of the place and it went halfway down to China." In no time he was telling us about the Dog Falls and Apron Falls and Indians Falls and said there was no other place in Nova Scotia could provide such interesting features. We told him we were interested in people and places and he said he could show us a spot to go not ten miles distant where we might get something "red hot." He went on to say that Segrim and his wife, Penora, were a topic when there had been no weddings or fires to talk about. For each had thought the other wellborn and possessed of money, and both had been mistaken. "First two years they was married neither spoke," said our friend. "They moved into a house that's seen its best days and roof leaks has loosened some of the ceiling plaster and wherever it's give there's bunches of red cow hairs sticking out, and Penora despises hairs. It seems the old fellow that built the house kept red cattle and he used plenty of their hair in his plaster. Segrim had a notion to keep breed cattle that fetch fancy prices and used up most of what ready cash he had sending for farm papers that has columns on the cow society. Penora didn't try to talk to him but got herself a dog size of a coon with silky red hair. She had an eight-cyclinder name for it and said she had its pedigree but it never took to Segrim and they tell he give it sly kicks now and then. She brushed and combed that dog half her time and kept ribbons around its neck and took it on walks and fed it the best meat. Segrim got so fed up he had the preacher come and talk to Penora about her wasting herself over a dog and they had words. Next we knew the dog took some kind of sickness and Penora phoned to town and had a vet come and do what he could but the dog died and Penora was melancholy for a week on account Segrim buried it back of the barn near the manure port. Her weepy ways got him down so he digs the dog up, puts it in a pine coffin he'd made and the two of them go over at night and bury the pet in the cemetery by the church. This pleased Penora mighty well and she started talking with Segrim as if she liked him. This made everybody somewhat happy and Segrim mentioned that some of his folks would like to visit. They filled a car and come every Sunday, hollow to the neck, for three weeks and Penora was worn out with cooking for them. Segrim harped about meat pies, too, and when they come the fourth time Penora had baked them a meat pie in an old iron pan her forefathers brought from England. They tell it's about two feet across, and she had it full. The catch was that the meat was a goat that got its leg broke and had to be killed. The Segrim tribe chewed and chewed and Segrim's step-mother near wore out her store teeth on a strip."

We finally learned that Penora has another dog much like the first one and has it as company for Segrim works in Middleton and is only home on weekends. So decided not to call, and went on to Springfield, a farming and lumbering settlement of comfortable homes and good fellowship.

There are lakes all along that paved way through New Germany and at Springfield there are picnic grounds twenty acres in extent at the lake. The biggest surprise was a nice beach of sand, ideal for those who like freshwater swimming. Two cars and a tent were there and one car had an American licence. It's owner was on a second trip to Nova Scotia.

"I heard about this new road when I was in the Valley," he said, "and decided I'd leave the main drag and see what off-trail places are like. It was dark when we got here and I had a flat, else we might not have stayed. But some folks took us in and when I had a look at this lake next day I drove to town and got me this tent. All my life I've read of people on a camping trip and here I am in the best spot I've ever seen. Best of all, my wife's beginning to like it and the way the owls and loons make nights interesting in your Nova Scotia really gets you. I'm ready to bet we'll be back here next year and if I have my way we'll buy some land for a place when we're retired."

The other car, he said, belonged to five girls who alternately went into the lake until they got wet, then lay in the sun until they got dry. "They haven't enough on to flag a wheel barrow," he said, "but with my missus around it's 'eyes front' all the time. Yep, I sure like it here."

At Albany Cross we left the pavement to go on a dirt road through Dalhousie West because someone at New Germany had told us of a cave that was six feet high inside and was one hundred and fifty feet long. They said Indians used to stay in it during the winters and that it had a dry gravel floor. We asked a man in a field where the cave was and he said he had no idea. He had lived in the place for ten years and had heard some vague mention of a cave but knew no more about it. There was, somewhere, he had heard, a huge rock weighing many tons so situated that anyone could rock it by hand. We left him to his weeding and went on, saw a woman at some yard chore and asked her about the cave. She said she had heard about it and that green moss grew on the walls of stone and that the floor was dry but she had no idea of where it was. In all we asked five different persons and not one could tell us where to locate the cavern. So at last we were back on the main highway and we thought of Ernest Buckler, the writer, who was born in the district.

We reached his farm and found him home. No, he did not know where the cave was and had never seen it. It was nice to chat with him in his comfortable home. Here was a man working with cows and chickens who could sit down to a typewriter and write short fiction that won *Maclean's* First Prize, short fiction that the slick American magazines publish, or a novel like *The Mountain and the Valley*. If ever he could be persuaded to give his full time to writing he would make an easy living but he has a love of the land and farm chores that keep him in labour's chains.

Buckler asked us if we knew we had travelled an historic road when we came by way of Dalhousie, and explained that it was the final stretch of the famous Dalhousie road leading in a straight line from Halifax to Annapolis Royal. It was to be settled by discharged soldiers, was surveyed by John Harris and laid off in one-hundred-acre lots. Demobilized soldiers at Annapolis were told to be ready on July 12, 1817 to go on their land. Lots were drawn and the lucky ones led off in single file as the new land was reached and posts marked each section. As the first man reached his land he stepped aside and stood on his holding as the others filed past. One veteran wrote of his experiences later. He had been eighty-fifth in the line so that when his post was reached he was a considerable distance into the wilderness.

When the others had gone from sight I felt I was alone in the world. There was no sound save bird song in the bush and only the forest around me, the blue sky overhead. I had some tools and set to work to keep from thinking, slowly chopping one tree and then another, bothered by black flies and debating whether or not I were a fool to be there. But we had been promised provisions and rum and seed so I kept at it and by nightfall had a space large enough in which to build my home of logs. I dug a cellar of sorts and put up the log walls and roofed my home with poles and soon had a shelter from the weather. Each day as I worked some of the others walked past on their way to Annapolis for some tools or blankets, anything that would serve as an excuse for their errand. For the isolation soon had one creating excuses and the military acted as if they had forgotten us.

The man stayed with the land for a year or more, planting quite an acreage, and gathering a good crop of potatoes. The rum ration came regularly and helped some during the winter months but the lonesomeness increased and so one day he went to town and sold what he had to buy a passage to New England. Fifty years later he returned and explored the region until he found, among the growth of birch and poplar, the stonework of what had been his cellar. No other had then occupied his land and within the hour he had the same feeling of loneliness and isolation. Today one can drive quite a distance along the road from Annapolis, and at the far end it leads into the interior by way of Hammonds Plains. Buckler told us of another portion leading from Dalhousie to New Ross and we determined to explore it later. Meanwhile we would go along to Digby and from there drive down the "Neck," an area that not one visitor in a hundred ever sees and which, we were told, had a fine new highway.

So we drove to Digby and stopped for the night at the Hotel Champlain, a very fine and friendly hotel serving good food. In the evening we wandered along the main street beside the water and found many others near old cannon that gaze seaward like grim guardians of the town. Soon we got in conversation with a trio of oldtimers dressed in Sunday blue serge and open-neck shirts, and learned one was from up the Valley and visiting his two cronies. Talk veered around to a young fellow who was to be married that week and one of the trio reckoned the young man would remember his uncle and take no chances. The uncle was full of hope in his younger days, had a steady job and good prospects. He was going with a girl who worked in one of the restaurants and always had his Sunday supper there when it was her turn to work the odd day. One Sunday evening he got talking with an American visitor who told him his marriage had been broken because he had neglected to check birthstones and dates. He said if perfect happiness were wanted the birthdays gave guidance and much depended on moon sway, etc. This so impressed the young man that he began to investigate and found, sure enough, that his girl was allergic to certain things to which he was endeared. He broached the subject timidly and as soon as the girl comprehended his meaning she gave him back his ring, went to Boston, got a job and soon was married.

The young man began looking for a nice girl with a correct birthstone and had no luck. Nine years later he was still single and went on an excursion to Boston. There his thoughts turned to the girl he had once known and he was downcast when he saw an advertisment in the Boston paper offering advice to those perplexed in love. Consultation with an expert could be arranged by appointment so he went to the address and saw signs saying: "Human Relations Counsellor. We Save Marriages. You Must Be Frank with Us. No Bride Should Be a Burden." He entered and found that the cheapest consultation would cost him thirty-five dollars, but filled out a card with his name and age and birthday. The receptionist took his card but returned to him shortly to say that the expert was booked solidly for the next three days, but his wife, also an expert, would give an audience for seventeen fifty. This seemed a bargain so the young man was quickly ushered into an office where a lady sat studying a chart, and the card he had filled in. After some time she began writing on a pad, consulting the chart as she did so and with great care. Then she pushed the result across the desk and the young man read that his proper soul mate would be a brunette, that her birthday should be about the middle of June, that she should be two years younger than himself. He finished reading, stared at the card and at the lady. Suddenly he jumped up. "Ella!" he cried. "I didn't know you till now. Gosh! You were what the card says?" "Correct!"

snapped the wife of the expert. "Only you were too stupid to know it. Give me seventeen fifty, please."

We laughed heartily at the tale and the second of the cronies at once said he knew a story just as good. A young fellow outside of Digby was girl-shy for seven years and finally got married, his mother practically engineering the affair. That winter he got a job cutting pulpwood and so was away from home a week at a time. His wife got the flu during an epidemic that engaged the services of all the available nurses and the doctor desperately sent for a practical nurse who was a deaf mute. She worked with a pencil and note book but was a smart girl. The doctor left her written instructions, and the wife made any request in writing. At the end of the week the husband came home but had not heard of his wife's illness. The lamp was burning low in the kitchen and the deaf girl was wearing an old dress the wife had given her. So the man entered briskly and gave her a hearty kiss. She jumped up and walloped him a good one, then realizing who he was and the natural mistake he had made, hastily scribbled explanations on a sheet of paper by her elbow, and handed the missive to the stunned husband. He read the message, and bolted from the house, sought a neighbour's help. The deaf one in her haste had written on the back of a message the wife had handed her, and the husband had read the wrong side, which read: "The doctor says it is all right for you to sleep with me but warm your feet before you get in bed."

This encouraged the man from the Valley to dig into his memories and he came up with a description of the quiet rivalry that existed between two leading ladies in his church. Neither was blessed with much money but both had ambition to be tops in all church affairs. Each was president of a church society. One reigned as head of the committee looking after church socials, and the other headed the committee looking after rummage sales. The good minister and his people did all they could to keep everything in proper balance. In March of each year they had a congregational tea and, naturally, each lady wanted the honour of pouring during the first hour. Their jealousy was so well known that it was arranged that they share the honour, one at each end of the table. Widow Amy had no nice dress for the occasion and was bitter about it when a merchant's wife phoned to say she had bought a dress in town that did not fit her properly and the widow was welcome to it. Soon the happy woman had got the dress and it proved to be a dark red in colour and of a style that seemed exactly right. Moreover, the dress fitted perfectly and Amy was filled with triumph. She would show her rival a thing or two. Meanwhile the doctor's wife had phoned the rival, Widow Blanche, and said she had bought a new dress that proved too tight under the arms. It was a dark red and Blanche was more than welcome to it. Over rushed Blanche, as she had been gloomy over the prospects, and soon she had tried on the dress and found it exactly right. Came the night and Blanche arrived in splendour and took her seat. Amy came a little later and was sat down before she raised her eyes to find Blanche staring at her in rage. The ladies were wearing identical dresses—for the simple reason that the merchant's wife and the doctor's wife had met at another function wearing the garments, and all the good preacher could murmur did not stay the merriment of those attending the tea.

5

Off-trail along the Neck

W E started down the Neck
from Digby town and found a fine paved road. On our
left were the waters of St. Mary's Bay, named by De Monts back
in 1604. The Indians called it a name meaning "the end." On
our right were the turbulent reaches of old Fundy and as we
came to Rossway, the first small settlement, we were fully
aware of a change in the atmosphere and we could understand
why visitors are intrigued by the influence of the sea. They
breathe sea air that blends with breezes from the inland frag-
rant with spruce. They find that no matter where they go
within the province they are never more than an hour's ride
from the sea, its restless tides and never-ceasing battle with
rocky headlands. They go for boat rides and find it a rich
experience to skirt granite promontories strewn with skeletons
of forgotten windships, and to tack into quiet harbours under
leaning sails.

Some consider the Bay of Fundy the most unique feature of
Nova Scotia. They never tire of its unconventionally coloured
waves and its acrobatic tides which rise and fall as much as
fifty and sixty feet. At various places they see the ebb tide
dwindle to a slim trickle on the mud flats, while vessels lean
naked hulls against dry wharves and little boats list sidewise
on the mud. Then the tide rushes back and every craft is soon
floated as if by magic.

Along the Neck one gets varied vistas of the sea. There are
the russet and amethyst waters of the Bay and the iridescently

green and blue of the Fundy. Here and there are chugging fishing boats and in places long fishing nets dry in the sun,
stretched from posts like great spider webs. Surf crashes on
sandy crescents behind which dream brackish lagoons. Velvety
fields reach down to the water. Bright cottages perch among
sea-freshened gardens. There are the salty odours of the sea, the
scent of ripening clover and the rich aroma of pine needles.
Along the way we saw spruce growth capping ridges rising from
the sea with straggling growths of birch and poplar and alder
following the course of streams that cut along the low ground
and always there would be black irregular fences rising from
the water, pole and brush markings of weir and trap. Visitors
love the little fishing villages that rim the coast line. High
banks sweet with clover lure them to bask in the sunshine and
watch the boats put out to sea, every stitch of canvas piled
upon them. Or days may be spent with the fisher folk, listening
to their odd tales so racy with humour, putting out with them
to lend a hand at the trawls, returning at night, tanned by
wind and sun, to rest in a clean, homelike chamber, there to
lie happily watching the stars through a window until one is
lulled into refreshing slumber by the hushing sound of the
sea behind the hill. We talked with a man and discovered that
Rossway was settled in 1785 by military officers from Annapolis
Royal, and that a road to our right would take us to Gulliver's
Cove, so named because in the olden times a pirate, "Cut-
Throat Gulliver," had his camp there.

"Yep," said our man, "and it's always told that folks here-
about took him a steer or sheep and hogs whenever he
demanded for his men were a hungry crew and they'd be quick
to come with gun and sword and fire the place if they had any
opposition. They tell, too, that his lady was a coloured woman
from the West Indies, near six foot tall and good features. She
had earrings with pearls big as chestnuts and a necklace of
diamonds, wore her own knife and pistol and could speak
English good as Gulliver himself. But she was unhappy up in
these parts and wanted the warm weather and when he made
too much fun of her she put her knife atween his ribs and

sailed the ship back to her island and there handed it over to Gulliver's men. And they tell every manjack of them was scared to death of her, and praying glad when she got from the ship."

Centreville was next along the way and many sheep grazed in the pastures and a small boy with countless freckles stood by the wayside and waved with one hand, pointing to his catch. So we stopped and found he had a young robin he had caught in some brambles when it could not fly. We asked what he was going to do with it and he said he wanted to sell it for ten cents. The dime was duly produced, and then he was given a second coin to take the bird back where he found it. He went gladly and as we watched he gave the young robin its freedom by a fence post and set off at top speed for home, his prized money in his fist.

We swung down a long grade and saw before us a scene such as some high-class postcards carry. It was Sandy Cove and though dozens of artists and photographers have spent hours trying to catch the elusive beauty of the Cove I have not yet seen a picture that does full credit to the scene. We turned right into a small street where there were stores and sat and ate ice cream and feasted on the vista of hill and trees and water. A small hotel was near and the shopkeeper told us it was full as was every boarding house. "More people are finding the Cove now that we have the new road," he said, "and all them that have found it come again, so I guess somebody will have to put up a real big hotel here."

A car from Michigan stopped as we talked and two ladies in shorts came in and bought fruit and candy and asked about accommodation. "It's simply out of this world," said one. "And to think we wouldn't have been here if those people hadn't told us about it yesterday. What's in those neat little boxes?"

"Nova Scotia minerals," said the shopkeeper. He showed them small specimens set in separate spaces and named, amethyst and agate and all the rest, a charming little packet prepared by a Halifax business man, Ralph Machum, who does it as a hobby. The ladies purchased three boxes at once and settled themselves to talk with the man so we went along another road nearer the water and talked with a few who had been fishing. It was a warm day in the hollow and lazy as a yawn. A collie slept in the sunshine, cocooned in a patch of tall dead grass, and we saw honey-coloured stubble at a line where climbing hours pruned the shadow of a clump of ragged spruce. Insects, stirred by the warmth, provided an orchestra thinned to a giant hum. A man was digging new potatoes beside the field and a lone robin hopped hopefully nearby.

We stopped to talk and were soon hearing the story of Jerome. No other person ever to reside in Digby County has had as much written about them, and yet no one to this day can tell you who Jerome was or where he came from. It was in the summer of 1866 that a strange ship was seen off the coast of Digby Neck at sundown, a ship that obviously did not want to make shore nor yet to leave the area. She hovered about, tacking here and there until it was too dark to watch her further and her rigging was unlike that of any other vessel that came up the Bay.

The next morning two fishermen of Sandy Cove, Eldridge and Allbright, went to the shore to gather rockweed and found, at the limit of high water, the huddled form of a man. Both legs had been amputated just above the knees and beside him was a jug of water and a loaf of coarse black bread. His legs had been amputated by a skilled surgeon and the stumps were still bandaged and bleeding. The man was also suffering from cold and exposure as if unused to cool weather.

The fishermen carried him to a home in Mink Cove where he was wrapped in warm blankets and given hot drinks. He was questioned but made no response save to grunt something that sounded like "Jerome." So they called him by the name. He stayed at the Mink Cove house for a time but was so unresponsive it was decided he would feel more at home with the Acadians across the Bay and he was taken to the home of John Nicholas at Meteghan. This for the reason that Nicholas could speak both French and Italian in addition to German and English. But Jerome did not give any sign that he understood anything said to him in any language. He ate and slept and acted as if he did not want to see anyone and had no intention of making his identity known. Nicholas tried in every way to get him talking but failed. Then his case was brought to the attention of the provincial government and an allowance was set up for the family, the princely amount being two dollars per week.

After a time Nicholas became convinced that Jerome understood Italian but he also surmised that the legless one lived in deadly fear of someone or something, and the only times the poor fellow spoke was when taken off guard. Once when suddenly asked in Italian where he came from he answered: "Trieste." Then he seemed to tremble with fear for days afterwards. Again he was asked the name of the ship that brought him and he answered *Columbo*. Once more he had a spasm of trembling and seemed absolutely terrified.

When the stumps were quite healed Jerome began to use them and learned to walk tolerably well but never went any place. He shunned all company and spent most of his time crouched behind the kitchen stove with his head in his hands. If visitors entered he always went back of the stove and would glare angrily if they tried to address him. He was seven years with Nicholas when the good wife of the home died and Jerome went to live with Mrs. Dedier Comeau of St. Alphonse de Clare. There were Comeau children and he seemed to be quite happy to be with them. When no adults were around he would speak with the youngsters but when adults appeared was as taciturn as ever. The children asked why he would not talk with their parents and he exclaimed "No—no." They asked how he lost his legs and he said "Sawed off on a table." One day someone came who wanted to have a look at Jerome but he was in his room and would not emerge. Mrs. Comeau tried to persuade him and he said in perfect English "I'll bite you!"

It was soon noticed that Jerome possessed extraordinary strength but he never offered to help with the chores. He also was short-tempered and was furious when anyone mentioned "forban," a pirate. Days on end he would watch vessels going up and down the Bay. Finally the government inserted notices about Jerome in various publications hoping someone would send in information about him. Many letters were received, mostly guesses as to his origin. One letter was from two sisters in New York, named Mahoney, who said their eleven-year-old brother, Jerome, had run away before he was eleven and had vanished. As it was surmised that Jerome was twenty-five when found at Sandy Cove, the age tallied perfectly and the chance took Mr. Comeau and his brother to New York where they conversed at length with the sisters but were not convinced they were kin of Jerome.

Not long before Jerome's death in 1908 Mrs. Doucet, daughter of John Nicholas, called to see him. She had played with him as a child and he had spoken with her. When she asked him questions he struggled visibly but long disuse of his vocal cords had made speech impossible and he died without saying anything. He had lived more than forty years in the district, a strange man, keeping his secret as if his life depended on it, arousing the curiosity of hundreds, and defeating every attempt to penetrate his armour of reserve.

On we went and soon were passing through Little River where scallop fishing and boat building seemed the only employment, and soon were blocked by the water at East Ferry known as Petit Passage. The ferry took us over and we were on Long Island, at Tiverton, a small fishing port much like Freeport and Westport farther along the Neck. Grand Passage separates Long Island from Brier Island and if you are nervous of small ferries stay away though there is nothing to worry about as the operators are extremely careful fellows who simply will not take any chance. If the tide isn't right they don't attempt the crossing no matter how urgent you may become. On the south side of Brier Island near the entrance of the channel the cliffs present a striking assemblage of regular columnar masses which sometimes descend in continuous ranges of steps for many hundreds of yards into the sea. Serrated ridges rising here and there above the surface of the water appear at first sight like so much pierwork reared in defence of the island, scenery that almost suggests that in the vicinity of the Giant's Causeway of Ireland.

To Freeport*

Come down to fog-bound Freeport at the end of dear knows
    where,
Where the undulant deck of the Digby Neck fades out into
    salt-rimed air:
Where the ocean clasps the age-worn rocks with a Lorelei
    embrace;
And the keening gulls, o'er the bobbing hulls, are lords of
    endless space.
This is the lair of the restless sea where the waves come down
    to rest,
After they've curled over half the world in their infinite rolling
    quest.
This is the land of the simple heart (that you dream of now
    and then —)
Where there's no demand in the outstretched hand, and eyes
    are the eyes of men.

When Champlain saw Long Island he gave it its name and stated: "At the end of the island there are some little retreats for shallops and three or four rocky islets, where the savages catch plenty of seals. The tide runs strongly, chiefly at the little passage." A man near the ferry told us the island was ten miles long and consisted of seven thousand, five hundred and seventy-four acres, that the first settlement was in 1786 when twenty-nine lots were laid out. In 1887 Deputy Surveyor John D. Grebon wrote of it: "The island is stony and covered with black and yellow birch, beech and some fir, but I saw none fit for His Majesty's use."

We did not want to rush back and learned much from chatting with various men around the ports. For one thing, Brier Island is supposed to be an ideal spot for bird lovers to make observations and more varieties have been noted there than elsewhere in the Maritimes. And there survive many tales of

*By Alec McGovern

the first old-timers who braved the fogs and weather and tides and lived largely on the abundance of fish. Scallops were not a high-priced treat with them but rather a poor man's dish. The first settlers wore cowheel shakers or poke bonnets and high leather fishing boots. One firstcomer got himself plenty of pelts and contrived a fur suit of mink and otter, a fur hat with the tail at one side in jaunty fashion, and a broad belt in which he daily carried a sharp hatchet. His appearance, and hatchet, saved him many arguments with those who might have liked to poke fun at him, and his ability to handle a boat in rough seas gained him much respect. A vessel carrying settler effects was lost during an autumn storm in the Bay but the man in fur put out in his boat and returned with a salvaged cellaret that had its corners neatly bound in brass.

We talked with a man in old shirt and trousers who said he was on holiday and came from the Valley. "My wife doesn't like the place," he chuckled, "so I've developed an interest in bird life and I get books on them and make out I'm keen on the subject. But I just laze around and take it easy. The wife will come for me Saturday. She has the car but I don't mind. I'm having a rest from chin music. Women's styles may change but their designs remain the same. Gab and chin and criticize. They don't know how to relax."

After a time he switched to other topics and finally talked about a fire on Long Island that burned a house in twenty minutes because it was during a dry summer and the old building had been insulated with birch bark. However the fire he remembered most was one that happened in the Valley. He had been motoring along when he saw smoke pouring from windows and an elderly man struggling to get a large horsehair sofa through the front door of the house. Stopping the car, our friend rushed to assist. He was told the well was almost dry so it was impossible to fight the fire and the only thing to do was save as much furniture as possible. The man had two elderly sisters and they were carrying out dishes and silverware.

After the sofa had been deposited on the lawn the two men entered the house and got a large armchair of the horsehair variety. It, too, was unwieldy and hard to handle but at last it was outside and then they went for a rocker of the same type. The smoke was getting bad but they worked hard and got the rocker out, re-entered and stumbled over another big armchair. The elderly man was nearly exhausted and could not help for a time but at last the chair was out but on their return they found another big rocker. Before they could move it the women shrilled orders about a big chest in the kitchen. It was very heavy but at last they got it outside and then went around to the front again. Flames were now shooting from the windows and our friend was astounded to see that not only had the chairs vanished but there was no sign of the sofa. He shouted the fact but the elderly man only shook his head mournfully. He said there was nothing more they could do about it. His sisters had always hated the horsehair furniture which had been brought from New England. It was well insured and they were determined it should burn. The two women, the old man said, were much stronger than they looked and had carried the chairs and sofa back inside while the two men took the heavy chest from the kitchen. So there was nothing to do but move other furniture farther from the heat and watch the rest go up in smoke. When the roof fell in, concluded our friend, those two old girls actually grinned at each other. The insurance money would help build a new home but nothing would bring back the hated horsehair sofa and chairs.

We drove back up the Neck and thought it a grand area for a quiet vacation. The road is perfect and there is no traffic. The scenery is "different" and we found the people friendly and filled with legends of the coast. It was the week-end so we had to go back to Halifax and when we started out again to get from the main highway, Route 3, we were glad to pull over to the left a few miles from the city and go along a new paved road leading to Shad Bay. New homes and canteens were mushroomed along the way and we took a turning from the hard surface that led us to Terence Bay. It's certainly off the trail, and the road is narrow, has to be driven with care or you won't have any car. But men were widening and smoothing the road surface and soon there will be a fine highway. The houses are small and are strewn over the rocky hills and hollows without any attempt at lanes or lines or levels. One man's front door may face a neighbour's back entrance. Paths wind in and around the boulders and climb or descend as need arises. Cars are parked where there is a chance and the owner walks the rest of the way.

We managed to climb a grade leading to open ground near the church and there we had our lunch. Two friendly youngsters came along and shyly accepted cookies as they explained they were going to a birthday party the next day and would have "loads of fun." Then we talked with an older person on the way to the church and she explained that for years the good folk of Terence Bay had turned out handcraft under a trade name "Star of the Sea" and made as fine scarves as a man could wish.

We drove back and turned left on the pavement again to continue to Shad Bay. Stopped at a small store for ice cream, where a dozen adults hovered around a radio broadcasting a baseball game, we asked about the place and were told promptly that there was more mystery about Shad Bay than many advertised ports. Everyone, from the first settlers onward, had known there was buried treasure in the region. Then men had come from New York to investigate rumours and it ended with their sinking a shaft a mile and a half from the village. Then the project was abandoned.

"No one knows what happened," said our informant. "They may have found some money or maybe something scared them away. Fifty years back three men found some cones of stone arranged to point like an arrow at a spot near the beach. So they got shovels and a crowbar and started digging. They struck a boulder under the sod and when one of them started to pry the stone out the crowbar started going down. The man called and both his helpers caught hold of the bar with him but it was wrenched from the grasp and vanished

in the earth. They ran from the spot and refused to tell anyone where they had dug."

Another man standing near told of a settler starting to dig
a cellar for a house. To his amazement he found it easy shovel-
ling for he was simply removing fill from a space about twenty
feet square and six feet deep. The strange thing was that one
side was filled with fine sand and the other side with coarse
gravel, placed as if a partition between the two had been
removed. He sounded the bottom of the working and made
tests but revealed nothing, and the site was in an area where
there had been no road or dwellings.

A third man said early folk had had a dread of the devil
standing on guard over buried treasure and none had searched
for it. There was no church at any of the smaller places for
some years and when a campaign to build one began it met
with some opposition. It was said the place was too poor to pay
for the upkeep of a building or parson. One who voiced
opposition was Aunt Sally who, it was said, sold the odd bottle
of watered rum from her kitchen. A neighbour warned her
that she had better change her ways or the devil would have
her in his chains.

"Trash stories!" snorted Aunt Sally. "There ain't a devil,
and if there is he don't have chains."

Sally owned a huge black cat that sometimes bothered the
neighbours and the next night it was prowling a backyard
when a lad caught it and decided to teach the feline a lesson.
He would scare it so it would not return. He got a short
length of small chain and fastened it to the cat's collar, hoping
it would snag on obstacles every time the big cat started to run.
Aunt Sally was home alone, and rocking in her kitchen, thinking of the efforts to convert her. Suddenly she heard a noise in
her cellar. Her nephew had cleaned the place that afternoon
and had forgotten to replace the cellar window.

Aunt Sally listened intently and heard a chain rattle.
"Bosh!" she snorted. "It ain't so!" But the sound came again.
No footsteps. Just the clanking of a chain. Goose flesh pimpled
her. Aunt Sally rose, weak-kneed, and forced herself to open

the cellar door. She gazed downward but could see nothing as she held the lamp. Then, very distinctly, she heard a chain rattling as something entirely invisible came toward her.

Wildly she stared, her hand shaking and—clank-clank-clank —came the chain on the very cellar steps. Aunt Sally turned with utmost speed. She slammed the door and bolted it. She put down the lamp, tore outside and headed for the nearest neighbour, about three hundred yards down the road. Gathering her skirts, she put her best foot foremost and was making fair time when, unmistakably, she heard behind her the clanking of a chain. The devil was after her and was catching up.

The neighbour was by her doorway, getting ready to go to a meeting regarding the new church, when she heard something, looked out and saw Aunt Sally coming along the road like a wind-blown hen. Such speed was unbelievable. Her feet seemed scarcely to touch the ground. And there came an anguished wail for "help."

There was no sight of anything in pursuit but the neighbour hurried to the road and Aunty Sally collapsed in her arms, gasping something about the devil and his chains. It didn't make sense but Aunt Sally meant what she said and at the meeting vowed to contribute all she could to the church and to be a faithful attendant at all services. Such a change in conduct was welcomed by her good sisters but all were mystified until the nephew did some explaining. He had remembered the open cellar window and had gone to replace it. Halfway to the house he found the big black cat anchored firmly to a root snag on which the chain had caught as the cat tried to join his fleeing mistress. The chain was removed, the window replaced, the cat taken home and Aunt Sally was thereafter a model lady.

Driving around the shore line from Shad Bay to East Dover and to Peggy's Cove is like being in a different country. It is all so rugged and strong and free. Peggy's being on solid rock, has no cemetery, so the dead are buried at East Dover. At one time there was a gate to the village where children waited to open the portal for visitors and a ten-cent tip, but that is gone and now you roll in and up over rock ledges and wind your way around a corner or so and park by a small wharf because you cannot get any further. A car with New Jersey licence was there before us and a New York one came behind us and all had cameras.

The house we passed first had fine postcard views on sale and there were many places selling various articles and the sun was bright and a dozen cameras were at work around the lighthouse. You can go a hundred times to Peggy's and you will be thrilled anew each time you go for the sheer rock ledges and great steps on grey granite, and the shore view, with fish houses on stilts, and boats in small havens, is just a bit more intensified, it seems, than elsewhere. And if you are lucky enough to be there in a big wind and see the spray flying house-high and hear the surf thunder in the rocks you'll not forget it. Peggy's is, as yet, utterly unspoiled, the most photographed spot in North America, known to tens of thousands. George Matthew Adams has written about Peggy's the way most of us feel:

I have read of the scenic splendours of the world, and I have sat and listened to people tell of them, who have visited them. A few I have seen. The semi-tropics, the desert, the Rocky Mountains, glorious Florida and California, the gigantic redwoods, the Grand Canyon—but all alone, on a separate page, in my memory book of beauty spots, I place all that I was able to drink into my being and paint upon the canvas of my heart, of Peggy's Cove. It's scenic unique!

I saw a sunset here. The soft, grey purple shadows crept across the granite of the great rolling rocks, leaping to the fishing craft in the little harbour, playing upon tiny beds of flowers that line the homes of these simple folk, and then melting into the water's edge to die in the moss and weeds about the base of the rocks and the foam of the sea. The rocks there are smooth, washed by centuries of sea waves, by some so mad that they have bitten into the face of the rock and given it a thousand dimples. And there are gorges and steps, and great platforms, so smooth that you could happily sleep upon them in a blanket. Some day I hope to see a sunrise at Peggy's—and some day to be there in a storm. What a sight that would be!

A distance from Peggy's we were back on the paved road again and then we saw Indian Harbour, beautiful as a painting. If there were not Peggy's beyond it is certain that hundreds of cars would go to Indian Harbour every summer for it has a beauty of its own that lingers in the mind. We saw several cars parked by a small building so stopped and went in. It was the Sadowski Studio and customers were buying pottery of odd shape and style that made all exclaim excitedly. Down the slope was another building, and a third, living quarters and the studio of Mrs. Sadowski where she would be busy at her weaving.

If you have any time in Nova Scotia don't overlook the drive to Peggy's and be sure to stop at this studio. There's nothing else like it in eastern Canada, and the story of this couple reads like fiction. Konrad Sadowski was a university graduate in his native Poland, of such high calibre that he was selected by his government to go to Brazil there to teach physical training to Polish immigrants isolated in frontier communities of that country. He arrived there in 1930 and spent several years in such work. Kryslyna Sadowski was sent to Brazil in 1937 to teach weaving to the immigrants. She was an artist of amazing skill and soon had sixty looms in operation and had to ride horseback from one area to another to look after her pupils. Konrad had not met her but carried a message for her after one of his trips home. He had to tell her that her mother had died, and that she had been awarded a Gold Medal for her exhibit in Paris. Soon they were married and were back in Poland when World War II began.

Konrad at once joined the Polish Air Force. Then came disaster and he was jailed by the Russians in a border town. A young Polish patriot helped the Sadowskis escape to Hungary, and then they were able to reach Yugoslavia. It was a case of continual flight and at last they were in North Africa. From there they reached England and Konrad joined the French Air Force but found time to study pottery with Dora Billington, President of the Arts and Crafts Society of England, while his wife taught in an art college and composed an illustrated book

of thirteen Polish legends for the children of the Duchess of
Kent. At war's end, the Sadowskis went back to Brazil to turn
out pottery and tapestry and painting. In 1949 Mrs. Sadowski
held an exhibition of her work and one effort was a tapestry
of reindeer in the snow and was titled "A Dream of Canada."
An official of the Canadian Embassy saw it and investigated.
He learned that the hot weather of Brazil made the artist long
for cooling breeze in a country she had never seen, and soon
after the Government of Nova Scotia invited the artists to
Halifax there to assist in teaching weaving and pottery.

They liked the country and were delighted with Indian
Harbour, bought an old house and transformed it into an
amazing home and workshop. But it caught fire and the Poles
lost all. So well were they regarded that a loan was available
for them the next morning and they at once rebuilt. Then the
head of the Ontario College of Art was spending a holiday in
Nova Scotia and chance took him to Indian Harbour. He saw
the pottery on display and knew at once that here was a master
hand. When he came the next summer he had an invitation for
the Sadowskis to join the faculty of his college. There they
serve eight months of the year but the remaining time is spent
at their beloved studio at Indian Harbour. The tapestry that
had brought about the change of fortune won another prize
at the International Textile Exhibition at Greensboro, North
Carolina. Its creator studied under Eleanora Plutynska,
Director of the Norwid School of Weaving, who rediscovered
the ancient Polish technique and cult of kilim weaving. She
uses an upright loom and develops design as the work pro-
gresses, never drawing a design in advance. She uses hand-
spun wool and dyes it herself in natural colours. She has
exhibited in Warsaw, Paris, London, Edinburgh, Rio de
Janeiro, Rockefeller Centre in New York, Syracuse Museum of
Fine Arts, the Henry Morgan Gallery at Montreal, and at the
Canadian National Exhibition.

Konrad Sadowski uses ancient Babylonian methods in
turning out the pottery that causes visitors to use up all the
adjectives and then gape in wonder. He does not mould his

work but shapes by use of the wheel, using one driven by electricity at one stage and a hand-driven wheel for the fine finishing touches.

The drive back to the main highway was beautiful beyond description. We saw the cars of visitors parked around almost every curve, on the hills, beside the small coves. We saw visitors with cameras of every type, engrossed in getting a correct view in their finder, exclaiming over the possibilities, comparing notes. There was Paddy's Head and Modesty Cove and Hackett's Cove and Salmon River and Glen Haven and Tantallon and Seabright and Frostfish Cove and, finally, French Village. The road curves obligingly and continuously so that you have different views and angles as you go, and each seems better than the one before. At the few small stores along the way cars were parked and visitors bought ice cream simply for a chance of talking with the natives. I doubt that any are disappointed for this is an area where stories are legion and none are allowed to wilt on the vine.

At one shop a youngster came in and asked for some special candy. "Fresh out," grunted the oldster by the counter. "Have some tomorrow."

He said that local candy makers were a nuisance in Nova Scotia. There was one up in Hantsport and another near Truro and one up in Pictou County, and why in the devil didn't they turn to something else to earn money and let the fellows who put candy in bars and cans have the business. After getting rid of his grousing he grinned and began telling me about Moody, a young chap of romantic nature who was named for the great American evangelist. Moody was good-looking to a degree and meant well but never seemed to have much ability and by the time he was twenty he had held and lost about a dozen different jobs. Then he met a girl who was working and who had put a few dollars by for a rainy day. She liked Moody's wooing and believed him when he said he had the chance of a lifetime to start in a new area and make candy, as the market for his product was wide open. So they were married and away they went. They furnished a small house and Moody did his best but things went wrong and it was only through the wife going to work again that he was able to keep going. One year was no better than another yet, strangely, the wife felt the fault was not his. He had won her admiration the night he paid eight fifty for her pie at a social when he was out of work and had borrowed the cash. But at last the hard drag got her down and she died just as Moody was striking a better market.

Folks watched him struggle a few months and then he began to pay off his old bills and get along better. He had struck luck with a new peanut fudge. He met another lady and started romance on the track but she had heard about him and though his gallant ways had effect she told him she hated the candy business and the area and there would be no marrying him unless he gave up both. When Moody was in love it was no halfway business with him and so he found a buyer for his little shop, got married and set off to some remote area that pleased his spouse.

The buyer of his place was told that the peanut fudge set exactly right on the marble slab that Moody had started using in place of an enamel pan not nearly so efficient. So the new owner kept on and had regular sales. He felt that the shop would stand a general clean-up, however, and set to work one evening. When nearly through he decided to move the slab and clean its table and in the doing happened to turn the marble over. He almost dropped as he read, on the reverse side, "Erected to the memory of darling Muriel by Moody, her sorrowing husband." Moody, needing a cooler, had used the headstone, found it right, and had forgotten its original purpose.

Back on the main highway once more, we turned left and drove down to East River where we again turned seaward on a narrow and rather rough road. Gulls sat on rocks and gazed at us with indifference from mere yards away. A lanky blue heron stood hopefully in one of the many narrow road ponds that lined our way. We saw great clumps of lush ferns at swamp heads and a silvery flight of shore birds wheeled and circled and wheeled again as if doing acrobatics. The road moved in to touch a point where spruce bush reached the roadside and there a pair of jays discussed us as we passed slowly, almost stopping as a large toad hopped solemnly from a depression into the wheel rut. We spared him and felt better and then came to a long curve almost under a cliff and a hairpin turn just beyond. A boat was lying at anchor but no one was around and the water of Deep Cove was like a mirror.

Around the next bend some men were working on the road as if they had no serious intentions and when we paused to gaze over a wide seascape one fellow casually leaned on the car and asked if we were headed any place in particular. We told him we were happy rovers looking for verbal loot and he grinned and allowed we might find some interesting names as down shore where he came from there was a lad went to school with him who was named Harden Widen Zinck. And when the school teacher got married, at thirty-middlin', she had a hard time with the first born and named the baby Alpha Omega. "Which she was," declared our cheery friend.

We pressed on despite the entertainment and saw Blandford ahead, sprinkled over the landscape in happy abandon, with a store at a dead end, beach bathers out in some surf and a sign indicating the way to "Out of the Way Inn." Gulls were everywhere and we would not have been surprised to see youngsters in the lanes playing with them. Blandford has a well protected harbour deep in a semi-circular cove which is lined with homes of hard-working fishermen. Beyond the village at the tip of the peninsula is New Harbour, small but holding enough water to float a battleship. Its narrow entrance and high rocky shores make another safe mooring spot for fishing craft, and on one side of the harbour is a solid line of wharves and buildings in which the fishermen store their gear and prepare the fish for market.

Visitors staying at the Inn were strolling around and when we chatted with one we were told that a Saturday evening in one of Blandford's general stores was the most interesting experience an outsider could have as the fishermen gathered there to swap yarns and take home the weekly provisions. They were easy to talk with and would answer any questions about their daily chore with the nets. In Blandford, as in other villages like it, cod, haddock and pollock are salted away during the spring and summer season and in the fall the catch is dried or sold green to processing plants. Herring and mackerel are pickled and more than three thousand barrels were shipped from the community each year. A considerable amount of fish of all sorts was sold to waiting trucks who came from many sections of the province and supplied retail customers.

On Sunday morning, said our friend, the fisherman who got up so early through the week and worked so hard was up and had his family on the way to the church. There was nothing slack in church attendance and the good folk were also interested in education and saw to it that competent teachers were engaged. And often there would be a dance and all hands would attend, young and old. We saw a fine bathing beach soon after leaving Blandford and bathers were coming from a nearby cottage while three trucks had brought a regular company of swimmers. Next we were at Aspatogan, picturesque to the last degree, offering everything in a marine view and including, for us, a glimpse of a deer vanishing in bush at the turn of the road below the village.

Next we were at Northwest Cove and we parked near a tar pot and gazed over as fine a cove vista as one could wish. A long planked way led to a small fish store where we talked with a man, Miller, who had been "raised to fishin'." His place had a hole in the floor we thought dangerous but he grinned and said it was handy when he used his brush broom to clean up. One gazed down into several feet of still water below and it was well in walking around the wharves not to think about it for there were many places where a greenhand might slip to a wet ending. We gazed in fascination at the boat hauls, and the toggles for the nets, at tiny piers like stilts, at the heavy cords and ropes and nets, at nets draped over poles for drying, and remembered an interview with a fisherman's family we had read in a magazine.

There are twenty-three families at the little horseshoe-shaped cove, and they live in square solid-looking frame houses on a band of clearing that rings the water. They work with nets and traps that have changed little in a hundred years, that is, the oldsters do. The younger ones are restless for they know the movies and radio and hear of big wages earned up in Ontario and in the towns. Some young men have entered the armed services and others have become plumbers and carpenters in Halifax as there is a steady demand for skilled workmen and usually a fisherman can turn his hand to any trade. But those who are raising families keep steadily at work, proud they are carrying on the traditions of father and grandfather, often using the same hand-carved buoys like oversize pencil stubs that have served two generations.

Our man showed us the trade mark of the cove fisherman, a bracelet of iodine-painted red lumps—saltwater boils—around his wrist, and told us of a day when he could scarcely lift the lobster traps they'd be so full. "And now," he commented, "we're lucky to get two or three at a time." He talked about close escapes he'd had, of losing two hundred dollars worth of traps during one storm, and admitted he could make more money working on the highway. "But it's in the blood," he grinned. "And a man's his own boss." We looked at his hands, thickened and calloused from hauling salt-soaked ropes in freezing temperatures, at his heavy sea boots in which he stumped around, at the tar pot by the road and its messy output, then at the sea line where the Atlantic washed up shimmering green, frilled with white, before it dimpled off in the distance, and thought of the many things we'd sooner do than go fishing.

And yet had we been raised there it would be different for on a day like it was then Northwest Cove is a pretty spot and the whole Blandford peninsula is like an invitation to relax and know a beach holiday. We asked about buried treasure and soon realized that this out-of-the-way region had its own stock of yarns and probably believed in them. Yes, our man said, he held to some beliefs and one of them is that never should a man wear gray mittens on a boat. It is asking for trouble, and one must never speak the word "pig" if you want to steer clear of disaster. "Then what could a man say?" we asked. "In our dories," grinned our fellow, "pigs are mentioned as 'Mr. Dennis'."

An American car stopped beyond us and back came a man with a camera. He stepped about and paced this way and that and finally said he had never seen a better spot for pictures. "We drove up the Maine coast," he said, "but I've never seen anything like this Northwest Cove. This is the third day I've come here from Hubbards."

"Many more would come," said our Mr. Miller, "but for that narrow road full of potholes. We keep after them to get it fixed but it's not for cars."

We hated to leave and were not conscious of the smell of fish and woodsmoke until Miller mentioned it, for it is a charming spot with the fish stores silver-gray from the salt-raspy winds, hoisted up on stilts like patient storks waiting by the shore. Beside them nets were drying in the sun and casting lacy shadows on the tiny landing stages. There were piles of lobster traps, their slat sides making them look like disused chicken coops, and between the sea and the line of dark green spruce was an uneven broadloom of grass broken by gray and black rock. Overhead gulls were circling and swooping and speculating, complaining now and then but we were unconscious of the symphony of the sea as we were of the smell, until we paused to listen. It is always there. The lapping at the wharves is the minor note; there is the murmuring, whispering, chattering overlay as the tide runs in and out among the timbers and in the distance there are the heavier notes where the surf kicks up at the outside barrier and the wind moans in a low key, uneasy and often mournful.

We went on to Mill Cove with more small piers and tar pots and then some bathers. And crows flew from the roadside fence cawing derisively at something they didn't like and we met a sports car in bright yellow filled with girls in bathing suits who were singing about Bayswater. It was good to get by them without losing paint and we were glad as the road widened and then we saw a lobster pound by the right where one could purchase a treat at any time. Soon the road wound into Hubbards and we debated about a place to eat and somewhere to spend the night for the strong air of Peggy's and Indians Harbour and Northwest Cove had made us both hungry and sleepy. So on we went to Mahone Bay and had our dinner at the Royal Hotel, a good fish dinner. Afterwards we crossed the street to The Teazer Handcraft Shop for it is a unique shop that reflects the skill of Nova Scotian craftsmen with weaving and hooked rugs and pottery and wrought iron and carved wood. We admired miniature lobster pots and ship models and old-fashioned cotton hooked rugs and handwoven skirts and stoles and scarves and tartan ties and handmade leather jewellery and character dolls and Indian baskets, a dozen and one items that we'd love to own. Everything is well displayed and you can roam at will, examine as much as you please.

However we had to find a place to stay and right there at the edge of the town found Lockie's Cottages with showers and everything. Our interest was one hundred per cent when we learned about the place for it goes back to the last century. Balthaser Weinacht came from Hanover, Germany, and bought the property November 30, 1763. It passed down through the descendants of Balthaser to William Weinacht who built the house that holds the main office in 1834. The old place looks as strong as a fort and had the old-fashioned bake-oven fireplace until the house was remodelled in 1920. The outside walls and some of the partitions have three-inch hemlock plank, twenty-three inches wide. William's grandson, also William, changed the spelling of the family name to Wynot, and the property passed from him to his daughter, Mabel, whom we discovered to be the wife of the owner of the Cottages situated on the property. But there was more than history to our location for the night. We discovered that three of the cottages had been built on the famous Oak Island and moved over seven miles of water in May, 1949. They had been constructed during a period when it was felt that great treasure pit was at last to be tapped, and cottages at the site would have earned a fortune. But faith had ebbed once more and the builder had sold.

In the morning we left the main road again beyond Lunenburg and soon were at First South with houses neatly painted and flowers in abundance. Ferns banked a pasture corner and as we slowed to admire them a fox slid from their cover and loped across the field as calmly as if it were a morning routine. Crows raised harsh voices as they saw the saucy fellow and a dozen lighted on a fence to caw anew, dipping and raising as if the vocal effort were strenuous. There were lawn ornaments that caught the eye and at one yard a life-sized postman held the mailbox. At another spot four ducks seemed to be flying through the ornamental bushes. Wives had already hung out washing and at one place the linen was spread on a windmill-like rig that whipped around with speed.

We reached Bayport and sat for a time watching a blue heron fishing from a stone at the edge of the water. It could lower itself with an amazing jack-knife performance and then thrust with the dagger bill. Twice we saw it come up with a small fish neatly speared. Then we saw an ox calmly cutting the grass of a front lawn, feeding most carefully along the edges of flower beds. Sea birds of all kinds rose in flight as we neared a shore line and three huge snowy fellows settled on a ledge as if they intended harmonizing as a trio. A car from Ohio pulled up near us and watched and the man used a camera at long range. Then we went on and saw a sign telling us to turn left to see "the Ovens." So we obeyed.

The road took us to a high arch surmounted by a huge Indian head and below it letters spelled "Welcome." A large sign inside the grounds explained what there was to see and soon we were at the museum which contains relics such as spinning-wheels from early days, handwoven rag carpet, quaint old pictures, gold panning equipment, old tools and shoes and ancient household gear. The canteen sells ice cream and drinks and if you want Adam's ale there is a fine pump nearby with ice-cold water—also a table and benches and stove, everything needed to make you enjoy a picnic lunch. Near the parking space for cars is a "fairy ring." It is about twenty feet across and at nightfall it seems to light to a brighter green than any of the adjoining knolls. A sign told us we were at Cunard's Cove, and the manager of the Ovens, Mr. J. Oscar Young, explained to us that a son of the famous Sir Samuel Cunard leased the entire beach from the Government when gold was found in the sand.

Before that time people had but a mild interest in the Ovens, a series of strange caverns along the rugged shore line. One legend had it that an Indian paddled his canoe into one of the caverns at low tide and kept on going, finally to emerge on the other side of the peninsula, at Annapolis Royal. However no one knows how deeply they penetrate as the sea is generally rough at the entrance and when a wind rises great clouds of foam shoot high as if someone had thrown in soap powders. After gold was noticed in 1861 a regular gold rush started and more than a thousand men flocked to the area to stake claims. They came in such hordes that the farmers in the vicinity made no effort to stop them, not even when doors were ripped from barns in the hurry to get any material that could be used in the construction of sluice boxes. Cunard's men used pans and cradles and for a time netted good returns but the method seemed too slow and so all the sand in the Cove, enough to load three ships, was placed in sacks and sent to England for testing. Stores and places of entertainment had mushroomed during the rush and digging and exploring went on feverishly but after a time all petered out. Lots on the shore had been sold at as high as forty-eight hundred dollars each, and eighty-two claims had been worked. From June until December in that boom year the Ovens had yielded one hundred and twenty thousand dollars in gold without the aid of machinery. But the workers drifted away and the buildings were taken down or fell in ruins and the farmers could once again carry on in a peaceful manner.

who free-wheeled with ideas and had a voice like a trumpet. Those who did not attend would go on a fine summer Sunday to Great Island across the harbour and sit there and hear every word. The church windows would be opened wide and our man said there seemed to be a sounding board that sent every word across the water.

He told us about an aged sea captain in the place, Captain Eldred Glawson, who was born in 1865 and always sawed four cords of wood for his stove each year. He read all the papers and had a memory "good as the records." He had sailed at the age of seventeen as one of a ten-man crew on a brig taking drum fish—dry cod put in barrels—to British Guiana. He received seventeen dollars per month for standing watch in all kinds of weather, climbing the rigging, to reef, furl and make sail, and to help with odd duties on deck. And board was added—all he could eat of hard tack, beans, salt pork and beef. The round trip took seventy-five days as they put in to Boston on return to unload sugar. Glawson sailed ten years on windships then went into steam and stayed with freighters until 1902. Then he went to command the yacht of John T. Pratt, one of the founders of the Standard Oil in New Jersey. He looked after the construction of the schooner yacht at Mahone Bay and the cabins were finished in mahogany and oak. There was a crew of fourteen and the maiden voyage was to Labrador where Pratt visited his friend, Dr. Grenfell. Then they stopped at Pratt's hunting lodge on the northern coast of Newfoundland. The captain served on an oil tanker during World War I but otherwise he was with the yacht. The years at sea and the hard decade at the beginning seemed to have given him an iron constitution, and he sawed his wood to keep in shape. He had no hard and fast rules about diet but would never eat any "fancy foods."

The road was rough as we went on and as we rounded a turn I had to brake swiftly. Ahead of us, crossing the road with nonchalant deliberation, was a doe and fawn—and the fawn was a dainty albino. We thought of the visitors with their cameras but they were too far away and so we watched as the dainty one muzzled a big yellow butterfly from a weed top, then shook pipe stem legs in a short jig, turned and had a long look at us, then finally followed mother who had become quite impatient.

Another turn presented us with a tableau that would make a magazine cover. At one time someone had lived near the road but the place looked long deserted. However there remained in a grove of tall spruce abutting the narrow road a strong stand made of timbers. It was to hold oxen when they were being shod. The big fellows were literally lifted from their feet and held in the air. But that had been in the long ago and now there was a wasps' nest in the tree directly above and the gray timbers looked rotted and falling apart. But right alongside it, chewing her cud in the shade, was a black and white cow, and she was watching with good natured tolerance her steer calf investigate the strange contraption of poles and beams. We imagined she would say to him in cow language to be thankful it was a motor age else he would find himself in the frame one day, getting iron shoes so he could spend years dragging heavy loads over field and highway.

The Rev. James Monro did not think much of the Port Medway area. He wrote:

> There is a shoal on the east side of the harbour that may be seen at low water. Not many vessels come as there is nothing to export but a little lumber, and few inhabitants to buy, there being no more than thirty families. They are of the same religious sentiments as those that settled Liverpool, to wit Congregationalists or Presbyterians or the descendants of the ancient puritans old England, but are now attached to the New Lights or Methodists at least some of them as the preachers of such descriptions are still going about among them corrupting their minds. From Port Medway to Liverpool a bad road, a path only, and cumbered with brushwood which greatly retards the traveller and after rain the road is exceedingly disagreeable and wets the person very much, also swamps and windfalls which not only retard but mislead.

Poor old Monro. To his Presbyterian mind a Methodist was a corrupted person on the verge of perdition, and no doubt he

waxed eloquent many times in trying to bring someone back
to the straight and narrow (very narrow) way.

Next was Eagle Head and a fog closing in. There are great
drifts of white sand in this area and along Beach Meadows,
banks of it that youngsters were sliding down like snowdrifts.
And beyond were countless gulls on wing, crying restlessly like
evil spirits most of the time unseen in the rolling masses of
mist. We stopped where an American car was parked and an
elderly man came to chat. He was kindly and had the stoop of
someone who had spent years over a desk or machine. He said
it was his first trip to Nova Scotia and sheer chance had placed
him on the road to Port Medway and then he had continued
to get back to Liverpool.

"I used to dream of getting away from whistles and car
horns and street clatter," he said, "for I was born and brought
up in a city, and now I've really reached a place where there
is quiet. Isn't the air soft and nice here? And those gulls
fascinate me, and I saw a deer in the bush. Look! I'd like to
take a boarding house and stay right around here till freeze
up." Then he sighed. "But my wife won't hear of it. She likes
noise. She wants people elbowing her. She wants to ride
elevators, to eat in a restaurant, to be in a rat race. But I'm
coming back here next summer for three months, if God
spares me, wife or no wife. I've served my time in the noise and
now I want quiet."

A man was cutting grass near us and I talked with him
about the sand and he said that years ago there used to be
hundreds of seals on the shore, lying in the sun. People would
come by horse and buggy to picnic and to watch the seals
play. But they damaged the salmon nets and the fishermen got
authority to shoot them. "Then crowds would come through
on Sundays," said our man bitterly. "They weren't fishermen.
Just fellows who wanted to kill something. They fired all day
at anything and most of the seals they hit they just wounded
and the poor things were alive for days after. I used to love to
watch them when I was a lad and I guess that's why I hated
seeing them killed. Now you'll never see a seal near here all

summer. But that's the way of life. Half our generation aren't happy unless they're killing something and they'll keep on until all wild life is like our moose and the caribou. There are gun-crazy fellows along these shores that will shoot anything on wing or on foot, in season or out of season, not because they need it but simply to kill it."

It was night again so we drove back toward our cabin and stopped for dinner at the Bluenose Lodge at Lunenburg, one of the better eating places in Nova Scotia. The dining-room is encased in glass, windows all the way around, delightfully airy, and the food is excellent. Fred Glover is an ideal host and Mrs. Glover is one of the best pastry cooks in Canada. In the lobby is the steering wheel of the famous schooner, *Bluenose*, a model of the ship, a picture of her captain, and three cups won in schooner races of 1921, 1922 and 1936. The Bluenose is an honoured name in Lunenburg, and in Nova Scotia generally, and Bluenose Lodge carries the name proudly, and is becoming as famous as the schooner.

6

Islands Off-trail

As we came out we were accosted by an American visitor who asked if there were any trips out to the islands he could take, especially to Oak Island. We sent him along to Western Shore and an address there in a happy frame of mind, then wondered how many might be interested in such expeditions. Any man along shore who owns a motor boat will gladly take you out if you are prepared to pay him for his time and trouble, and he can give you enough local legends to add all the glamour necessary, and will prove a delightful companion. Of course you can only go in decent weather. You could not land on some of the islands during a blow no matter how much you wanted to get there. We thought of this and had a couple of tours off shore.

Perhaps the most exclusive of the islands is Ironbound. It is hard to land on, is three miles off shore, and was written about in a book that did not prove popular along the South Shore. Less than forty people live on Ironbound which is about a mile long and half a mile wide. There are six houses only and no accommodation so you must go over and back during the day. On the way you will pass Flat Island where a spouting rock regularly sends up a fountain of spray. Ironbound looks from the distance as though it rose straight out of the sea but when you get nearer you will see it is not so abrupt and that its headlands are a dazzling green. Whether this is due to constant moisture from showers and fog or to the nature of the soil I do not know, but Ironbound has a beautiful shade of green. You

get from the boat at the government breakwater and soon
smell fishtubs and see the trim fishhouses where men in oilskins will be cleaning the morning's catch. As at other places
along the shore, the tar pot will be cooking or the big
cauldrons steaming with spruce bark being boiled for the
tanning of nets. You will see the poled launching slips up
which the boats and dories are dragged each night above
high-water mark to avoid the slap of angry waves.

Next you will notice that the six houses are snugged
between two hills and that a winding sandy road leads toward
them between pole fences on which nets are hung to dry. Your
best act on the island is to climb to the top of the lighthouse
for the view is breathless, taking in all the wide panorama of
Mahone Bay and a hundred islands sprinkled in all directions.
Oxen move around the fields with their slow solemn pace and
there is not a bell or whistle or train or traffic of any sort to
alarm. You look around a dozen times from the tower and
then come down and wave to the watching children and go
back to the motor boat, wondering how it may be there in
winter, and glad you can say you have been on Ironbound.

The trip to Oak Island is not thrilling in any sense of the
word. In fact, I am sure that a good wader could get across at
low tide. But no other island has had so many people from
the far corners of the earth, come to inspect and suspect and
prospect for a hidden treasure that has defied all the efforts of
man for a century and a half. It was back in 1795 that three
men, Smith, McGinnis and Vaughan, were over on Oak Island
on a simple prowl to see what might be there. They came to a
clearing where plants like heavy clover grew in profusion and
as they examined the glade one of the men spied markings on
the trunk of a huge oak, then saw an old ship's block hanging
from the stout stub of a limb that had been cut off three feet
from the bole. They looked down and saw a large circular
depression in the soil and surmised instantly that something
had been dug there and filled in. Excited, the men went home
and arrived the next day with shovels and picks, ready to dig.
They soon realized they were simply removing loose soil easily

shovelled and the walls of the shaft were of solid clay that would need a pick to loosen. So they scooped away the earth with ease and piled it high around the head of the shaft until they were down to a depth that needed a different mode of action. They had to use a rope and bucket to hoist the soil.

When they had gone down ten feet they came to a flooring of logs that had been inserted into the walls of the shaft with considerable care and in such manner as to provide a strong support for the earth later piled in the cavity. This, those who dug the shaft had planned, would not allow the surface to subside and thus indicate the excavation. Wondering still more about the persons who had done such work, the trio kept on and at twenty feet uncovered a second layer of logs. But it now became most difficult to use the windlass and so superstitious were the shore people that not one could be hired to help with the work. So the three young men decided the project was beyond their means and gave up the operation. A Dr. Lynds in Truro heard what was going on and after investigating became quite eager. He formed a small company and hired competent men to sink the shaft. Down they went and at thirty feet found the usual layer of logs but these were covered with charcoal.

At forty feet there was a coating of putty over the logs, such a quantity that it was said that sixteen homes along the shore used the putty for windows in building and still had pounds to spare. At fifty feet the layer was of seaweed like a matting, a sort not seen along the Nova Scotia coast. Sixty feet brought charcoal again, as did seventy feet, then more of the matting at eighty. The next stop was at ninety-five feet where the diggers uncovered a large flat stone bearing strange characters that had been etched by some very sharp tool. The stone was taken out and many tried to decipher the markings but without success. At last a bookbinder in Halifax bought it and used it for years. The markings became blurred and finally the stone was lost, the stone that carried the key to the mystery that has baffled all diggers for so long.

A long iron bar was used to sound and the diggers were feverish with anticipation when they discovered that something hollow and wooden existed at approximately ninety-eight feet. But it was then Saturday night and no one thought of continuing the few feet to explore. On Monday morning when the men returned to work water had risen in the shaft to within ten feet of the surface. Everyone was astounded as they had not seen traces of water in the shaft. Buckets were obtained and bailing operations began but were useless. The water could not be lowered.

After considering their problem from every angle the Lynds company decided to sink a second shaft fairly near the pit, and then to tunnel under and so reach the wooden compartment. They drove down to a depth of one hundred and ten feet and seemed likely to achieve their purpose when all at once the sides gave way and the water poured in at such volume that two of the workmen barely escaped with their lives. The workers were now confounded by the water barrier and when a new company had been formed it was resolved first of all to test the treasure pit by boring. A drill was placed on a platform directly over the original shaft and at ninety-eight feet the steel drill went through inches of heavy spruce timber. Then it dropped twelve inches and bored through four inches of oak. Next the drill wormed through twenty-two inches of loosely packed metal and three small gold links came to the surface. Another eight inches of solid oak seemed to be the bottom and top of two chests and once more the drill worked in loose metal. After four more inches of oak, the bottom of the chest, the drill entered heavy clay and scraped the side of what seemed to be the bulge of a large cask. After that there was more clay. There was now all the proof needed about treasure, and from the last chest a piece of parchment had come bearing a few letters, not enough to form any sentence. So plans were laid to come at the treasure from a new direction by another shaft. This was sunk and careful exploring drove toward the chests but down came the water again and all was lost.

The company had no more funds but other companies were formed and the best possible pumps were imported and put to work. They made little headway against the water. Others had the idea of driving in sloping tunnels instead of sinking shafts but the water stopped them as well. One after another companies with different ideas and different equipment tried and failed until the whole area about the original pit had been honeycombed and cave-ins had been so numerous that no one dare try further. Then it was that a farmer noticed his cow in trouble at a point on the island and found she had fallen into an air shaft constructed by man. This led to investigations and someone discovered that the water in the shaft was salty. A line was run from the pit via the air shaft toward the beach and there excavating took place. Soon a circular area over thirty feet across was found to have a strong seaweed bedding inches below the sand and the bedding was over stone loosely set that afforded good drainage. The workers followed this up and located a channel leading inland. It was filled with stone but had been about four feet high and two feet wide and water ran in and out freely. The air shaft led directly down to it and thus it was seen that the workers who buried the treasure had been expert engineers. They had driven a shaft one hundred feet below the surface toward the sea, using air shafts, had arranged the water trap to defeat any digger who did not first close out the ocean.

A new company thought it now had the key to the situation. Explosives were put down the air shaft into the water channel and exploded. It was fondly hoped that the earth would settle into the water conduit and block it completely. But when pumps had been installed they could not compete with the inflow and once more funds gave out. However another company took over and cleaned out the main pit and at one hundred and eleven feet discovered the water shaft filled with beach stone and rubble. They tried to block it off but eventually the inflow was so great that the pumps were once more defeated.

A question arose as to whether or not any diggers had recovered the treasure over the years and so eventually more boring operations were undertaken. A two and one-half inch pipe was swung from the pit mouth and at one hundred and twenty-six feet below the surface the drill bit into solid oak wood. This was a surprise as it was not thought the treasure was at that depth. A puddle of blue clay was found at this point though the other centres showed brown marl. Then the drill went down unpiped at another spot and at over one hundred and fifty-three feet struck soft stone. Samples were sent to England for analysis and the British firm declared: "From the analysis it is impossible to state definitely but from the appearance and nature of the samples we are of the opinion that it is cement that has been worked by man." There proved to be seven inches of cement and under it the drill went through five inches of oak, then through two feet eight inches of metal in pieces. Other borings went through four feet of cement at one depth. This company sank no fewer than six shafts in two years but were foiled every time through water rushing through previous workings.

No one knows how many companies have been at work at Oak Island but not one has succeeded. In recent years experienced engineers have figured it would be an easy nut to crack if proper methods were used but, so far, no one has the right method. Last year a cigar-chewing petroleum engineer came from Texas to spring his ideas and solve the problem. He sank four holes, then packed his gear and said he would be back with a bigger rig and a mineral detection unit. He said: "These holes haven't proved or disproved the legend about buried treasure. But they have convinced me that I should come back again. I've found everything I expected to find, with the exception of that confounded concrete vault. I worked mainly with the results of an expedition of 1850 which found wooden platforms well below one hundred feet from the surface. I found the platforms, but not the vault. The tough part is to find the treasure. If I find it I'll get it out, flood waters or no flood waters. Water doesn't bother an oil man."

Time will tell, and many men have said what they would do at Oak Island but the years go by and the treasure is never taken. The great mystery is who had the time and the skill to construct so elaborate a cache at such a depth, and the ingenuity to protect it with a water trap?

If you are not interested in buried treasure and don't want to hire a boat but would like to visit an island just for the experience, there is the very spot you want just six miles off Chester—Big Tancook Island. It's a mile wide and three miles long and about three hundred and fifty people of the finest you'll meet live there carrying on shore fishing and small farming. In season they net herring, mackerel and pollock, and they handline cod. Then there is the special time—lobster fishing. Along the South Shore if you mention Tancook the people say "Sauerkraut" automatically, for Tancook has been famous for its cabbage and sauerkraut for generations, and when you are on the island you'll see fields of the wide-leafed cabbage. About half the cabbages raised are sold to two firms on the shore, and these make sauerkraut and wholesale it in household packages. The balance is either sold as cabbage or made into sauerkraut on the island and shipped to customers in small barrels. No other part of Nova Scotia of comparable size has ever raised as many cabbages, and Halifax is a good market for the annual crop. In years gone by thousands of cabbages were shipped to the West Indies and Bermuda and it is ever hoped that some day the maritimes will renew the old trade in that area.

The folk from towns and cities would not last long on Tancook as they would be finishing breakfast at a time when the islander would have put in four hours hard work hauling nets and lines seven miles out in rough water. Gradually, of course, the younger ones are viewing the greener fields and better pay ashore and the population is about half what it used to be. Don't think you leave the conveniences behind when you go to Tancook, though. They have electricity and you'll see a washer and refrigerator in almost every home, radio and television and electric ranges. The ferry makes a daily run back

and forth and you can have the security of a snug cabin on
the boat. There are no cars on the island but fourteen trucks
use the island roads that have "just growed." Little Tancook
is not far off and many families live on it, and then there is
Green Island with its lighthouse. There is no hotel on Tancook
but you can be put up overnight at several different homes and
it's an outing that you will enjoy.

We stayed again at the Leckie Cabins and got to talking
about "collectors," for every summer a swarm of them arrives
in Nova Scotia looking for old stamps, old coins, old pipes,
dolls, bells, guns, arrowheads, knives, salt shakers, shaving
mugs, etc. "Go out to Oakland and see Albert Wagner," said
our host. "He collects Indian relics, and he's got the finest
collection of spear and arrowheads in the Maritimes. He works
with the Mersey Paper Company and has been all over the
Indian Gardens along Lake Rossignol. The Indians camped
there for centuries and he knows just where to look." Our host
was right. Wagner has found his relics within a three-mile
stretch. The Mersey River was dammed for hydro developments and this caused the water to back up and lakes at the
head have overflowed their banks and the Rossignol shore line
in places is half a mile above the original mark. And where
the overflow runs the mud and sand is washed away
occasionally uncovering arrow and spear heads that have been
hidden in the earth for hundreds of years. On off hours Wagner would walk along the shore line and watch for the glint
of quartz or flint in the sun. He has got one hundred and
twenty fine items, and says that others have found a few but no
one has had the same interest in it. Sometimes he searches for
a week before finding an item but he likes the tramping. He
has a tomahawk as well as the arrow and spear heads and some
pieces of ancient Micmac pottery. Then there is one piece
that fools everyone. It is a smooth worn three-cornered bit of
light-brown stone about the size of the handle of a dinner
knife, and a tiny hole has been made in each end. The flint
came from North Mountain and Mr. Wagner points out the
amount of tramping the Indians would have to do to acquire

the material. At the Gardens he found a spot where they had a
sort of workshop. There were stone chippings two feet deep in
an area about twenty by twenty feet. Of course there are
summer visitors who want to buy Wagner's collection, and
that's easy to understand, but he wants to keep the relics, and
points out that there is a grand chance for any person who has
a few days free to go to the area and have a nice camping
expedition as well as finding a few real treasures.

We stopped for gas as we entered Queens County and
talked about the arrowheads to the wrinkled old chap who
stood by waiting for a bus. "Them things is nothin'," he said
scornfully. "I had a dozen or more and sold 'em for five bucks.
There's bushels in the woods if you know where to look."

This seemed possible, we agreed, but few knew where to
look. "I had a collection, too," he said. "Snowshoes. My
granddad had an old Indian pair that was round as a plate,
and another pair that was nearly square. So I started collecting
and I had seventeen different pair in our woodhouse loft when
the danged place burned down. I wouldn't have sold them for
five hundred dollars."

We mourned the loss with him and inquired where he had
lived. "New Albany," he stated with some pride. "Good fellows
lived up there in my time. They're all gone now. Men that
knew how to do things. Men you couldn't lose in a woods. Men
who could tell the weather ten times as good as them chaps in
Halifax that tell you wrong and then wiggle out of it with
jokes and the like. You take the moons to steer by, but how
many knows about them? March moons start hens laying.
April moon brings the fish. May moon's the right time to sow
oats. June moon's the first time the water's right to go for a
swim; July moon ripens strawberries. August moon always
brings the eels in, and the September moon is just right for
moose calling."

"It's not likely anyone knows about moons today," we
ventured, and we expressed our admiration for this small man
with wrinkled cheeks and faded blue eyes.

"I reckon you've heard of moonshine, too," he ventured. "I was only a youngster—and I was seventy-eight last Friday—when they started a Temp'rance Society where I lived in Shelburne County. Women did it, with the help of the preacher. They'd meet and discuss books—and they only had 'bout ten or 'leven in the whole place—and 'bout doctorin'. I 'member my old mother got the idea of usin' stewed burdock roots for boils at one of them meetin's. Well, we had an old chap who'd read up on history and it told about makin' spruce beer. You take the tenderest tips of the branches and boil them three hours steady. They take out the tips and put in molasses and add wheat yeast till it froths. When it don't froth no more put in the plug of the keg and after four days it's ready to drink. They used it for scurvy and we didn't have it but all hands got so pie-eyed on that spruce that it near broke the back of the Society. I heard after that my uncle feared the molasses and yeast wasn't enough and added a quart of other brew."

Our friend paused to remember and his face crinkled in a grin. "That drunk upset the preacher so that he had one of the 'New Light' fellows come to do a revival. They used to roll and sweat and shake and sing and shout. I heard my dad say a reg'lar cry they had was 'Lord, come down and shake these dry bones.' Often the women would faint, or pretend they did. Then there would be baptisin' at mill ponds and brooks and everybody would be saved. We had one old customer, George, who worked hard and hadn't too much time for courtin' so it was well along past his thirties afore a school teacher who'd had ideals and missed 'em decided George were better'n none, and married. After three years and three youngsters I reckon most of them ideals had gone out the window. Then come this revival, one fall, and somehow she got George, who never went to more'n the odd school meetin', to go to church. It was Thanksgiving time, and the preacher got them all to saying what they was thankful for. Some for good crops or good fishin' or good health and the like, till it had gone pretty well around. Then the preacher said is there no one else and up got Mrs. George. She said 'I am thankful I am not a man . . .' Then seemed to realize what she was sayin' and dropped back in her seat. There was an awkward pause and no one knew what she had meant and the preacher was fair stuck for what to say. But George remembered something about them school meetings and he jumped up. 'I second the motion', he says, and that was all of it. Three of us just had to git up and go out."

By this time we were in no hurry to go along and soon our friend was telling about the moose hides he'd seen in his settlement in one spring, often thirty or forty. "They used to soak them," he said "and stretch 'em and heat 'em so the hair come off easy with a old knife. Then they'd rub 'em with bird's liver and a little oil and work 'em over polished wood till they was soft as cloth. Then the women would wash 'em till they left the water clean, and put 'em to dry. Some houses they could colour patterns on them in red and vi'let and blue by usin' isinglass. My granddad used to make moccasins out of moose knees and there ain't a tougher hide. We made most anything and one spring a neighbour who'd lost his horse traces fastened four layers of mooseskin together and hitched up. He went to haul a load of wood home and it come on a rain and that mooseskin stretched till the horses walked off the pole. That made old Jim madder'n all get out so he off the sled and held up the pole but his place is on a hill and that hide kept stretchin' and time the horses turned in the lane Jim and the load was at the foot of the slope. Jim yelled whoa and went up and turned the horses around a big elm that grew near his back door and did a half-hitch of the traces around the tree. Then he put his horses in, did the chores and went to bed. Next forenoon the sun come out real hot and danged if them traces didn't take in and haul that load clean up to the tree."

"It would seem," we murmured, "that amazing things happened in the long ago, and we have missed or are missing, much. Did you do much hunting?"

"Some," the old man said brightly. "Mostly I used to have fun with dogs, till I made a mess of my old Mike."

"And who was Mike?" we asked.

"A yellow dog I once owned that had a quarter hound and a quarter bull and a quarter setter and I don't know how many other quarters in him. He could out-run anything on legs and I had pure fun settin' him after a fox. I reckon Mike and me got more'n fifty-sixty foxes in our time. But there was an old he-fox down back of New Albany that stood shoulder-high to Mike and he could out-smart anything. We tried for him a dozen times but he tricked us till one day we got him by surprise and Mike was off to a fair race. I soon saw the fox would run in a circle and waited for my chance to shoot but Mike put on a great sprint as he neared where he figgered I'd be and dang near caught up with the fox in a little more'n a hundred yards. Well, that had the fox really worried. He was doing his best and it wasn't enough. Mike was overtaking him. Just ahead was a tree that had been splintered by lightning, an oak, and a part of the stump was left with a wide piece left thin as a shingle and sharp-edged as a razor. The fox headed straight for it and Mike put on a spurt that looked like the end. But the fox veered at the last split second and went around the oak and poor Mike couldn't make it. Next I know that danged sliver had split him clear to the tail, fair in two halves. I hadn't had a chance to shoot and I just run and picked up the pieces, knowing I was sure going to give Mike a decent burial anyhow. Then I clapped them together to make easy carrying and next I know that Mike was out of my arms and after the fox again. Only I'd never thought of such a thing and had put him together wrong, with two legs up and two legs down. Well, sir, he run so fast and that fox was so surprised to see him that he caught him, but his head was wrong and he couldn't bite and I up and fired and killed the both of them—Mike and the fox. Well, sir, if I hadn't been there and seen it I wouldn't have believed it myself." The old-timer wiped an eye. "Here's my bus," he sighed. "It was good meetin' you. Good day."

The filling station man grinned at us. "Too bad that bus come," he said. "He gets better the more he tells. In about an hour he'd have you believing them stories same as he does."

Timidly, we asked about the snowshoes, and were assured that the old man had really owned the collection he mentioned. But if we were interested in collections, said the man, stop at Brooklyn and see Henry Maillette.

"Henry the Clockmaker," his friends call him, and it takes him forty-five minutes to wind the clocks before he goes to bed because he has sixty-five of them, wall and mantel, and says they average about one hundred and twenty years old. They all have wooden cases with fancy scrolling and scenery of some kind on a glass panel below the dial. Mr. Maillette bought a clock at an auction six years ago and took it to a jeweller to get it repaired. But the man couldn't do it and so Henry tackled the job himself, was successful and thereby got the bug to tackle more such cripples. Not one clock in his collection was in running order when he acquired it, and in the majority of cases he could not purchase the defective parts but had to make them himself. So he became adept at turning out small cogs and gears and wheels. The older clocks worked by weights, generally catgut wound around an axle, and the weight provided the power as a spring does today . . . There is an Ives clock that has a spring at the bottom of the case. When the clock is wound by key two pieces of gut at either end of the spring pull it into a bow and thus create tension enough to keep the clock running thirty days. Every clock in the collection is American made, mostly at Bristol, Connecticut, with brass the chief metal used. Mr. Maillette works at the Mersey Paper Company and clocks are only a hobby with him. But this is the part to remember. He has only one arm! He lost his right arm when a boy in a car accident."

We got away from the clocks and arrowheads and kept on the main highway until we reached Birchtown, then swung left toward the sea and had a wonderful cruise around by Gunning Cove and Roseway and Port Saxon and Greenwood and Ingomar back to Port Clyde, then West Port Clyde and

Thomasville and Cape Negro and Port La Tour and Baccaro and Coffinscroft and back to the paved road at Barrington. It was a windy day by the time we got turned down by Gunning Cove and shaggy hillsides seemed to hunch their rumps like old horses in a pasture. Hens by a farm were a clump of speckled feathers blown off course. A weather vane spun around as if it were hysterical. We saw a shingle flip from an old barn roof and sail high into an apple tree. A dog came out to bark at us and the bark was blown back in his teeth and the wind parted his ragged fur to show hide pink as puppy skin. Two red cows, wise as old women, had backed into shelter between two old stacks. Only their tails were being wind tossed and almost tangled.

The railways ran alongside at many points and the road is not built for speeding but we thoroughly enjoyed seeing the country and the rugged shore line. We tried to get a picture of a pair of steers, white-faced, gazing at us from a spruce covert and then found a sheltered spot and parked to have our lunch. A thin little old lady came from the farmhouse nearby and invited us in for a cup of tea, saying she was fond of company, especially when the company was strangers. So we went along and were regaled like royalty and heard stories of storms in that area, of fires and boat wrecks, and the pleasures of a trip to Boston years before. We were shown snapshots and old treasures that were family heirlooms and it was three o'clock and the wind almost gone before we realized how kindly we had been treated.

Our kind lady had gone to school in an old building where the desks and seats and all were handmade, the ink bottles were stone and froze and burst in winter, and often the school teacher, a man from Halifax, would appear drunk and after hearing one or two classes would fall asleep. "We had spelling books and a copybook that we wrote in only on Fridays," she said, "and we had to learn many of the pieces in our old reader by heart. I can still recite 'Mary, Queen of Scots'." Then she talked about the sea birds, coot and whistlers and gulls, that she loved and said that spring was the best time of the year as more birds sang then. So we sat back in our chairs and listened as she told us she always got the first pussy willows of any person in the Roseway area because she knew where to go, and she also had a calendar of dates when she had picked first mayflowers, with April 14th the best or earliest. She said she loved watching fox sparrows pulling over the winter's leaves in thickets and giving their one sharp note at the same time "Seep!" The old lady could pucker her lips and imitate almost any bird call to perfection. The robins and song sparrows were next, and the juncos. She trilled like one and then had us guessing her next call and we had to confess we did not know the chipping sparrow. Robins, she said, did not sing until they had been back a week or so. She talked about yellow hammers and said where you saw them you could be sure of plenty of ant hills and dry stubs around. Then there was the purple finch and she had found the nest of one, and had it on a shelf alongside half a dozen others. She also had a dish filled with different birds eggs, each with a tiny slip of identification. The pine grosbeaks were old friends, and she talked about the ruby-crowned kinglet and suddenly inspired us with "Hip-a-tee! Hip-a-tee! Hip-a-tee!" so realistically that we knew we had heard the bird without knowing its identity. However her favourite, she said, was the white-throated sparrow that always sang about "Dear Canada." We just had to go much as we enjoyed the talk and hearing the bird calls but we received a hearty invitation to return some day and go a mile with her through the bush to a place where she has a seat made and where she listens to nature's choir that features two soloists, a hermit thrush and a veery. Her wish for years, she said, has been to visit the Seal Islands as she had been told of many different birds that nested there.

We drove on along the narrow road and only met a truck in five miles, went through Round Bay and into Greenwood and Ingomar. At one place an old gentleman was puttering around some flowers and we stopped to ask about Seal Islands. He said we would be a long time getting there by car, that many ships had been wrecked on the islands until two

families had gone there to live just so they might save those
who were shipwrecked. Finally the government had put up a
lighthouse and then everything had been better. But he said if
we would wait he would go and get his "Barrington Bible"
and we would know the truth. The Bible proved to be a book
entitled *Barrington Township,* by Edwin Crowell, and it
carried an account of Seal Islands written by M. Denys who
visited the place in 1672:

Between Cape Fourchu and Cape Sable, three or four
leagues out to sea are several islands, which are named Seal
Islands. They are somewhat difficult of approach because of
the ledges about them, are covered with spruce and other
trees which are not very large. They are called the Seal Islands
because those animals choose the place to bring forth their
young who are large and strong. They give birth about the
month of February, climb up on the rocks and lie around on
the islands where they have their young, which at birth are
larger than the largest swine, and longer. They remain on
land but a little while before their father and mother lead
them into the sea. They return at times to land where the
mother suckles them. Monsieur d'Aulnay used to come there
from Port Royal in vessels for the seal fishery in the season
when the young seals are there. The men go all around the
islands with big clubs; the father and mother flee into the
water, and the young ones attempting to follow are intercepted
and killed by a blow of the club on the nose. Sometimes those
as old as six, seven or eight years are killed. The little ones
are the fattest for the father and mother are thin. In the
winter it takes only three or four young seals to make a barrel
of oil, which when fresh is good to eat, and also as good for
burning as olive oil. In burning it has not the odour of other
kinds of fish oil, which are always full of thick dregs.

On these islands are great numbers of birds of all kinds,
especially in the spring when they come there to make their
nests. On anyone approaching they rise in such vast numbers
as to make a cloud in the air which the sun cannot penetrate.
To kill them it is unnecessary to use guns as they are sluggish
in rising from the nests. Of the young birds, as many are taken
as desired to load the shallops, and the same with the eggs.
Crossing Tusket Bay, we came to Cape Sable, then to Sable
Bay which is very large. About the year 1635, I passed there

and went to see young La Tour, who received me very well and gave me permission to see his father which I did. He received me well and pressed me to take dinner with him and his wife. They were very nicely furnished. While I was there, a Récollet Father arrived, who told me about his garden and invited me to go see it. We embarked in a canoe. The Father set his sail and trimmed it by the wind, then had to lower it lest he drive ashore too hard and stave in the canoe. He told me he had cleared the garden himself. It was perhaps an acre and a half of ground. He had a great many white-headed cabbages and of all other kinds of pot herbs and vegetables. There were some apple and pear trees which were well formed and fine looking. It delighted me to see the height of the peas. They were poled but so covered with pods as hardly to be believed without being seen. The young de la Tour also had a garden near his fort, of wheat and peas, which was not so well taken care of as that of the Récollet. The land is flat at the head of the Bay. The trees are very fine. There are several brooks which flow into the bay, in which can be caught small cod, mackerel and flounders. There is a river where one may fish for salmon and trout; and drawing toward Cape Sable there are to be found numbers of shell fish, mussels, clams and lobsters. A great deal of fine meadowland is found on ascending this river and along the brooks which flow into it.

Coming out of Sable Bay one perceives a little cape or point and some islands along the shore, covered with trees. There are numerous birds all around, which come there to make their nests in the spring. The shore is also lined in like manner with them. Three or four leagues from there is a harbour, called the Port of Cape Negro.

We thanked the old man for letting us see the book and drove on to Port Clyde. At first glance someone used to driving only on pavement might be alarmed at the view of the highway but all that is needed is common sense. Just go along quietly and carefully and there is no trouble whatsoever and the absence of traffic makes the drive enjoyable. We spoke with several persons who were about for after the wind died down a warmth seemed to spring up that brought everyone outdoors to enjoy the air. Three persons out of four we accosted were in the place for a holiday and when two were from Vermont and one from Boston we realized that some Americans at least knew the trick of getting away from car horns and juke boxes to quiet and peace. The fourth one we talked to was a lady who looked warm and after she had chatted a time she brought out fresh doughnuts and a glass of cold milk. I never tasted anything better. "See some old men around and they'll tell you about shipwrecks," said the lady. "I think we can feature them more than romance down in this area. But that reminds me of my scrap book. You know we in these out places keep such things, and autograph albums." Away she went into the house and came back with a wedding write-up that we had to admit was original:

John Jones, son of Mr. and Mrs. Sam Jones of Pleasant Villa became the bridegroom of Miss Elizabeth Smith at high noon today. The ceremony took place at the home of the groom's parents. Mr. Jones was attended by Mr. Brown as groomsman. The groom was the cynosure of all eyes. Blushing prettily, he replied to the questions of the clergyman in low tones but firm. He was charmingly clad in a three-piece suit, consisting of coat, vest and trousers. The coat of dark material was draped about his shoulders and tastefully gathered under the arms. The pretty story was current among the wedding guests that the coat was the same one worn by his father and grandfather on their wedding days. The vest was sleeveless and met in front. It was gracefully fashioned with pockets and at the back held together with strap and buckle. Conspicious on the front of the vest was the groom's favourite piece of jewellery, a fraternity pin, and from the upper left hand pocket was suspended a large Ingersoll watch, the bride's gift to the groom, which flashed and gave the needed touch of brilliance to a costume in taste and harmony. The groom's suit was of dark worsted and fell from the waist in a straight line almost to the floor. The severe simplicity of the garment was relieved by the right pantalette which was caught up about four inches by a Boston garter worn underneath revealing just the artistic glimpse of brown holeproof above the genuine leather shoes, laced with strings of the same colour. The effect was chic.

Beneath the vest the groom wore blue galluses, attached fore and aft to the trousers and passing in graceful curve over each shoulder. This pretty and useful part of the costume would have passed unseen had not the groom muffed the ring when the groomsman passed it to him. When he stooped to recover the errant circlet the blue of the galluses was prettily revealed. His neck was encircled with a collar characterized by a delicate pearl tint of old-fashioned celluloid, and around the collar a cravat was loosely knotted exposing a collar button of bright metal. The cravat extended up and down under the left ear with the studied carelessness which marks supreme artistry in dress. Mr. Brown's costume was essentially like the groom's and as the two stood at the altar a hush of admiration enveloped the audience at the complete harmony. Actually one could hardly have told one from the other had it not been for a patch of court plaster worn by the groom over the nick in his chin made by a safety razor. Neither Mr. Jones nor Mr. Brown wore a hat at the ceremony. As Miss Elizabeth Smith led the groom from the altar it was noted that she wore the conventional veil and orange blossoms.

When we had copied the item we had to sign the autograph album and we scanned some of the entries such as: "Alice is your name and single is your station, happy be the handsome man who makes the alteration." Another read: "Before you are married it's all sugar and pie, but after you're married its root, hog, or die." A third said: "Never marry an old man, and I'll tell you the reason why. Only a young man will rock the cradle and sing a sweet lullaby." There were many others and I would like to have read them all for the good folk who took pen in hand for our lady of the doughnuts seemed to have been blessed with wit and brevity. We humbly penned: "In your memory's long woodbox drop a heavy stick for me. Let it lie and age and ripen till I come again for tea."

Standing on the bridge at Lyle's Falls, by the Port Clyde post office, one has an impressive view of the river and surrounding countryside, and our hostess told us the Indians used the stream to reach a camping place just below the bridge, and that wild ducks and geese are still found in Goose Bay above the bridge. Years ago the Powell Inn was at Port Clyde and the proprietor was annoyed when the Indians kept hanging around his place. One day he dug a grave by his

orchard and his help aided in carrying out something heavy
and sagging which was placed in the grave and covered over
quickly. Both the proprietor and his man wore handkerchiefs
over their faces and the curious Indians asked what had happened. They were told the cook had died of smallpox and two
others in the house were sick with the dread disease. The
Indians packed in a hurry and departed, never to return to
that area. But the proprietor did not trouble to excavate the
sack of rotten turnips he had buried in a blanket.

Many ships were built at Port Clyde in the old days. One
was the *Mary Jane,* built in 1869. Six years later this vessel
left with a cargo for the West Indies and Captain Edward
Nickerson was in command, with his brother, Harvey, the first
mate. After discharging their cargo, the crew sailed to San
Domingo City where they loaded sugar for New York. Some
member of the crew contacted yellow fever which broke out
when they were at sea. The captain at once headed for
Bermuda but a storm rose and the main sail was lowered. By
the time the gale died the men were so sick they could not
hoist sail again and the vessel drifted helplessly for days until
a passing steamer investigated and found two men lying
unconscious on the deck, two others dead. The captain was
dead in his berth and the cook was dead at the stairway. The
two living men, the mate and a crew member, were taken to
hospital at New York and recovered. The mate was twenty-
three and had jet black hair but when he recovered his hair
was snow white.

The *Cod Seeker* was built at Port Clyde in 1875 and sailed
to Halifax to fit out for a fishing trip. She was under command
of Captain Phillips Brown of Bear Point and was running light
before a strong wind when she ran on a shoal near Port la
Tour and capsized. Three men and the captain got away in a
dory, landed on Cape Sable Island and told their story. Several
ships put out in the strong gale to rescue the rest of the crew.
They discovered the sinking vessel and took off three men
who were clinging to the ropes. Several days later an American
fishing vessel sighted the wrecked ship west of Seal Island. As

the day was fine some of the crew rowed over in a boat. The side of the vessel was out of water, kept afloat by air in the hull. Hearing sounds inside, the visitors got an axe, chopped a hole in the hull and found the remaining crew members still living in the berths in the forecastle. They had survived six days without food and with very little air. Then the *Cod Seeker* was towed to port and repaired.

People in the Port Clyde district looked forward to the event of the year from 1908 to 1952—the annual "Temperance Picnic." For many years special trains ran in from Liverpool and Yarmouth taking as many as five thousand to the picnic grounds. A brass band would meet the trains and escort the crowd to the field. Ladies organizations of nearest communities would be busy a week before the event, preparing food, and items for sale, for much money was made if the day were fine. The "drys" waged great campaigns back in the old days and eventually drove out the rum sellers. The majority belonged to the Temperance Society, and had slogans to fit any occasion. Some wrote verse about it and the following appeared during a temperance revival in 1827:

TO A CASK OF RUM

Here, only by a cork controlled and slender walls of wooden
    mould,
In all the pomp of death repose the seeds of many a bloody
    nose,
The chattering tongue, the dismal oath, the hand for fighting
    nothing loath;
The passions which no words can tame, that burst like nitre
    into flame;
The face carbuncled, glowing red, the bloated eye, the broken
    head.
The tree that bears the deadly fruit of misery, mischief and
    dispute;
The rage that innocence bewails, the images of gloomy jails;
The evil thought on murder bent, the midnight hour in riot
    spent,
All these, within this cask appear — with Dick, the hangman,
    in the rear.

We told our hostess about the old lady who could make the bird calls and she walked down a lane with us to point to a huge black-backed gull that winged overhead and shouted down at us something that sounded like "Ha, ha, ha, ha!" "I'm a caller," she said. "I've called that gull everything I can think of. Its heart is as black as its feathers. Twice I've caught it getting a baby chick, and he's been around here as long as I have. It takes them four years to grow adult size and then they just seem to last forever."

The gull soared away over a field and came back like a plane, swooped low and settled out on a flat stone. The lady told us about gulls. The one she hated had a surprisingly short tail and wings were so long they had to be folded across like closing a pair of scissors.

"I think gulls are the smartest birds there are," said the woman. "I wish you could see them hurling."

"What on earth was hurling," we wanted to know. "Sometimes a school of herring will be chased by larger fish," we were informed, "and then they head in for the shelter of a cove or shallow water and in the rush some get squeezed, and if the squeezing is around the head the fish dies. There is nothing as tender as a herring's head. The dead fish at once start floating inshore and a gull sees them. It never drops down like a fish hawk but circles and the other gulls notice and join in the spiral that lowers over the school of fish and scares them right into the shallows. Dozens are dead in no time and the gulls have a feast. The herring gulls are those smaller white ones over there, and they are the best swimmers in rough water I've ever seen. They can ride the big rollers sweeping inshore and never come in closer or go further out. They just ride one wave after another with perfect poise and when a big wave is about to foam they'll raise their wings a few inches and overtop it every time. And when they find a clam at low tide they'll snatch it up and go over there by those flat rocks and drop the clam from about fifty feet in the air. Sometimes it will miss the rocks and drop on the mud between but up the gull goes again and it doesn't miss twice in a row. The clam shell is broken and down comes the gull and has its snack. I've seen them catch a dozen clams and eat them, then hurl a school of herring and eat two or three fish as if they were starved. Appetites on wing is what father calls them, and he's right. But that old black-backed fellow will eat anything, and he'll kill young gulls and tear them to pieces as quickly as he would a fish. He'd even kill young gulls of his own kind."

We drove on to Cape Negro and before we knew it were at another collector's. Lloyd Swaine has one of the finest collections of firearms in the province. He and his son, Allen, always had a few old muskets around and got to repairing them and then started to acquire more and more. It is no easy task to put an old muzzle loader back into condition when the pan is wrecked but Swaine simply makes a new one out of brass pipe and soon is ready to shoot. The Swaines always test their weapons with a hearty charge tamped down by ramrod and only once has there been any trouble. Allen fired a musket that blew apart but no one was hurt. They make their own lead balls and can guess pretty well what charge is safe. One would think, looking at their collection, that they had enough guns but they said they wanted a four gauge shot gun, a type made in England. This would be a far lighter weapon than the long heavy muskets that were once issues to the Shelburne Militia, the 12th Barrington Battalion and the Clare Militia. The oldest firearm in the collection is a pistol of 1740 engraved with the name of a famous English gunsmith, and bearing the broad arrow of the British Government. Another item is a muff pistol that was fired with a percussion cap and ball. The name was given because this was a weapon that could easily be fitted into a muff once so popular with people who wanted to keep their hands warm. Some of the muskets have quite a history. Captain Everett Nickerson who once lived in Port Clyde was sailing a three-master in 1900 when he put into the island of St. Thomas in the Virgin Islands. The port authorities asked him if he would take some of the old muskets that were taking up space in the old fort and dump them overside when they were out to sea. Nickerson agreed but kept two for himself. There had been another captain in the island port at the same time and when he met the man in New York Nickerson asked him if he, too, had had to take away a load of muskets. "Sure," said the captain, "but I ran an ad in the paper here and sold the lot at ten dollars each!"

The muskets had been used by Danish soldiers as St. Thomas was Danish property once and was sold to the United States in 1917 for twenty-five million dollars. The muskets were made in Belgium and were only half as heavy as the old British issue. One interesting specimen is a .52 calibre Spencer rifle made in 1879, and there is one of the first repeating rifles ever made, with the magazine in the stock. There is a Swiss army rifle, a Colt Burgess with a lever action, a Sharps cavalry carbine, and a U.S. Navy Remington percussion cap revolver made in 1861. Other pieces are a breech loader of 1831 and a Royal Navy cutlass. Not much is known about the weapons but there is no doubt that many of them have been in action, would have amazing stories to tell.

Away from the Swaines, we met a man who said he had fished for more than forty years and once was in a boat that was attacked by a shark. The big fish bit so savagely that teeth marks were left plainly in the heavy wood. He said that often he made less than three dollars a week but kept going as there was no work ashore that paid as much. His leathery skin and eyes with distance in their depths made me think of the old chap at the filling station, so I asked many questions about fishing and hunting and gulls and boats. Somehow fog was mentioned. "Do you have any bad fog here?" I asked. He settled back against the hood of the car and wanted to know if I remembered the fog of thirty-eight. I said I did not.

"It come in the last week of June," said our friend, "right out of a clear sky. The day before was decent enough with plenty of sun and we thought nothing of a report that Yarmouth had been blacked out. Well, the day before a bride and groom come here on their honeymoon and they wanted to go fishing over in that trout brook you crossed on your way here. A cousin of mine, a young fellow then, offered to go along as

guide and take them over by a short cut. He told them to be
ready to start early in the morning as the fishing was at its best
before the sun got hot. Well, Jim, my cousin, got up to find a
fog so heavy and thick it almost pressed against him. He hadn't
gone ten yards before he was straying and the only way he got
to where the newly-weds were staying was by following the rail
fence. But he had thought to bring along the rope horse lines
from his barn and when he found the bride and groom ready
to go he told them to hold to the rope which he tied around
his waist. Then he started but had to get down on his hands
and knees and feel for the path. As they went along the girl
screamed and pulled Jim off his knees. She declared something
had brushed her face. Jim said there couldn't be a thing as
there wasn't a tree inside the fence. Then the groom jumped
and yelled and said something had rubbed his chin and it was
wet and cold. They were both so jittery that Jim had to turn
back but as he stood something touched his neck. Jim grabbed
and got an eight-inch trout. That fog was so dense that at
water's edge the trout never stopped swimming but come right
along on it, and Jim grabbed till they had a mess big enough
for breakfast."

We agreed soberly that we had never been in a fog so
dense, and drove along to Reynoldscroft and then to Port la
Tour. A few crows sat on a fence and seemed to be deriding a
group of gulls standing sentinel along a gravel beach. An
elderly woman with a basket on her arm came along and we
asked about the location of the cairn marking the old fort site
at La Tour. We had a paper saying the inscription read:

Fort Saint-Louis. In 1630 Claude de la Tour arrived here
with an Anglo-Scottish expedition, and strove in vain to induce
his son Charles to surrender this last foothold of France in
Acadia. From the consequent displeasure of the Scots at Port
Royal, Charles later offered him refuge near this fort.

The lady indicated the direction we were to take to reach
the spot and said we were on very historic ground. We agreed
and chatted with her and she said she was going to help a

friend with a quilt, and intimated that quilt-making was quite an art in that section. We asked some questions and were quickly told that quilt-making was begun by Dutch and English women who quilted bed draperies and window hangings to keep the cold out. She said every country had its own patterns and she found it fascinating to compare with relatives she had in New Hampshire but added sadly that in many areas quilts were becoming an item of the past. She said that, when a girl, all the beds in her home were of the old spool variety, with the striped blue and white denim used for ticks. After the oats were threshed in the fall the bed tick was stuffed with crisp golden straw that rustled for a week or so every time a sleeper stirred. On the straw tick reposed the feather tick and this generally held goose feathers. "Father shot nine wild geese one fall," she remembered, "just after we had killed the six we raised and I never picked so many feathers in my life." As to patterns, well in that area The Mariner's Compass had been a favourite and there was also the Square and Compass, the Four Doves, the Spider's Web, the Old Gray Goose, Aunt Dinah's Delight and the Wandering Foot. Never was a Wandering Foot quilt allowed on the bed of a son of the household but it was purposely placed on top when a visitor overstayed his or her welcome.

"I had an uncle who lost his leg in an accident," said our friend, "and as he didn't like reading he got started to making quilts, and he made sixteen before he died. I don't know what his family ever did with so many. But I like working at them now the way we do. It's like a social affair. We go around to each other's homes and always have a cup of tea and nobody works hard at it as no one is short of quilts these days. And I always recite my piece." After a little persuasion she recited it for us:

> A patchwork quilt, now mellowed with age,
> Reflects a story of life, a page
> Of a quilting bag with bits of cotton;
> The silks and satins are not forgotten;
> As squares are blocked by quilting mold,

Hand stitched together in pattern old,
In colours bright, of red and green;
As children sit by fire and screen.
In pink and yellow and purple hue —
For a quilting party, there is much ado.

We went along and found the cairn and stood there a time
and walked about to visualize the old days, so long ago, when
Charles de la Tour had his strong fort of timbers so well placed
that the English force which brought his father over could not
capture it. Claude de la Tour, the father, had headed for
Acadia but had been captured and taken to England where,
being Protestant, he soon found favour with the king and was
created a Baronet of Nova Scotia. He petitioned for, and
received, a like appointment for his son, but when they were
arrived the son would have nothing to do with the bargain,
declared himself loyal to France. So there was the attack that
failed and Claude had to go away to Port Royal. There he was
in trouble and came back to Port la Tour where Charles
established him in a smaller post at some distance from the fort,
and looked after his needs.

The place was mentioned by most explorers and traders
and the Indians were great friends of Charles. Notes from
Diereville's *Port Royal* tell of his trip along this area and about
the Indians. He says they relished biscuits more than meat or
fish and were very partial to the white man's brandy. They
buried their dead with knees nearly touching the chin in a
round grave five feet deep covered with logs. The houses along
the shore then were built of logs and had clay chimneys, were
roofed with poles and reeds. Some roofs were of rude planks on
which fish were placed to dry. The Indians showed the French
how to get seals in abundance at Cape Sable, how to melt
down the fat for oil, which was used for burns and other heal-
ings. Sealskins were used for shoes and clothing. Partridge and
rabbits were plentiful but Diereville says the rabbits ate too
much fir browse which gave the meat too strong a taste. The
Acadians at Port la Have as in other places liked white-headed
cabbages and turnips. The turnips were kept in cellars covered

with poles and sod, and cooked in ashes. The cabbages were pulled and left in the field, heads down, stems up, to be covered with snow and only taken as needed. The Indians trained dogs to catch wild ducks, and also drifted at night among wild geese and ducks killing them with clubs. They raided bird nests on the islands off shore and ate quantities of duck eggs, goose eggs, gull eggs and ate most of them raw.

It all belongs to the past now. The Indians are gone long since and so are the French and only the black-backed gulls and the herring gulls have stayed in succeeding generations. "Go down to the point, if you are not afraid of the road," said an oldster who watched us take some pictures. "That's the end of Nova Scotia."

It looked it as we wormed along to the most southerly tip of the mainland. The Baccaro light is there, defying the turbulent Atlantic that battles the rocky point, and houses are there and families are there, and at dawn the men put out to sea and don't let bad weather bother them much. The fog horn helps them hold to direction and they know the sea. There are fourteen boats going out regularly, and about twenty men doing the work. Many ships have gone to watery graves on the ledges off Baccaro, and the man we talked with spoke of Half Moon Ledge as a monster responsible for at least ten ships, and Shot Pouch Ledge that they call "Old Shotty." The wreckage of a ship can be seen in clear weather by this last ledge. It seemed quite an adventure to get down there by car and to meet those men who dare the sea day by day, and we felt sure that if some of those spinning along the pavement from town to town would only turn off and visit some of these coves and points and tiny ports they would have an experience to remember, for some of the finest folk in the country live in such settlements and know far more of life than the average inlander.

The road took us along to Villagedale and to Coffinscroft before we arrived at Barrington. We talked with a man who carried a tray of fine strawberries and tried to buy a box but he said all were promised. He asked which way we had come and seemed surprised when we told him about Port la Tour and Baccaro. "Some of these tourists," he said, "get lost soon as they're off pavement. Down below Shag Harbour if they get off the road half a mile they're done. The gov'ment should put up signs at every turn, and a big sign at the first saying that if you can't read stay on the main road. That would fix them."

We agreed it might be a help, looked at his berries again and suggested he must have a green thumb. "Could be," he agreed. "My father was a hand sower and one of the best. He'd make apple trees thrive, too, where no one else could, and he was cook at sea for twenty years. A man of parts."

Not too many men were good cooks, we ventured, and he reckoned we were right. He said when he was young baked porcupine was quite a dish at some logging camps but one cook, Dish Bennett, was upset by the very thought of such meat. He was a bachelor and always had a warm eye for the schoolma'am, but old Tom Kenney also warmed to the school teacher and there was rivalry until Dish gave her a lamb which she at once named "Adorable" and after a time she had a piece in the Shelburne paper about sheep being friendly. Then Tom went over and give her a young pig. He told her sheep were foolish animals and carried ticks, while pigs were clean. Then came a Hallowe'en and both lamb and pig vanished and Tom found the lamb in his pen in the morning and booted it across the field, and Dish found the pig in his shed and sent it down the road squealing like a fire whistle. The preacher was much put out about all this fun which made hard feelings between the two men and at Christmas he asked them to his house to a real good turkey dinner. He made them shake hands and talked about the Christmas spirit and they ate till they could hold no more and then started for home as if they had always been pals. Just as they reached the crossroads Dish said he had not remembered so good a dinner and wondered where they got the turkey. "Turkey!" sniffed Tom. "Did you get fooled with that? Man, that were porcupine!" Dish gave a groan of anguish and all his Christmas dinner poured out on the snow in a rainbow display, while Tom hustled home chuckling to himself.

We drove from Barrington back to Clyde River and turned inland on a country road that required care, going up to Middle Clyde River and Upper Clyde River and over to Lower Ohio, seeing much that was woods, a ruffed grouse in an old apple tree, a fox running on three legs as if a fourth were shortened, and a deer that did no more than jump the ditch to get from our way. We met a woman who carried a bowl of berries and asked if there were tame deer around but she did not think so. She had been living in the area ten years, she said, and found it quite all right as the winters were mild compared to her previous home in the Valley. "Best of all," she added, "there's not been a tramp in here, nor any of the like. When I was a girl at home we had to keep the barn locked against tramps and they were always pestering around if the men were away, and there was tin pedlars, too, going round with a wagon piled with tin pails and pans all shapes and sizes. Once a tramp came right into our kitchen without knocking and shouted he wanted some money. Mother was a big woman and she grabbed him and banged him against the doorpost and then swung him outside. 'Go and earn money if you want it,' she cried, and she took up the potato masher and went down the kitchen steps and that tramp put around and run for the road as if a policeman was after him."

We looked at the brook in the pasture and the lady said it was a fine spot for mint which she often got, and at the run-off there were bullfrogs that sang a deeper bass than any she had heard elsewhere. "Them are grandma's flowers over there," she pointed toward the farm she had left. "Lily of the valley, and orange lily, and bleeding heart. And that snowball bush is old as I am, and by that back fence is hollyhocks and pinks, and a climbing rose that smells like raspberries. They had some hard times, my husband tells. They had a black mare that was worth two ordinary horses and she broke her leg in a woodchuck hole. Then a fox took the ducklings one summer but grandfather caught him in a snare that fall, and two others, and said it fetched as much as the ducks would have done. Grandfather had a muzzle loader that shot true but had a tremendous kick unless you held it right. A hired man tried it one day when grandfather was away and a bear was chasing the sheep. When they came home they found a dead sheep by the pasture gate, a dead bear by the brook, and the hired man was on his back in the grass, knocked silly."

We thanked the woman for her information and drove up to the Ohios, going much further than we had thought as the day was so fine and now there was no hint of wind and it was intriguing to picture the first pioneers going into the wilderness to carve a home and farm. The houses were different, to, just the difference between a sprawling farmhouse of an inland settlement and the usual salt box near the shore with small casement windows. It was hard to think of an excuse for going to a door, and no one was in a garden or field. So finally we rapped and asked for a drink of buttermilk. The woman looked at us as if she knew we didn't really want buttermilk, smiled and said she did not have any but if we would wait a moment she would get us a cup of tea. So we explained that we were really looking for items of interest about the region and she said there were plenty, that two old men who had died within the last year's could have filled a book with what they knew. One of them had fallen into a bear's den when chopping in the winter and had killed two bears with his axe. This man had often told her of a camp he had back in the woods for hunting and fishing and Indians were always using it and leaving it in a dirty condition. One day in the fall as he went back he heard sounds as he neared the camp and soon discovered that old Mike, the Indian, was snoring in the top bunk. So he opened the door softly and went in, climbed into the lower bunk, placed his double-barreled gun just under the top bunk and fired both barrels. The report inside the camp was terrific and Mike bounded clear to the pole roof automatically, dropped to the floor and had both feet going fast as he landed. He ran out and whooped through the woods like a wounded blue jay for as far as the man could hear him. And thereafter no Indians invaded the camp.

"What about the other oldtimer?" we asked.

"He was chased by a moose," said the woman, "and managed to reach a camp. But the moose was so close behind as he jumped into the camp that the door only slammed into the face of the moose and didn't latch. Then the bull charged inside and the oldtimer just vanished into the top bunk in time. The roof was low over the bunk and the bull's antlers hit the roof as it tried to rear and strike at the bunk with its feet. But it continued its efforts so strenuously that the oldtimer kicked a roof hole and climbed out. He was just in time. The enraged bull tore the bunks to the floor, then swung around as the oldtimer slid down the roof. But the door had swung shut and so the bull charged at the window, took out the small sash and all, but was held by the cross beams above and below, and could not get its head in again. So the oldtimer calmly took out his hunting knife and cut the bull's throat and though it made a messy job butchering in the small camp the meat seemed especially good."

We asked if the road went on or ended, and were assured it ended not far beyond where we were, so that the good folk were never bothered with traffic. Then she told us about preacher, the Rev. Thomas White, who had been stationed in Shelburne back in 1836 and had attended to the whole area, building five churches in his sixty years service, marrying seven hundred and eighty-seven couples, burying one thousand and six persons, and baptizing thirty-one hundred and five babies. It was estimated he had travelled by horseback and rig over one hundred and thirteen thousand miles during the sixty years, and he had been a great temperance man. In fact she could remember as a girl the old temperance society that was flourishing then, and was a social affair really, where the lads could escort their lassies and wind up the meeting with some hearty singing.

She asked if we had heard about Abigal Bowers, one of the early settlers. Her husband, Philip Bowers, had walked from

Shelburne into the bush carrying a bag of flour on his back
and an axe and cooking pot in his hands, had crossed the river
five times by means of fallen trees. Then he had cleared land
and erected his cabin. Abigal had seventeen children and there
was no midwife even when three of them were born. She had
helped clear the ground and plant the grain and potatoes,
could skin a mink as readily as Philip, shear a sheep or butcher
a steer. She washed, carded and spun the wool for cloth and
made clothes for all hands. Philip made greenhide footwear
for the family but in later years they were able to afford shoes,
made by the cobbler who stayed three weeks at the Bower
home before all were properly shod. In summer they often
walked the eighteen miles to Shelburne to attend church and
Abigal saw to it that each one carried his or her shoes until the
town was reached, this to save undue wear, and legend had it
that one pair of shoes was worn in succession by four of the
boys. As house room was limited a round bed was built in the
loft and the eleven boys slept in it, feet to the centre, heads
out, and Abigal made round quilts to cover all. Philip often
chased bears from his sheep pen with an axe and one of the
boys shot his first bear at the age of ten. Abigal herself was
treed by a bear when coming home late in the afternoon, and
was still up the hemlock when Philip arrived with lantern and
gun to look for her. Bruin did a sneak then and, with the
assurance of the firearm, Abigal wanted to go after him. It was
said that in fifteen years they never killed a cow or steer for
their own use, but always had moosemeat in abundance,
ruffed grouse and porcupine. When the blueberries were ripe
Abigal and the children would go picking and always had a
small brush fire going to scare the bears away from the scene.

One of the Ohio men had married a Shelburne woman and
moved into the town where he had employment. The wages he
received were larger than he had expected and he was worried
about having so much cash on hand, and worried that his wife
might become a spender. So he had his money changed to
pennies and had a large chest almost filled with them. Everybody was thrifty in the old days, our hostess said, and her

mother had made hats for the family from wheat straw. Her grandfather had worn a cap of foxskin for years when a younger man, with the tail hanging down the back.

There were blue jays in the apple trees by the house as we left and when we remarked about them the woman said she fed them through the winter and they stayed around all summer as if they belonged. We saw many flowers in Ohio gardens and at one place the hollyhocks were grand, the roses luxuriant. There were a dozen excellent spots for camping or eating a lunch and once an owl crossed the road ahead of us like something old thrown from a tree top. We saw fireweed and ferns and sheep laurel in the pastures, and yellow hammers were everywhere, darting to cover with their one shrill cry of alarm.

We had dinner at Barrington and then drove on to spend the night at Lakelawn Lodge in a nice pine-panelled cottage. A man at a filling station gave us many directions about off-trail roads and we were amazed to know there was another Ohio on our way to Deerfield and Carleton. Soon we found a maze of roads, got bewildered, saw many lakes and many deer and eventually reached Kemptville, the only place no one had mentioned. But it was a grand outing and if any visitor wants to see the country, the woods, lakes and Yarmouth county's best, just drive from the pavement at Port Maitland or Hebron or Yarmouth or Tusket.

We got so many moose and bear stories that we did not try to use them but it was easy to see that wild life dominated settler stories in that region. One man told us it was comparatively new country according to Nova Scotia history but another less than two miles distant said it was old, that there were many cellars to show where earlier homes had been. He said his father had been born in the area in a house that had birch bark insulation, and a fireplace with a bake-oven. The furniture had been made by hand, and his father had told him that as a lad he had used only wooden pails and tubs and bowls and had eaten from a wooden plate. The earth was good for cabbage and turnips and potatoes, and soups and stews

were popular on the menu. Roads had been little more than
horse paths for years but now there were so many summer
camps at places like Carleton and Lake Annis and other areas
that a car could go anywhere. We were surprised to find that a
factory at Carleton had made washboards and clothespins, and
wondered about the washboards now with nearly every home
owning a washing machine.

One man we talked with had shot five deer before they
stopped coming to his garden. "I was too late, at that," he said.
"The beggars just about took everything worthwhile. They'd
come as soon as it was dark and they'd even eat the pea vines—
clean out a row in a night."

7

Ex-soldiers Poor Settlers

BACK we went to the Leckie Cabins at Mahone Bay and next morning set off on another narrow and rutted off-trail north through Lunenburg county to Walden and Lantz and Parkdale, to Dalhousie Road and Forties Settlement over to New Ross. It was a road for dry weather, and we had it, and no traffic. We saw the usual old white horses in some fields, and sheep and geese, and crow congregations, and jays and robins, and wash on lines, and some boys with Davy Crockett ideas. We spoke with six different persons and were told each time that nothing unusual had happened in that section of the county and everyone lived a normal life. But the seventh was a man with a curious hair cut, very high at the back of his head, who said he was half Scottish, half English and half Dutch, and had continual inward quarrels. "My Scottish blood makes me squeeze every dime," he grinned, "but the English part of me keeps spending it, and the Dutch part of me says I'll not amount to anything because I'm not Dutch enough."

He said he hadn't any relics of consequence in his home as his parents had sold their grandfather clock for two hundred dollars before he was old enough to have any say in the matter. "Father wanted to buy a horse and harness and needed the money," our friend said. "And I guess a good horse is of more use on a farm. Time doesn't mean a thing.

194

But I do have some dishes that were brought to this country back in 1802 and I've salt and pepper shakers of solid silver that came in 1753. I saw them in a store at Lunenburg about a month before I was to be married. Money was scarce with me but I wanted something nice for my girl so went in and priced them. The merchant wanted five dollars each and when I explained he said to take one then and he would keep the other and suggested a verse to go with it. The verse idea got me so I made the purchase, and he wrote: 'I want the best for my dearest but my purse hasn't much for to cheer. So I'll give you one silver shaker and promise the other next year.' When I gave it to my wife she laughed and produced the other one. That merchant had talked her into buying it and had given her the same verse. We got the joke later. He'd bought them as a gift for his bride when he was married, and he'd had a fine verse with them, but they had parted and she married someone else. He went out of business soon after because he gave all his time to writing verse. They tell he had a half-bushel basket filled with poems he'd written on wrapping paper in his shop. Do you like verse?"

We admitted we were rather lukewarm about it but he was not discouraged. "You try going over to Springfield," he said, "and in places you'll nearly meet yourself coming back. So I recite about it at parties and the like." He bowed and began:

One day through the primeval wood, a calf walked home,
  as good calves should.
But made a trail all bent askew, a crooked trail, as all calves do.
Since then three hundred years have fled and I infer the calf
  is dead;
And thereby hangs my moral tale.

The trail was taken up next day by a lone dog that passed
  that way.
And then a wise bellwether sheep pursued the trail o'er vale
  and steep.
And drew the flock behind her, too, as all bellwethers
  always do.

And from that day o'er hill and glade, thro' those old woods
   a path was made.
And many men wound in and out, and dodged and turned
   and bent about.
And uttered words of righteous wrath because 'twas such
   a crooked path.
But still they followed—do not laugh—the first migrations
   of that calf.
That soon became a forest lane that bent and turned and
   turned again.
A hundred thousand men were led by one calf near three
   centuries dead.

After the verse our friend showed us his garden and he
had some unusually advanced tomatoes and large cucumbers
and excellent squash. We murmured about a green thumb
again but he said the earth was rich enough to grow a
Roman toga, if he had the seed for one. He said that his
house was built on a cellar that had been there a century
before, and the well was lined perfectly with stones as no
man of the present could do. "And she never goes dry no
matter what weather we have," he insisted. "I do believe
this place was one of the first cleared in this part of the
county. By the way, do you know how the first old fellows
lived?"

We admitted we did not. "Just a minute," he said. "I've
got accounts in an old scribbler that were taken from records
that are out at Chester." The first one was written in 1878
and our friend read in a good clear voice:

There was no preaching around the country except at
a funeral. My father was poor and I often walked to town
barefooted. The people used to be so thick in the taverns
they would tramp on my feet and hurt me. At last I gave
up going till I got shoes. In those days we had German schools.
It was my hurt going to them; I should have had English.
We went early in the morning and left at five o'clock. The
master was very strict and would not allow any noise. The
Bible was read every day. Wedding times were kept up a
day and night—sometimes longer. The people often walked
miles to town to get married. I took great delight in clearing

land, and used to work very hard, but I was never crazy at it like some folks, working day and night. People were much stronger in the early days than they are now, and wore less clothing. No flannels were worn, and linen for shirts was very coarse. There was no such thing as a fine Sunday boot. Low shoes, sharp in the toes, were used in walking; I have worn them in the snow. Short jackets were the fashion and coats were not much used. I got my first coat when I was married; it was a rather short coat with a split tail. In those days a coat had to last a long time. I am over ninety-one years of age—name Peter Zinck.

Miss Catharine A. Arenburg was ninety-two in 1887 and lived on an island. She said their house was solid:

The wall is four feet thick and eight feet high. Two of us women and a nephew about twelve carried stones on a hand-barrow and a wheel barrow to help build it. I helped shingle it and they said I did as good as the carpenter. I planted the first tree. I wove that cloth that's on the table thirty-three years ago and it's good yet. I wove a plaid dress twenty-two years ago and that's good yet. We worked hard and were very saving and the Lord was good to us.

In 1888 John Thompson gave his story. He was born in England and came through the woods from Annapolis to Lunenburg county:

Wagons were not owned then. Sleds were used in summer with runners of rock maple hewed with an axe. The Dutch yokes used then were roughly made. Lumber was sawed at the next settlement, piled and left for a year to make it lighter to haul. I had a small log house thatched with straw. I cleared land for five years and raised my own provisions. At first we used herb tea. We steeped branches of hemlock and drank it as tea, sweetened with maple sugar, and also used the box berry. We often went to church at Lunenburg twenty miles from home. I had to walk there to post letters for England. There were trees more than two feet across the stump, and over sixty feet high. What was called "petticoat and bed-gown" was worn by females, and they had something like a handkerchief for the head. Men wore moccasins of moose skin, which was washed and dried and pounded with a mallet of wood to make it like leather. All my clothing was made by my wife. The girls used to go to Lunenburg with eggs, in a basket made by themselves. They walked barefooted to the lakes where they washed their feet and put on shoes and stockings made of old woollen petticoats.

There were three other accounts, telling of rum drunk to excess and causing deaths, of otters that killed dogs, of a herd of caribou on the lake ice, of moose putting hunters up a tree, of trout caught with hooks made of pins, of making half a thousand puncheon staves from one tree, of bears tearing out a window entering a kitchen and taking all the food, of being more terrified by the cry of a cat-owl than from meeting a wild cat. It was all most interesting and we thanked our friend and kept on until we reached New Ross, where roads to Lunenburg and Kings and Annapolis cross. It is a pretty situation with a fine view of Gold River and Lake Lawson. In 1816 the Earl of Dalhousie was Governor of Nova Scotia and he was anxious to plant settlements around the province. He persuaded Captain William Ross to take in hand a number of discharged soldiers of the Nova Scotia Fencibles and start a colony between the coast and the Annapolis Valley. Rations were promised for three years and much assistance so we find the record in the *History of Lunenburg* as follows:

On the seventh of August, 1816, Captain Ross, having arrived at Sherbrooke (New Ross) with one hundred and seventy-two disbanded soldiers, cut down the first tree, probably the first ever felled by him. It was a rock maple, and at the request of the Earl of Dalhousie he sent the butt junk to Halifax. His Excellency had a dozen egg-cups made from it, beautifully trimmed with silver. A dining-table and a mounted egg-cup, made from the wood of the same tree, are still preserved at New Ross, as are also a drawing by Captain Ross of the house built by him—the first one erected in the settlement—and the whip-saw used in cutting out the boards. For three years all went satisfactorily. The disbanded troops were amply provided with ration biscuit, ration beef, and ration pork, while ration rum, arriving in puncheons, kept their spirits from flagging. The number of settlers was increased by disbanded soldiers of the German Legion who had seen active service under Napoleon, by some of the Newfoundland Fencibles and a few of the Fourteenth Foot. As long as rations continued to arrive it was "high day and holiday and bonfire night." There were no roads and the only method of conveying the rations from Chester was either on sledges in winter or on horse's backs or men's shoulders in summer. Sometimes when supplies were slow in coming the soldiers would use strong adjectives to the sergeants and the latter would indulge in earnest remonstrances to their superior officers. But the three years expired. Some left in disgust, threw up, sold for a trifle, or deserted their claims. A few had their little cabins burned, and sought assistance from the charitable to repair their losses.

Captain Ross and Paymaster Wells having settled on opposite sides of Lake Lawson, had a code of signals by which they communicated with each other, and the code book is now in a New York museum. A path was blazed to Kentville and Mrs. Wells rode through on horse back. Then a road was made. On December 22, 1819, Ross was granted eight hundred acres and sixty-seven others received grants averaging three hundred acres. The rest had gone. The Governor liked the Ross family and he presented Miss Mary Ross with a piano which had to be carried in to New Ross by four stalwart soldiers. This piano is now at the Archives at Halifax. The Governor promised the settlement a road through to Hammonds Plains near Halifax and in 1821 Ross reminded him of the offer, and pointed out it would be a matter of only forty-two miles to market. So Ross with an Indian guide undertook to lay out the road but they were overtaken by a violent rainstorm and had to spend the night in the woods. Ross received a chill from which he did not recover and he died May 2, 1822, leaving his young wife and children to get on as best they could. They did get on and the wife reached the age of ninety-two despite all the hardships she endured.

We saw the Ross homestead, looking as capable of defying time and weather as it did when built. It is only one and a half stories high, but has a commodious kitchen with a large fireplace fitted with a crane, pot hooks, etc., and there are fireplaces in the other rooms. The old melodeon is there, and the maple dining table. The original grant is framed and hanging on the wall as well as a plan attached to the grant showing a road from Halifax to Annapolis via Hammonds Plains. This crossed New Ross and the descendants of several of the original grantees still occupy the lots which were granted to their forefathers. Looking over the list of items supplied the settlers in 1817, I wondered if any of the articles were still around New Ross. Each man was given a hoe, axe, and whipsaw; a hand saw, chisel, drawing-knife and auger was given for every five men; a cross-cut saw for every ten men. And every male in the lot received a spade, hammer, gimlet and nails. Each family was given five bushels of seed potatoes and a quantity of turnip seed and red and white clover seed, a rake, shovel, grindstone, Dutch bake oven, rope, lead, twine, wax and thread.

We drove back to the town hill to look over the wide expanse of field and lake and river and could understand Captain Ross liking it beyond any other place he had seen. While we were there a car from Vermont came up the grade and a man got out with binoculars and gazed over the area. "Even better than home," he grinned at me. "I took a chance and came from the paved road and, brother, am I ever glad. I've been around Nova Scotia on the main highways and now I just realize there's half of it that I've missed."

He was most interested when we gave him some of the history of the place, asked information as to getting to the Ross house, turned his car and headed for there still wearing his happy grin. We drove toward Chester and reached Sherwood, about a mile north-west of the New Ross road. The point of departure from the highway is clearly marked by a small white church, built as a joint church and schoolhouse in 1877, and well looked after by interested friends. Sherwood was situated on the old Halifax-Annapolis road, the lifeline for military settlements, and the village and road lie today as the unfulfilled dream of the Earl of Dalhousie. It was one more place where free rations and rum, seed and tools attracted disbanded soldiers. Captain Evans and a number of men with the lot that formed New Ross saw a likely-looking hill nearer the ration point and stopped there, forming Sherwood. However these soldiers faced a virgin forest that had to be cut down, rocks that had to be moved, and a siege of cultivation that meant hard labour. So only nine stayed on to receive grants and nine separate locations of habitations are discernible at Sherwood today. Only two have houses on the original site, the others are marked by abandoned cellars. Four had sold out by 1822. Evans stayed until his death in 1840. It is the old story, so often repeated along that fabulous military road, of soldiers who had no experience presenting themselves as settlers in order to get a year or so of easy living. The Earl of Dalhousie got to know, finally, that of all men available for the establishing of colonies, the disbanded soldier was the poorest choice. We came out near Chester Basin and there were many dwellings along the way. Two women, walking with rather painful steps and slow, gratefully accepted a lift. They had been at some sort of a church society meeting and were talking about a visiting clergyman who was a dear. "And his wife is so perfectly frank," remarked the other lady. "I just love the things she says. When they were invited around last Thanksgiving I think someone had them to dinner every day of the week. And each woman gave his wife a basket of leftovers as they were leaving. So Saturday they had dinner at home and when he started to say grace she looked at him and shrugged. "Never mind it, dear," she said. "You've already blessed every bite on the table."

We took them to where they wanted to go in Chester Basin and then turned on to Route 14 going through to Windsor. It was a rough road in spots and there are long stretches of bush and spruce and ragged clearings. We met two or three vehicles raising the usual amount of dust and decided that we would not recommend the route to visitors unless they were wanting to visit Windsor. There was Waterville and Vaughan and Smith Corner, and not a soul we talked with had anything unusual to tell us, so we kept on and near Windsor had to stop to let a man driving cattle get his cows from the road. He smiled in a friendly fashion and thanked us for our courtesy. "It's generally the strangers who give a chap a chance," he said. "Nova Scotians don't seem to think."

"Looks a nice cow you have there," we ventured. "She's fine," he agreed, "and gives a lot of milk, but we have to handle her with kid gloves."

"Temperamental?" we asked.

"All good cows are," he returned. "I got one that wants to be by herself and I tether her by the orchard. She's ugly as sin if she's been with the rest all day. Now this one I spoke about has to be handled exactly like I said. We have to wear kid gloves to milk her. It started back when I had a sore thumb and had an old glove on my hand. Before that I often had to tie her legs in order to milk her, but I noticed she liked the glove, or seemed to, and one night, just for fun, I put on the other glove and didn't tie her. She never raised a foot, and since that I've worn out two pair of kid gloves milking her."

We asked him about old settlers in the place and he shrugged and said he was never interested in history but his grandfather was from somewhere in Ireland, and his father always recited a piece a fellow wrote to his girl:

I'm yours to command, both in weeping and laughter
I'm awake all the night that of you I may dream;
I'd hang myself now, if you'd marry me after,
and though I may change I'll be ever the same.

Then he said he had been told that first traffic from Halifax to Chester went by way of Windsor, and he suspected the road was much like it was in those days. Roads were his interest, he said, as he had worked on highway construction for a year after leaving a job as clerk in a store. He wanted to know if I had written about the plank road at Milton.

It ran four miles, he said, smooth plank road, built as an experiment and wonderful to drive on, no bumping or ruts, but it rotted out inside of five years and was deemed impractical. Then there was the slag road at Londonderry, as good a road as a man could want, and why wasn't more slag used in building country roads. To get away from the subject we asked if he had liked clerking.

"Good enough," he said. "You talked with a lot of people, even if some were cranks. It was back at the beginning of the twenties and our boss hated the Income Tax idea as he avoided bookkeeping as much as possible. So he sent in no returns and always watched strangers who came, wondering if they worked for the Tax people. Then half a cheese was missing from the cellar, and it was the third such loss we had had. It was plain that someone was in some way, getting in and out of the cellar without us knowing it. So that noon the boss took a basket of food and a shot gun down cellar with him and he told us to report he had gone out of town for a few days. Late in the afternoon a stranger came and insisted that he wanted to see the boss. We did our best as we lied to him but I think he guessed we were bluffing and went out in the back shop to look for himself. We'd been getting in some potatoes and the bags were just sent down a chute into the cellar. The door was closed and the stranger never saw the dark opening but stepped into the chute and shot down at high speed. The boss had been sharp as it became dark and was ready with the shot gun but the stranger shot down like a bolt from the blue, knocked him over, and the gun was discharged. Its contents shattered a keg of vinegar and the stranger was soaked in it. We rushed down cellar with lights and saw the mess as the stranger sat up, felt of a bump on his head and announced: 'I'm an Income Tax Inspector.' 'I knew that devilish tax would come just like you did,' swore the boss. 'Who pays for the vinegar?' The concussion in the cellar had loosened a window we thought solid and as we shone our lights on it we saw someone had cleverly loosened it from the masonry so it could be taken out and put back as often as needed. Iron bars were set in and the window put back and there was no more stealing. And that Income Tax fellow was so stiff the next day he could hardly move, but he was so glad he was still alive after that gun blast that he was mighty easy with the boss."

In the morning we drove up Highway Two from Halifax and turned right at Shubenacadie after going to the Wild Life Park to look at the beaver and foxes and racoons and other woodland characters who are so much at home in their true environment that I think they enjoy seeing visitors as much as the visitors enjoy seeing them. There were forty-three cars parked at the entrance at nine-thirty which gives an idea of the popularity of the Park.

The road we were on was good and gave a general picture of inland Nova Scotia. Farms and woodlands and brooks and trees and gardens and cattle and crows. There was a small store at Gay's River, and geese were on sentry duty at the crossroads where a road came in to join ours from Milford. There were pleasant intervales and some areas looked like excellent muskrat ground. There were some small homes that had TV aerials, and homes that had flowers galore. One farmhouse had the four windows in view simply jungled with geraniums. Then we came to Middle Musquodoboit and pavement for some distance, with stores and churches and a sawmill. There was a fine school and nice homes and we kept on going as seven different persons we talked with had no stories for us. Then came Greenwood and we were on a slope and saw nice homes and a unique mailbox holder. It was a bear sawed from wood, life sized. There were many sheep in the pasture and then we were at Upper Musquodoboit and walked around a store while a friendly cat purred against our legs and, outside, we began talking with men who were loading lumber near the station.

Soon we were getting history. First settlers in from the main road had cleared land at Stewiacke and Upper Stewiacke, they said, and then three Fishers, with Horton, their brother-in-law, a Holman, Reynolds and Geddes, had taken goods and axes and tramped through the wilderness, crossing gullies and climbing hills, with one man or another taking turns in climbing a tall tree to look ahead. Finally after about eight or nine miles as the crow would fly they saw big natural intervales and joy lifted their heels. They took up land in the area and soon others had followed them to the site, and those firstcomers were granted fifty-three hundred acres. They sowed seed and built log cabins with pole roofs thatched with birch bark, got cooking gear and their wives and began to make a settlement. A log meeting-house was erected and they were a good people. For years they had to go out via Stewiacke to buy any unusual supplies. But they grew their food, made their own footwear of moosehide, and made their furniture. Soon they were raising enough sheep and flax to provide their clothing. There were soon settlers at Middle Musquodoboit and a settler named Archibald established a tannery. One of the men said we could go back and find a building that had been in use at the time and it still had some old equipment in the cellar. They built a log school and one William Muir was the teacher. He kept mighty busy as he taught children in the daytime from nine till five, and in the evening by candlelight had classes for the young folk, as many had grown full size without learning to read or write. Muir maintained strict discipline and always had some reading of the Bible daily. Once a fortnight he had to shift his boarding place as he, like all early teachers, had to board around, two weeks at each home in turn. His pay was about forty pounds for the year.

As they had no heat in the meeting-house the occasional preacher who came in winter had to hold services in the homes and this state of affairs lasted until 1829. But a church was built and a preacher came whom everyone loved. He was the Rev. Sprott, a short, strongly-made man, who had strict ideas but loved everyone. He served the area for twenty-four years and we were told that dozens of stories about him and his doings could be had if we cared to call at the homes. When the new church was built it had box pews with doors, a gallery, and the pulpit was up thirteen steps, the sounding board above it. The precentor had his desk up three steps near the pulpit. The building was beside the Holman clearing and one fall Holman had a fine crop of wheat which was in stook on Sunday. The day had been fine until preaching time and then thunder clouds began to roll up. Sprott noticed them and pointed a finger. "Go home and put your wheat in," he ordered, "and as there isn't much time you," he pointed to two able young men, "and you go and help him." The men went out gladly and the wheat was in the barn before the rain came.

At another time the Rev. Sprott was preaching at a settlement where two churches stood almost together, and as the service in the other church was to be much later in starting people intending to attend there went in the other church first to hear the visiting Rev. Sprott. As his sermon got well along it was time for the other service to begin and members from that church started to tip-toe out. This annoyed the speaker who did not know the circumstances and so as more started he paused, then said: "Oh, well, the more fools that go the fewer there will be left." After these words the others dare not get up to go and there was no further disturbance.

The Rev Sprott had no time for musical instruments such as the violin and fiddle, and did not think they should be allowed in churches. But one congregation held to the fiddle and he had to preach there on one occasion. So at closing he announced. "We will fiddle and sing to the glory of God in the 119th Psalm. Basil—Basil—get my horse." Basil was his aide and as the fiddle wailed the first of the one hundred and seventy-six verses of the Psalm the good man walked out, and the congregation was left to wonder whether or not he would be back as it struggled through the entire length of the Psalm. Then, worn and exhausted, it had to disperse as Sprott was far away on his good horse.

Once he was holding a service at Middle Musquodoboit when a terriffic storm arose and as the Rev. Sprott was praying there came a blinding flash of lightning that filled the church, then a clap of thunder that fairly shook the building. The good man stood for a moment with his hand upraised till the last rumblings had died away, then said. "When God speaks let man keep silent." When he grew old his legs bothered him much and one day as he climbed laboriously the high steps to his pulpit he gasped: "I'll have a new set of legs on resurrection morn."

We were told that Matthew Burris built the first Presbyterian Church that was permanent. Another had been started but was burned to the ground before the roof was finished. Burris came from a family of much fame as settlers and sailors and medical men. An ancestor was one of the strongest men in Colchester County and legend had it that at a Fair held at Onslow he picked up a hefty steer that was loose in the yard and dropped it over the fence. He was said to be six feet three inches in height and weighed almost three hundred pounds. Burris went to Musquodoboit with little more than his tools and died a citizen of considerable means. After building the church he built several homes and made furniture so strong that several pieces are still in daily use in Musquodoboit.

Bears were a menace for the first hundred years. One day when her husband was absent Mrs. Henry heard their pig squealing loudly and knew something was wrong. It was a pig of much value, almost pure bred, and as she ran toward the pen a big bear backed from the shed dragging the pig by a foot. Mrs. Henry snatched up the splitting axe from a block in the yard. It was a large and heavy tool that Mr. Henry kept whetted to razor sharpness. She never hesitated but swung the weapon with all her strength and sank the blade deeply into the bear's neck severing the spinal column and killing the animal. Then she sent the pig back into place and fixed up the pen as if it were an ordinary chore.

Young Billy Burris was curious about everything he saw and when he was sent to the store at Middle Musquodoboit for matches the first time he could scarcely believe what was told him. No one had seen the sulphur matches but they were real, people said, and saved all worry about fire. So away Billy went on the long walk with his precious shilling and arrived back with pride. "They're real," he declared, "and every one of them is good. I tried them all coming home."

In the fall of 1844 the last wolf pack troubled Musquod-oboit Valley and reached as far as Dean Settlement. Mrs. Grizzel Dean was riding home that night on her fine black mare when suddenly the mare became nervous and started to run. Mrs. Dean was unable to check the mare and then fear made her cower in the saddle as she saw nine, ten, eleven, twelve shadowy forms emerge from the woods and close in behind the mare. Soon they had sped up nearer and then were to one side but the gallant mare had her head down and was running for her life and the wolves could not get a chance to leap. The race lasted a full two miles down the road and then a last sprint carried the mare into the home yard where a large dog set up its baying and the men rushed out with lanterns. The wolves immediately slunk off to the woods, frustrated, but they lingered in the vicinity and before dawn had killed twenty-seven sheep. This angered the men of the settlement so that a hunt with horses and dogs was arranged but the crafty animals seem to sense their danger for the pack fled the entire area and were next seen up in Cumberland County.

We were quiet a time as one of the men told us where we would see the road over which the wolves chased Mrs. Dean, and then another chap spoke up.

"You a Grit or Tory?" he asked. "Well, it don't make much difference, only up here we're mostly Grits. I can show you where to go to see the spot where the Annand House was a pride in its day, and it was there that the great Joseph Howe spent two years and declared they were the best years in his whole life. After his election in 1847 people went on horse-back twenty miles to meet him and the parade kept getting bigger as others joined in and they put Howe in a big cart drawn by six horses, and the whole body of it was filled with

flowers and they had Howe in a big chair taken from somebody's parlour. He was like on a throne and they had a big
sign reading 'Welcome Howe—The Victory is Yours.' Nobody
was a Tory that day, not around here. It weren't safe to be
one."

"There was lots of noted people around here," said an
older man who had been listening to all we were told. "You
should have something about the McCurdys. They come from
Onslow and there were seven boys and seven girls in the family
and every one of the boys was six feet tall or more. And all of
them were preachers or elders, and not one used tobacco or
liquor. I've heard they wouldn't let their wives put a ribbon
in a bonnet or a fancy comb in their hair. They went around
sober as judges and it's hearsay that one of them never laughed
but once in his life and that was when he and his wife came
home from church and found their old sow had got out of her
pen, had pushed in the kitchen door and made her way at last
into the parlour where she was fast asleep on her side on the
Turkish carpet under the parlour table. They said he laughed
fit to hurt himself and his wife was so mad she got the broom
and cleared both him and the sow out of the house. After he
died they tell his widow went to Truro and bought a bonnet
with all the colours of the rainbow and ribbons by the yard
and a fancy comb four inches high. Then she used to invite
folks in to tea and tell jokes and laugh. She said there were
so many grey corners in the house that needed something
merry that she needed nothing but fun for the rest of her life."

We drove to Dean to see where the wolves had run and
liked the country very much, saw that the road continued and
a man told us we could go on to Eureka but its a long distance
on a doubtful road and we decided to leave it to later and
drove back to Upper Musquodoboit. At a store we were given
direction to a man who had some old papers and he showed
us a statement by Howe to the effect that he had spent the two
best years raking, hoeing, reaping, calling moose, doing all
sorts of farm work until he was in the very best physical
condition. But there was also an article he had written about

the area in 1839 and it had to do with the very road to Sheet Harbour that we intended to take. So we read with interest:

If you are fond of wild and romantic scenery you can go from Middle Musquodoboit to Ship Harbour for the most part by water. A chain of freshwater lakes runs back for more than twenty miles and comes within five miles of Mr. McConkey's Mill. The best road to Sheet Harbour is by Upper Musquodoboit, the distance from St. James Church there to St. John's at Sheet Harbour is twenty-seven miles. Twenty miles of this road is without settlers. It appears to have had a sprinkling of population most of the way; but the settlers have moved off and left their homes empty like beacons to warn future adventurers of the folly of seeking a living in such a dreary region. In the heyday of the war, while Halifax merchants did not know what to do with their money, large sums were expended in clearing land and building homes; the new tenants contrived to live as long as their masters supplied them with pork and flour for supposed improvements; but when the provisions were withheld would not put a nail in a shingle. They gradually moved to more favoured situations and with regard to any real improvement the farms might well have been tenanted by Orang Outangs. The large farm of Mr. Robert Hartshorne has all gone to ruin. Brushwood has got possession of the Patterson farm. Bishop Burke's shingle palace has been pulled down by the Indians. The best establishment on the road is the farm belonging to Mr. Esson and its dwelling house occasionally affords a shelter to the benighted traveller. In good hands it would cut plenty of hay for a large stock of cattle. The office houses went to ruin but the Mansion House is a decent-looking ruin and were it situated in a remarkable part of the country would easily maintain a ghost.

He dwells on the subject of ghosts in lonely places and advises a man to have a tomahawk on his saddle, a feed of oats for his horse and a few crackers for himself before starting through the bush as it is wild and lonely and all he will hear will be a woodpecker hammering at a rotten stub. But we swung into the road and after a first narrow mile or so found it wide enough and in good condition as trucks were running plaster and lumber to Sheet Harbour. There were many

parked cars here and there for a gunning season had opened
and as we sat in some stretches admiring the foliage a ruffed
grouse walked into the road beside us. Now and then we saw
a porcupine. Twice we saw cranes rise from a brook and
several times a deer crossed the way. In all we met four cars
during the twenty-seven miles through the woods and it was
as lovely a drive as one could wish. The road was a bit rough
just at Sheet Harbour but over twenty miles of the way was
all a person could wish. And anyone who likes to photograph
wild life would have a wonderful time.

We turned right and drove along to Musquodoboit
Harbour, turned right again off the paved road and drove
through Gibraltar and Meagher's Grant and Elderbank back
to Middle Musquodoboit. The road was not as good as that
to Sheet Harbour but a careful driver will have no trouble
and it is interesting back country. We came to a man who
had a flat tire. His car looked old and tired and so did he
so we cheerfully got out our jack and raised his rear axle and
showed how much we knew about changing tires. He was
very grateful for it all and said he would be glad to get home
before his wife started to worry, and then he said he was
known around the district as "Schemer John." We asked why
and he said that he had had trouble deciding which girl to
choose for a wife. Alice was a pretty blonde who was clever
with a needle and made her own hats, which would save a
man some money. Jennie was dark but played the organ at
church and was an excellent cook. One night he was taking
them home from a party when the old Ford he drove ran out
of gas. He told them to sit tight till he borrowed some from
a neighbour a mile up the woods road. Alice was terrified as
there were only side curtains on the car and begged him not
to go. Then Jennie said that she would go and that would
solve the problem. Whereupon he got his spare can from the
back and poured gas into the tank, took Alice home first and
proposed to Jenny. "And I've never been sorry yet," he added.

We drove along as it was getting dusk when we neared
Elderbank and then we slowed to low speed and passed with

care for on our left a mama skunk headed a family parade and her four children were almost as big as she. There would be a powerful barrage if trouble brewed and we used every caution. It made us recall that the Hon. Joseph Howe was not long in his beloved Musquodoboit when he saw a pretty kitten one evening and went to stroke the dear. What happened was sickening and it was a week before the air was properly cleared. He thereafter knew the striped animals as "Tory kittens."

Lights were glowing from various homes as we passed along and then in a wooded stretch we saw eyes glowing and three racoons watched us from a glade like so many young dogs. Out we went to Stewiacke, taking the long way simply to chance seeing more wild life but none appeared and we remembered vividly a wild night when we had been to Middle Mosquodoboit to a meeting that lasted until eleven. When we were outside the rain was pouring down and the wind was a power, but we wanted to get home and started via the Milford road. We stopped in a narrow part as a huge tree fell across the way. Then we backed half a mile to get a chance to turn, swung around and started out the Shubenacadie way. Soon we saw lights ahead and here was another tree down, a car stopped and some angry men chopping with axes. When they had severed the upper part of the blow-down we could just get by and then came a third tree down but we could drive in the ditch and get past. It was surely a night one would not forget.

8

Through the Garden of Eden

THE next day we drove up Highway 7 to Sherbrooke and then started more adventuring. We turned left at Melrose and headed along to Caledonia and up to Sunny Brae. Some might get nervous in spots but one can get through all right on a dry day and it is grand scenery. We talked with one farmer who said his grandfather had made a map of the country showing every cart lane and farm bridge but it had gone with a relative to the United States. He had grown up with five other lads in the community and not one had stayed. Three of them were in New England and the others were in "Canada." He had no desire to travel, however, as he did his roaming in books. He said that when a lad he had to bucksaw the birch and maple hauled in from the bush for cooking fires and generally on Saturdays would have a book of some sort propped in the sawhorse crotch, and minutes at a time his saw would go to sleep in its white notch. His father was easily angered at sight of the books but his mother encouraged his reading. "I reckon," he observed, "I'd read everything printed that was in this settlement time I was fourteen. Then I had a fine Newfoundland dog an uncle gave me and I never got lonesome when the other lads left. I never had another dog before or after I liked as much as 'Blackie.' He could do everything but talk. Stories around here? Used to be some, but mostly yarns, I think. There was an old woman lived at a lane end up the road fifty years ago, and she got mighty lonesome after her man died. Weeks on end hardly anybody went to see her and she got no mail so the postman didn't stop. At last there came a fall night when she got desperate and went out and lit sixty candles, sticking them along the pole fence a foot apart. They were all she had for a few month's supply but she lit them, and the glow in the sky—it was a real dark night—sent a dozen of the neighbours hot-foot, they thinking her place was on fire. When they saw the candles, and she cried and told them why she'd lit them, the folks felt ashamed, and they say she never wanted company after that."

We asked if he could remember when candles were used, and he brightened at once.

"I was one single soul in all this county I guess that didn't care about oil lamps. It always seemed kinder than any other kind of light, and made a person's face look as if it had a kind of glow. And we used to read about candle light on armor and satin and pewter and in secret passages and tower stairs and the like, and you could see it in fancy, but you never read about 'lectric light on anything. No, sir, give me the good old candle any time."

He followed us to the car and seemed reluctant to see us go and we asked if the winters seemed long. "No," he said quickly. "No longer'n the summers. In the winter we've got 'hockey night in Canada,' and I do love them games."

We drove up to Bridgeville and Springville, learned there was paved road on a left fork up to Eureka and Hopewell and drove that way. It was a lovely fall day, and we were almost wishing we had waited for fall to do all our exploring, and along that drive that day, and the next day's drive from New Glasgow down through the Garden of Eden we met more grand old-timers of excellent memory and kind words and hospitality than we had thought possible. We did not see half a dozen American cars in the two days and it is a great pity that this wonderful area belongs to the half of Nova Scotia that is rarely explored. We heard a song sparrow and stopped the car near an old farm. It was warm for the time of year and some "cracklers"—locusts—were making themselves heard by a bare clearing. Crickets helped out in the afternoon's music and an old man came out and asked if we didn't want to rest a while. I said I'd like to walk a distance up the slope back of his house where there was scattered growth and traces of an old road, and he eagerly insisted that I go. I saw yellow hammers and a large woodpecker, and chickadees, saw scarlet berries above the yellowing leaves of the painted trillium, and china-white clusters of the white bane berry, pigeon berries and part-ridge berries, wintergreens and a patch of blackberry bushes. A brown snake rustled underfoot and stuck out its tongue at me. A squirrel raced frantically up a birch and scolded, and I saw some of those long "loopers" or "measuring worms" that I hadn't seen since a boy.

The old man asked if I knew that Bridgeville fostered the first debating club in Nova Scotia, and that Pictou county had the first agricultural society, that Pictou had produced more doctors and preachers and lawyers than any other two counties. He had facts and numbers and names galore and told me that as a young man he had graduated from Pictou Academy. The good folk of Bridgeville were proud of the number of books they possessed and it was decided that a debating club should be formed. Rules were established that three speakers per side should argue, and three judges be elected. The first debate was to be held at the biggest house in the district and the subject was: "Resolved that anticipation is greater than realization." The good wife who was to be hostess was worried over the fact that hubby had procured a jug for the occasion but she dare not say anything about it. However when the debators and others were assembled she had more fears and took every chance to fill the dipper from the water bucket and pour it into the jug. The debate was lengthy and she did what she could. Those supporting Realization won. Refreshments were served and then the jug was passed. The first old-timer who hooked a practised thumb into the handle and drank, lowered the jug, shook his head, and stated loudly that the decision of the judges should be reversed.

The debating society lasted two years. There had been a shortage of men debators when spring planting was in swing and women who took their places had proven so smart that when the third year rolled around it was decided that the women were to debate against the men, that all would have the same chance as the topic would not be known beforehand. Each member could write a suitable resolution and these would be placed in a hat and drawn by the president. This was done, and it was evident that some wag was in the group. The paper read. "Resolved that wives will not be with their husbands in heaven." Soon there was a perfect clatter of tongues as angry women wanted to know how the husbands would get there in the first place. This brought many retorts and it ended with no debate being staged and the society disbanded.

"Learning is a wonderful thing," said the old man. "Two neighbours along the way here to town quarreled over the line fence, and one set out for town in the morning. He went to a lawyer in one of the blocks, and told his story. When he was finished the lawyer said he was sorry but he could not take the case as the other man had been in already and engaged him. This rather stunned the farmer and he asked where he might get a good lawyer. 'Right on the next floor,' said the lawyer heartily. 'And I'll give you a note introducing you, to make it easy'."

This seemed a kindness and the farmer took the note, climbed the stair and found that the lawyer had gone away for the day. This meant he would have to return in the morning and as the farmer drove home he thought of the note and looked at it. But the message was in Latin, and it made him wonder. He stopped at a watering trough as his horse was thirsty and while there a preacher drove up and exchanged greetings. "Do you know Latin?" asked the farmer.

"Quite a bit," said the preacher. "Anything I can do for you?"

"Read this." The farmer handed over the note and the preacher deciphered it at once.

"I don't understand it," he said, "but it says 'Here are two fat geese. You pluck one and I'll pluck the other'."

"Thank you, reverend," said the farmer. "It was a joke that I wasn't sure about."

He drove home and went to the man he had quarreled with, showed him the note and told his story, and there never was any more trouble, or any fat geese plucked.

There were other stories as the old man was full of them, and then he had steered us to the house and his good wife was insisting we stay to tea. "There's just we two after all these years," she smiled, "and we do love having company. I won't fuss any, and don't be alarmed about the stains on my fingers. I was putting up some herb juice I keep on hand for chilblains".

Soon she was telling us of dandelion leaves she used to clean poor blood, of cucumber juice for sun burn, raw potato juice for rheumatism, hot onion soup for bronchitis, the good of tea of caraway for nursing mothers. We said we doubted any doctor would have business in her area, and she said there hadn't been one in the house in forty years and her family had coped with most of the ailments that came to mankind. Then she talked of her family and relations, of a cousin who was a professor in Ontario, of another who was a doctor in Ohio, of an uncle who wrote for the magazines. "He began when he was at school," she related proudly. "He was only eleven when he got a prize for an essay. Now, dad, don't bother the people with your scrap book."

But we urged to see it and the old man had a large book of wallpaper samples pasted full of clippings on all sorts of things. Many were essays and some were humorous. We liked one a small boy wrote about geese:

A geese is a low heavy-set bird which is mostly meet and feathers. His head sits on one side and he sits on the other. A geese cannot sing much on account of dampness in the moisture and he is always out when it is wet. He ain't got no between-his-toes and he's got a little balloon on his stomach to keep him from sinking. Some gooses when they get big has curls on their tails and are called ganders. Ganders don't have to sit and hatch but just eat and loaf and go swimming. If I was a goose I'd rather be a gander.

The old man put on a coat and we had supper. It was a meal we enjoyed to the full as the biscuits were delicious as was the blackberry jam and sweet-apple pie. And we sat and talked and they told us about old times, legends handed down of first settlers along Hopewell and Springville and Sunny Brae, of Macdonalds and Camerons and Murrays and Mac-Kays and Sutherlands. There were giants in those days, as it was the best and brawniest of the Highlanders who had crossed the Atlantic to make new homes in New Scotland. There was Farquhar Falconer of Hopewell who stood six-foot-four, and weighed two hundred and seventy, and had hands that could grip a tree and twist the bark free at one wrench. One night at supper a bear came in the yard and grabbed a small pig and Farquhar rushed out. He had no time to get an axe or other weapon and the bear was still trying to drag the pig away so he straddled the big animal and grabbed it by the ears. The bear dropped the porker and struggled wildly and they were back and forth over the yard but brother Alec had seized a pitchfork and he reached bruin's heart with the tines as Farquhar never relaxed his grip. And a neighbour who was passing told the story and half the settlement rode in to see the bear that had no other mark than the punctures made by fork tines.

And there was Alex Mackay who was a perfect athlete, a big man built in proportion. He could out-stunt the sailors when a lad as he came to Canada, doing his tricks aloft in the ship's rigging. Then when accustomed to the woods he started after a young caribou one day and ran the animal to earth and dragged it home with him. This caribou calf was a great prize as one was wanted for the London zoo and it was sent

overseas, remained healthy and lived to old age in captivity.
A bull in the neighbourhood became vicious and no one dare
go near the barn in which it had been fastened. So they sent
for Alex. He came and opened the door and as the bull
charged he caught it by the horns and twisted it until it fell
to earth. He held it there by sheer strength and so mastered
the beast that when he finally let it up there was no more
fight in it, and no trouble thereafter. When Mackay was eighty
he swung his scythe all day with the other men and never
lagged a step. He lived to the age of ninety-seven.

We went to look at the scrap book again and the old lady
showed us the piece she liked best. It was by Leslie Nelson
Jennings, in the *Christian Science Monitor:*

THE PARLOR

> All things that had been cherished down the years,
> Too odd or choice for using every day.
> Knick-knacks and ornaments and souvenirs,
> Were gathered here and safely shut away.
> Blinds drawn on rosewood cabinet and plush,
> The gilt clock mute, the wax flowers still in bloom
> Under their dome of glass; a solemn hush
> Hallowed this almost legendary room.
> Only by special favour could we hope
> To spend a rainy Sunday afternoon,
> Looking at pictures through the sterescope,
> Playing the music box — we knew each tune.
> If there were places where a child could find
> More sheer delight, they're faded out of mind.

We talked and talked and then the old couple were plead-
ing for us to stay and sleep in the spare room under the eaves
where a great maple whispered at the window. So we did for it
was another world in that old house, a bit of the past carrying
all its aroma of long ago. Before we turned in we walked the
hill path again. The Dipper had swung low in the north and
in the east stood a moon verging on the full and promising
colour like a pumpkin in the field. We heard an owl making

queries of the thickening darkness, and after it had hooted a
few times some distant dog set up a clamour, for we imagined
the night was full of scents no country dog could ignore. Fox
scent, racoon scent, a mere man mightn't know a piece off, all
he could smell in a still September night. There was a smell
of apples, the sweet, winey smell of an old apple tree set with
ripeness, and the tangy smell of crabapples we had seen by an
old sheep fence, the cidery smell of windfalls left to ferment in
the grass. There was, too, the rank fragrance of goldenrod and
clover coming from where the old man had scythed weeds and
grass by the roadside. There was also a pond smell and as we
detected the mucky sourness of margin ooze we remembered
seeing stiff cat-tails in ranks against a background of banked
alders. Then as we walked back we caught the sweet wind from
the hilltop, slowed down to a night breeze, the sweetness of
September. You smell it in places like that old settlement in
Pictou county, and you feel it, and it seeps into your blood.
And you know why the owl hoots and why the dog barks, and
you almost wish you could, too.

In the morning we had breakfast in beautiful sunshine and
tasted real oatmeal porridge with real cream. Then we were
off and and around the first turn saw something belonging to
boyhood, now forgotten, a cow wearing a V-poke. And there
were some sheep, too, with pokes, and that day we saw so much
that belonged to fifty years ago that we felt the road should be
advertised as a tourist drive. Then thought that it might soon
be spoiled should everyone go that way and too many visitors
would change everything.

We talked with many, tarried less than an hour in town,
and were back on the Eden road in no time. Heard more
stories of Alex Mackay and about many others, of a woman
that made all the square nails used in a church and many
homes, a woman blacksmith who was better at the trade than
any man. We heard about the West River Agricultural Society
formed June 1, 1817 — fees one shilling and threepence
quarterly. Anyone who swore or used indecent language at a

meeting would pay a fine of five shillings, and their minutes
were headed by the following verse:

> Let this be held the farmer's creed,
> For stock seek out the choicest breed,
> In peace and plenty let them feed;
> Your lands sow with the best of seed,
> Let it not dung nor dressing want,
> And then provisions won't be scant.

In those first days settlers lived on Blue Mountain and
McLellan's Mountain, where there was a cave among the
many deep interstices in the limestone. It was 100 feet long
and a settler made it his summer home by inserting a door
and window and using a vent as a chimney. Then as more
people came a move was made toward East River St. Mary's
and there was only a blazed trail in most places and the first
year came the plague of the mice. The rodents were everywhere
in hundreds of thousands. They chased cats out of fields. They
ate everything including the potatoes and kept advancing in
millions until they reached over every bit of planted ground.
Many reached the sea and were drowned and made ridges
among the seaweed at tide reach and codfish swarmed in to
eat them as the tide rose.

There was always excitement in the early days as wild
animals and the Indians kept around in numbers. One hunter
chased a big moose on a cold winter day and shot the animal
just as a snowstorm started. The hunter was afraid he might
lose his way so after he had skinned the animal he wrapped
himself in the thick hide and crawled into a brush shelter.
When he woke hours later the storm was over but the hide
had frozen and he was firmly imprisoned. It took him hours to
work a hand free to use his knife and then hack the frozen
hide enough to gain freedom. And another hunter shot a
moose, saw it fall, leaned his rifle against a tree and went to
cut the animal's throat. Just as he reached it up jumped the
bull and charged him. He raced to a tree, got around it just in
time. He could dodge much quicker than the bull but had to

manage to reach the tree where his rifle stood, then to circle other trees at full speed while he handled powder and ball and ramrod. Eventually he had his rifle loaded and then put an end to the sport. He had encircled, his tracks showed, thirty-two different trees.

Donald Mackenzie had a small hunting camp in Eden and one night came and stood his rifle by the door, then went for fuel for his stone fireplace. As he returned he met a bear coming from the cabin. He dropped his wood and ran at top speed in one direction while the bear footed it a different route. Needless to say, the supper Donald anticipated was vanished. Some time later he was spending a night in the camp when he heard a wildcat leap on the pole roof. It clawed at the poles and snarled. Then he heard others outside and they ran round and round his camp, clawing now and then at the plank door and walls. But no entry could be effected and when daylight came there was a path beaten around the camp as if a flock of sheep had patrolled all night.

Then there was Donald Mackenzie who owned a big black bull with sharp horns. One day when the family was away a bear chased sheep in the pasture and had killed two when the bull broke down the fence of his field and charged in. There was a terrific battle but it ended in the death of the bear and though the bull was somewhat battered it survived. William MacDonald was the first man at the Garden of Eden and so, naturally, was called "Adam" by his friends. He planted six apple trees for his "Eve" and they flourished in good soil but the first year they bore fruit the Indians, watching closely, picked the green apples at night and ate them. The resulting agonies kept the redmen from the trees the next year, and they were amazed that the MacDonalds ate the fruit and suffered no pangs whatever.

The first settler going to East River St. Mary's from McLellan's Mountain borrowed four horses and tied his children on the back of one. They made their slow way through the bush and by blazed trail and when at last they reached the promised land "were too tired to go anywhere else." The cabin was erected and land cleared and in due time all was well. But one of the four horses was old and had been a family pet from coltish days so at first opportunity Dobbin hit out for home. It was hard to recall all the valleys and Dobbin could not watch for a blaze on a tree but took as direct a course as possible. It was unfortunate that a swamp extended across the way chosen, and that the old horse would not trouble to detour. Weeks after they found the bones, picked clean by bears and ravens. There were no roads for years and when a beef or pork had to be taken to market a horse drew two long poles which had crosspieces at the end and long pegs held the load being taken for sale. Many salmon in the river proved a boon to the first settlers and a dozen could be taken at a time in a set net. The great trouble was eels. These would eat all the meat and never crack the skin. Eel spears were made by the blacksmith and one drive during one afternoon netted more eels than could be carried from the river.

There was the story of the ambitious young groom who borrowed a sled and travelled on snowshoes to Pictou to make purchases for his bride. He bought an oven, two large cooking pots, two teapots, cups and saucers and knives and forks, large plates, a platter, a pitcher, three bowls and a jug and frypan. His return journey was all right the major part of the distance but when nearing home snow fell to the depth of eight inches, light fluffy snow that made the going too hard to pull the sled. So he made use of a length of rope he had purchased for himself and tied about him everything that had a handle, put the other items in a large Indian basket he borrowed and made the rest of the trip on snowshoes, looking, his bride said afterward, like a walking store as he arrived. But not even a cup was cracked, and a generation used the dishes without a mishap.

There were great trees in those days along the area through which we drove and there are records of elms along the Garden of Eden that were sixty feet high and more than three feet across the stump, being clean of limbs for thirty to forty feet. And there were pine and hemlock twenty feet taller and four feet across the stump, and Angus Cameron felled one great pine that was hollow toward the top and no fewer than five racoons emerged from sleeping quarters within. The first houses were made of round logs with moss stuffed between and plastered with clay, while the roof of lapping bark was held in place by poles tied down with strong birch withes. The men used the axes and adze, draw knife and auger to construct stools and benches, table, chairs and cupboards. Wooden dishes and wooden bowls were used until better could be had. Beds were of straw until the families acquired a flock of geese and feather beds added to warmth. Fires were never allowed to go out as no matches were invented and it was said that some of the first settlers became so accustomed to the chore they would rise and throw a log on the blaze and get back in bed without ever waking. The hardest chore was getting grain to the mill for grinding, and often this meant a two-day journey on snowshoes, hauling a sled over high drifts and through hollows. No one wanted to sleep out as means for making a fire were rare and so it was planned to stop over with someone at the halfway mark, and Sandy Fraser recorded having three different men with grists bedded down beside his fire on one night. These men slept on the floor of hewn planks and it was their duty and concern to keep the fire burning. The only other way to obtain flour was by the use of hand mills, a contraption with a heavier stone at the top, turned by main strength, a task so tiring that often a family would go without flour sooner than try operating the mill.

Many places were plagued by too much use of rum, and temperance societies were formed quite early in some parts of Pictou county. At one settlement the dry and wets were about equally divided and when a barn raising was to take place the builder, a temperance man, announced that no rum would be served. The drys assembled but the pushing up, with poles, of the framed side of a large barn, was a heavy task and the good friends were unequal to the occasion. A number of the opposition had arrived and these watched the attempt with amusement, then stepped forward and joined forces. Up went the framework and when the job was finished by nightfall, with much of the roof boarded, a jug was slyly brought from where it had been hidden as refreshments were being served. The owner accepted the situation with a smile, as the "rummies" had worked hard. Soon after, it was recorded, all but two families joined the society. On another occasion the owner refused to accept help from those who indulged in rum and his men were inadequate but the barn raising was postponed to a later date when distant friends of the drys attended and the work was accomplished. It was said that inside of twenty years one could go through the settlements and see roofs fallen in and land abandoned where king rum had ruled, while the homes of the members of the temperance society were enlarged and in good repair.

We saw the ghostly remains of the roadbed of what was to have been the Guysborough Railway. Much work was done, spurred at election time, but finally the undertaking was abandoned. And the visitor today will wonder what happened as he sees how far the track had proceeded, and he will puzzle, perhaps, at a monument bearing verses from Kipling's poem about the "children of Martha" who had to give their lives to toil. This was erected to the memory of some workers killed by accident during the building of the railbed. When we reached Aspen we could not resist going back a distance on the paved road to Sherbrooke and then turning off on another dirt road leading to Indian Harbour and Port Bickerton. We had loved the country and the woods and the people but wanted another whiff of salt air and a look at the sea. They are fine shore communities and we talked with several at Port Bickerton. Fish prices was a main topic and one oldtimer insisted that the government should fix two days a week when hotels and restaurants would serve nothing but fish.

"If it was Russia or some of them countries that ain't catering to the big shots we'd have such a rule here," he said, "and once the people had to eat fish they'd get to like it.

Half the trouble is that a lot of girls getting married these days hardly know how to boil water. They want to buy everything from the store in a packet with directions on how to use it, and they've got the funny idea that fish is a lot harder than meat to cook or fry. Fact is, it's much easier. And in them eating places you hardly know, toward the last of the week, what you are getting, and that makes me think of a verse you had in that gov'ment paper that run a time, called 'Hospitality' ":

> The wee-wee pigs and Mary's lambs all find
> their way to the table,
> With the little sons of Ferdinand, each bearing
> a "fresh meat" label.
> As veal or pork or prime lamb chop, they
> appear on the printed menu,
> Rare, medium, or well done they come, with
> many a change of venue.
> They all go along in a sausage roll that a
> hot dog may resemble,
> To meet once more in a Monday stew, where
> the strangest things assemble.
> No man knows as he cleans the bones, were
> the owner smooth or woolly,
> Were they soft with lard or tallow-lined, were
> they pig or lamb or bully.

Fishermen have a hard life. They live by the sea because it is their choice, and inheritance. They learn to handle a dory while others boys are learning to ride a tricycle. They become accustomed to having their income ruled by the luck of the market. The magnificent scenery that is spread before them each time they leave or enter port they take as a matter of course, and can never understand what visitors see to exclaim over where tiny piers dip stilted feet into the salt tide and ancient wharves are piled in picturesque confusion with lobster traps and fishing gear. Their wooden homes are weathered sea-grey in colour, with windows looking widely out to sea and doors built to stand the strain of winter storms. Their talk is always of the tide and wind and outboard motors but in summer they scan with pride the flowers the wife has planted around the house, the best blooms to the windward, and take hoe and spade to make vegetable gardens wherever there is earth sufficient. When we went in to inspect some relics brought back from South Sea islands by an ancestor we saw a good radio and record player, and noted a shelf of books, and some nationally-known magazines. One of the books was the poetry of Charles Bruce, and the man smiled as he saw me point to it. Then he opened it at a well-marked page and read, almost recited:

EASTERN SHORE*

He stands and walks as if his knees were tensed
To a pitching dory. When he looks far off
You think of trawl kegs rolling in the trough
Of swaying waves. He wears a cap against
The sun on water, but his face is brown
As an old main sail, from the eye brows down.
He has grown old as something used and known
Grows old with custom; each small fading scar
Engrained by use and wear in plank and spar,
In weathered wood and iron, and flesh and bone,
But youth lurks in the squinting eyes, and in
The laughter wrinkles in the tan-bark skin.
You know his story when you see him climb
The lookout hill. You know that age can be
A hill for looking: and the swaying sea
A lifetime marching with the waves of time.
Listen—the ceaseless cadence, deep and slow.
Tomorrow. Now. And years and years ago.

We went back by Route 7 to Antigonish for the night, then back on Route 4 to Sutherland River and away we went on a quite good secondary road to Merigomish and Lower Barney's River and Lismore and Knoydart and Doctor's Brook and Malignant Cove and Livingstone Cove to Cape George— every place interesting and filled with colour. We did see three or four American cars proceeding like explorers but the

---

*From *The Flowing Summer*, by Charles Bruce. Published by The Ryerson Press.

great majority never know of this drive which should be paved all the way and the main route for visitors. For the scenery is grand and the people are grand and one gets the full flavour of Nova Scotia by knowing all of it—not one-half.

When American privateers were roaming around Nova Scotia looking for the places likely to offer least resistance one lad had the bright idea of running around to the Northumberland Strait where his kind never reached and he came to Merigomish where a vessel loaded with West Indies produce had been fast in the ice all winter. Rations were scarce so a part of the crew had gone inland to Truro. A settler named Earl who was in full sympathy with the American cause set off after the vessel was fast and in some way got word to the privateer. It appeared suddenly to make the seizure and, unfortunately for them, James and David Patterson were making oak staves near the port. They were forced to go on board the privateer so they could not give alarm and were put in irons until the looting was completed. When the privateer sailed with the booty they released the two men but David had large wrists and the handcuffs would not release. So a burly lad put his hand on the rail and struck at the irons with a marlin spike, hitting David's thumb and shattering it for life. They then put the two men in a small boat with a few biscuits and a small toggie of sugar. The privateer was then far out in the Strait and night was coming on. The Pattersons rowed desperately and at last sighted land. Alarm had been raised too late and armed men were at the seaside when the boat was sighted, and James Patterson had to shout with all his lung power to halt the intentions of an officer who was ordering a volley fired at the intruders. The first settlers at Merigomish found plenty of salmon in the streams, great flocks of geese along the shore and game in the woods. There were many Indians, too, for Merigomish had ever been a favourite spot for the redmen when they held their annual sports in summer. The settlers' children played with the children of the Micmacs and it was said that several of the young Scots that were raised in the settlement could speak the Micmac perfectly. George Morrison was the second man at the colony and he was a big man, and able. While he was away from home one day two Indians came to his house and made his wife cook most of the food she had in her larder, which they ate until they could hold no more, and all the while they sat in comfort by the fire and would not let the Morrison children near it. When George arrived home and heard the story he was so enraged he started at once for the Indian camp. Luck had him meet up with the two culprits at the first wigwam, where they were still resting and digesting the feast they had had and which they had boasted about. Without any arguing, George set at them and threshed the pair within an inch of their lives, then stood there bare-handed and dared any man of the tribe to face him. It was enough. That night the whole lot struck camp and vanished. Another settler, Walter Murray, walked to Truro and carried back with him a bushel of seed potatoes. When he reached home he removed the eyes with a quill, and planted them, then ate the rest of the potatoes, so that ever after he would tell of "planting a bushel" and "eating a bushel" and "carrying both from Truro."

The Indians did not like the intrusion of settlers at Merigomish as they claimed it had been their headquarters for years. They came in July in large numbers and staged foot racing and jumping and dancing and mock battles, with much orating and feasting in the evenings. But none made trouble save with Murray who had taken land that had been the site of an Indian encampment. One chief came and planted corn in Murray's potato rows. So Murray went to him and with great ceremony paid him five pounds cash for the ground and had the Indian make his mark on a paper purporting to be a deed of the area. The Indian was so pleased to receive the money instead of an argument that he made his mark without delay and hurried off to Pictou to spend his riches.

The post office at Merigomish has unusual boxes and a man told us we should see them. There are thirty-two, all without keys, but each has a lock opened by a combination. On the top of each box is a plate and knob like that on a safe, and each owner uses his own code to open the box. The postmaster keeps a record of all the combinations in case someone forgets, and there is never any problem of lost keys. The postmaster, W. F. Smith, got the boxes from Timmins, Ontario. He has been postmaster for thirty-three years and has a scrap book in which he keeps a local history. It was amazing to know that approximately fifty vessels had been launched in the Merigomish area.

Lismore was the home of the woman blacksmith who knew metal better than most men and could make the finest square nails in the country. And somewhere beyond there or near Knoydart we talked some time with an oldish man who was splitting wood, a fall chore that men used to enjoy. There are several reasons for the enjoyment. It is not a pressing seasonal job that has to be accomplished by the dictate of time. The wood is got out in the winter by sled and then the saw comes around when the time is suitable and the neighbours give a hand and when the pile is finished the man goes along to the next house to return the assistance. Much later in the year, when the crops are harvested, the man starts splitting wood and wheel-barrowing it into his shed, working at a comfortable tempo and taking pleasure in the fact that he is prepared for another winter and independent of coal or oil shortages. The feel of his favourite axe is pleasant—an axe just the right heft and balance, not too heavy and with a razor-keen cutting edge. The secret of efficient work is not brute strength but an art that one learns by experience, and the use of a solid splitting block that is exactly the right height to get the full power of the blow. Each chunk of wood presents a separate problem, and each must be studied for its run of grain. Clear pieces of maple and beech split easily. It is when there are knots and twists to contend with that a man takes a minute to ponder, then, perhaps, tosses the chunk into the pile that will be used in the Quebec heater that stands in the hall. As we chatted we noted the clean aromatic fragrance of the split wood blended with the spicy pungency of the disturbed sawdust.

"I got a sister in Antigonish," said the splitter, "and the 'lectric power went off when I was calling and it was like the end of the world. She hadn't any light or heat and couldn't cook. No, sir, them 'lectric gadgets is all right when all's fine but you're stuck when they go out of kilter. Now you can rely on good wood for furnace and stove, and long as you've got kerosene the lamps won't go out." He paused and sniffed. "My woman's cooking a batch of ginger cookies," he mused, "and there ain't no harm in us seeing how they turned out."

He was no more than started toward the kitchen than his good wife appeared with a plate of lovely cookies hot from the oven, and there is nothing that tastes better than cookies from a woodstove on a farm. There seems to be some ingredient not included when the baking is done on an electric range in town.

Lismore means "great sight" in Gaelic and when you see the green meadows with a mountain in the background you will understand the term. An old man told us about Mrs. Moses Priest making the square nails for the church, and another told us about an old mare coming to the farmyard on Sunday afternoon and pawing at the gate until the man went to see what was wrong. Whereupon she turned and headed back over the pasture, looking to see if he were following. So he went along and found her mate with his head through the pole fence in such a position that he could not withdraw. The fence had to be taken down to release the horse and the mare stood by and watched with obvious approval.

The *Malignant* was carrying troops from Prince Edward Island to Quebec when a wild, blinding snowstorm descended while the vessel was in the Strait and visibility was almost nil. The storm was such that there seemed no hope as the gale increased but the captain glimpsed a cove and did what he could, managed to swing the ship into the cove stern first and get to shore. It was bitterly cold as the men landed and there were no habitations near, so all started to walk to the nearest village and many reached homes at Barney's Brook. The doctor found the going hard and collapsed and died by a brook ever after named "Doctor's Brook." The majority survived the storm and afterward men went with sleds to salvage the ship's cargo.

The scenery around Livingstone Cove and around Cape George and Ballantyne Cove is remembered by all who are fortunate enough to drive that way. Land and hill and water blend in vistas of unusual beauty and the drive down along George Bay is interesting. We stopped half a dozen times and chatted with kind folk and were told of heroic sea captains and intrepid settlers and moose hunts and old-time barn raisings and chopping frolics and quilting bees that made life bearable in the good old days. "We used to have plenty of company in the days when I was a girl," sighed one white-haired old lady. "Everyone come on an afternoon if it were stormy or a Saturday, for mother owned a pair of real barber's scissors and was the best hair cutter in the county. She cut the hair of near every man in twenty miles of our place, and that was all the barbering they wanted for nobody shaved. We built where we were, I've heard my father tell many times, because there was a good spring. And before the fire, before the bread, he would say, drinking water comes first. It's first of all the bedrock things that keep a farmstead strong. He put half a molasses puncheon down where that spring was by digging deep, and it never went dry the hottest summer we had nor froze in winter. We used to call it a boiling spring. He had other notions, my old father, and always had every bed in the house with the head turned north for restful sleep. He said it was the way the world went around. And he always said bones should be saved from the roast as there was as much good from bones boiled for a broth as in the meat itself."

She asked us to call on her sister who lived two miles on, and we did, because she said there were racoons in the farm-yard every evening and her sister often fed them. The sister proved to be a kind-voiced, kind-eyed lady who scorned all frills and favoured us with accounts of a mink that got into her chicken pen and created havoc, of a deer that came to the garden for fresh lettuce until she put sugar on what was left and the deer wouldn't swallow another mountful, of a crow that came to feed with the hens in the yard and finally lighted on the window sill one day and made off with a thimble. The more she talked the more interesting she became as wild life was her hobby and she had a scrap book filled with pictures of moose and deer and porcupine and beaver and dozens of other animals even to tigers and elephants. And the back part of the book was filled with animal stories she had clipped from provincial papers. She insisted on us reading one choice bit— *The Diary of a Racoon,* by Gertrude Ryder Binnett:

Here on this ancient open book of sand beside a fern-bound brook. Inscribed by paws all silver-tipped upon a moonlit manuscript, in writing cuneiform and bold the racoon's diary is told. Here in a silent pool of night the polliwogs were stirred to fright—a score of comets, fat and black, scooting away and wriggling back. And here the grottoes of the trout were searched and morsels raided out. Tracks, retraced and blurred, express his ritual of cleanliness. With etiquette of innate laws he gripped each bit in eager paws, and washed it, feasting all alone. Then, here beside a moss-grown stone, he paused, content with his repast. He left his signature at last, in ink of night, and he was gone. His page concluded with the dawn.

We had buckwheat pancakes for tea and an apple pie almost too good to be true. Then we sat and waited two hours and not a racoon had grace enough to put in an appearance, causing our hostess much impatience. She made threats of letting them go hungry the next time they appeared, and we reluctantly left her after she had proudly told us of a famous teapot at Ballantyne Cove that was shown to visitors for years. It bears the inscription: "Presented to Captain Angus MacDonald of the brigantine *Trust* of Maitland, Nova Scotia, in acknowledgment of his humanity and kindness to the shipwrecked crew of the ship *Coronet* of Liverpool, which was abandoned at sea in November, 1881." Our hostess told us it was a handsome silver pot with an ebony handle and had been presented to the brave captain by Queen Victoria.

It was a lovely drive in bright moonlight to Antigonish, and we thought of the roads we had travelled the last day or so and wished that motor visitors could have such an experience. The road map handed out at Information Bureaus shows these roads in brown lines, and one cannot get lost. We loved the shore roads that wound in and out to the whims of cove and inlet, and we liked as well the quiet roads that wound around the sloping shoulders of hills the natives call "mountains," and then meandered along the sides of upland ridges. From open places one has a down-hill view of boulder-dotted pastures and brook-traversed intervales where elms stand sentinel. Sometimes the road dips to shady ravines where small brooks tumble over grey-white stones and sing muted songs below old plank bridges. On some of the open stretches the roads are sandy; in the wooded places they are firm and moist. Generations ago men trekked through virgin forest looking for favourable homesites. One could write part of the nation's history in terms of its roads. At first there were blazed trails followed by horse paths, then by rough roads for ox carts, with stumps here and there so big they had to be by-passed; then came the better roads good enough for farm wagons and buckboards loaded with grist, and the mail driver's two-wheel road cart. Spring and fall men worked out their statute labour with log drags and shovels, digging occasional drains at low places and taking out stones on the grades. Each road had the wheel ruts and the hollowed centre that was the horse path where plodding hoofs scuffed the dust and tramped the earth to powder. Now the more remote off-roads drowse through the changing seasons. Some seem to dare the motorist to venture on them. Rock maple, poplar, birches, hemlock, spruce and pine lean over them. Squirrels and chipmunks race along the tops of stonewall boundaries, and woodchucks dig their dens underneath. From spring to frost wildflowers flaunt their blooms by the roadside and raspberries and blackberries fruit and ripen in full view. Year by year these old roads are more forgotten as Nature recovers that which man once wrested from her. Traffic follows the paved arteries in endless rush but for a long time yet there will be roads in the back country that are a reminder of pleasant times when life was less hurried.

We reached Antigonish and found quarters for the night. When we spoke of where we had been the clerk expressed his regret that we had not driven from the Cape in time to visit Crystal Cliffs, eight miles back, were a colony of cormorants had become so used to visitors that one could get real close to them. Dozens of folks had gone to get photographs of them, he said, and on the beaches there one found stones of every colour. "More people have carried away pink rocks from Crystal Farm than from all the other parts of Nova Scotia," he declared.

But we had to miss something, and so we made our plans to drive over the new causeway to Cape Breton in the morning and start more adventuring off the trail at Grand Anse.

9

Cape Breton Corners

IT was another bright and sunny morning and we crossed the causeway in a line of cars bearing American licence plates, kept up with some of them, and then turned from Highway 4 at Grand Anse. In a moment we were by ourselves through the road was paved and the scenery promising better things ahead. We drove onto Isle Madame by bridge and were soon in historic territory. French Hugenots from Jersey were first settlers and the place was called "Sante Marie." Later it became "Isle Madame" in honour of Madame de Maintenon, second wife of Louis XIV of France. We drove along by open fields, saw distant water and flocks of crows almost merging with soaring gulls. Next came a slope and there we met a lad with a steer hitched to a small toy-like wagon. He said it was the family conveyance, in constant use for various purposes and gladly accepted a quarter for posing beside the young steer for a picture. Soon we were at Arichat, corruption of an Indian word meaning "split rock," an old town that wears an aura of history and age and peace. It goes back to 1784 and is so spread across the rugged ground that artists come each summer to try and trap the elusive beauty on canvas.

Rock Loaf Farm is one hundred acres spread about half a mile from the village main street. It's on the other side of the hill and offers a fine view. The name comes from a huge, loaf-shaped, scrub-covered pile of rock which shades a natural artesian well which never goes dry and is ice-cold during the heat of summer, as it is believed to be fed from Bottomless Lake, several hundred yards away, a water stocked with trout and fed by scores of springs. On the shore side of the farm is a salt water lake offering good swimming, a sort of inside beach, and at the entrance to the farm are depressions that show traces of gypsum mining in the long ago. J. Emile Benoit owns the farm and is a progressive farmer. He has a herd of the famous Bowater cattle, imported from Newfoundland. The original stock came from Scotland but these Bowater Ayrshires have been developed on the big farm of the Bowater Pulp and Paper Company at Cornerbrook, Newfoundland. Mr. Benoit uses modern methods on his farm, using a new-type harvester that cuts and loads grass into a feeding cart, which takes the pasture to the cows. He also uses a Doane-Pole barn, called a "loafing barn." This one has room for fifty cattle to roam around and help themselves at self-feeding silos. This cuts labour costs and an opening is never closed, allowing the cattle to come and go at will.

Among the firstcomers to the Arichat area were the Robin brothers who settled on what was soon called "Jerseyman's Island," at the mouth of the harbour. John came first and Charles came soon after, but he would go home for the winter. When he stayed on Jerseyman's Island the first winter he was almost frozen despite the fact that they had banked their rude dwelling high with turf. The wind carried all the heat up the stone chimney, it seemed, and Charles declared in his diary he did little other than chop wood to feed the fire. Their bread would freeze so solidly overnight that it took an hour to thaw it after the fire was made up, and not once was the fire allowed to go out over a period of five months. Each brother took turns in getting up to place logs on the embers whenever the fire got low.

A barrel of beer was rolled into their room and stood near to the fireplace but it had frozen and did not thaw out until

March. The brothers were energetic and established other fishing posts in various parts of Cape Breton. They continued to prosper and eventually the firm became Robin, Jones and Whitman. Then they had trouble with a "Jones." The fellow is featured in a new American novel entitled *Gallant Captain,* but John Paul Jones proved anything but gallant when he came as a pirate and sacked Jerseyman's Island, seizing two vessels, the *Hope* and the *Bee,* and loading his booty on the *Bee.* However he spent much time exploring about the permises to make sure he was not missing anything and two British warships were sighted on the horizon. Jones was a terror when those he preyed on were unarmed, but he had no stomach for dealings with armed men. So he hastily set fire to the *Bee* and fled.

The fire on the *Bee* was extinguished and the goods saved and placed back in the storehouse. Then cannon were brought and established at a point from where fire could be brought to bear on any intruder. All the workers at Arichat at the beginning were brought from Jersey, carpenters, coopers and blacksmiths, and soon they had settled the place. They also brought out Jersey lilies, a stately flower with red petals that can be seen today in dozens of gardens all over Isle Madame. We drove on around the island and saw lobster traps piled in precarious array at Little Anse. And there was wool hung to dry on fences, and fish nets. Petit de Grat is very old and the seascape attracts many painters. At Cap la Ronde we were told that at one time the place supplied half the cabbage used in Cape Breton, as the soil was exactly right for such planting, and that a vegetable farm run by a woman had operated for years. D'Escousse dates back to 1752, an old man claimed, and said that each year a number of artists and photographers are there. He also told us about the old cannon at Arichat.

This cannon had been placed on a hill above the town and was used on special occasions. During World War One a British warship that had been badly battered during a storm steamed in the harbour for respite and a loyal citizen urged that the cannon be fired as a salute. This was done and the warship responded with a salvo that broke every window in the house walls below the town. So the man who had fired the cannon was called everything but a hero. The cannon's roar could be heard all along the shore and was used to call farmers and fishermen and their families to such events as church celebrations. There came a Saturday, however, when the old gun would not fire. Some thought that the gun powder was too old so a new quantity was purchased and poured in and more matches struck but without avail. It was a wet and drizzly day and others suggested that the powder had dampened. Dried powder was poured in but it was all the same and at last word had to be sent along shore by men on foot. Sunday came in very warm, a hot sun soon drying the ground and causing everyone to shed coats. After the morning service a fish hand and his friend wandered up the hill to the cannon, and the fish hand used it as a seat. He was smoking a pipe and when he finished he carelessly tapped it clean on the breach. Boom! There was a terrific report. There were at least four large helpings of gun powder in the cannon and it rocked on its ancient platform like a bucking pony. An onlooker said afterward that the fish hand soared about ten feet in the air as the blast was released and that his feet were going like pistons long before he hit the ground. He never stopped running, it was said, until he was in Grand Anse.

We drove back on Highway 4 to a small place called Cleveland and there took a road that led to West Bay on the Bras d'Or Lakes. The road was narrow as we went on along the coast but the views were simply magnificent. In places great parapets fronted the lake with sublime austerity. Then the road would descend to a glen of exquisite artistry. And there seemed to be forest life in every dim retreat as we counted no fewer than five deer by the time we had reached Marble Mountain, and also saw a porcupine and a flock of ruffed grouse. Sometimes we were high up where we could look over rippling seas of tree tops, a dozen different shades of green blended, in places, until all looked purple. The road was narrow and passing another car might be tricky but it was a long winding path of dreams come true as far as scenery goes. We stopped at one spot where bright waters danced down moss-lined terraces of darkstone, and a faint path led to a ravine. There was the inexplicable lure and magic of a silent winding woodland trail but we had to go on as there was no place to park, and then we emerged on a shelf-like ledge with the lake stretched in blue panorama and dotted with islands. To our left were great quarries like hollow ghosts of the past. A few long-deserted buildings were grey spots here and there and a huge rambling old building that was the community store loomed on our right. We climbed to the top of the hill by the quarries and gazed up the lake almost in awe. Cape Breton is the most beautiful part of Canada and there are vistas around Ingonish that baffle description but from that hill top one has a view that is unforgettable. The lake is a lovely sapphire in an emerald setting, and, far up, where the light breeze caused ripples, the colours seemed to deepen. For years the marble was quarried and shipped to many places. Two of the finest buildings in Halifax at the turn of the century were faced with this marble. Large crews had steady work and the quarries had their own cutting mills and rubbing tables. Then, in 1900, the Dominion Steel people leased the quarries to obtain material wanted for fluxing. When the lease expired it was not renewed and blight descended on the village. The workmen had to move away. They left their homes to the elements or the neighbour's chickens. More and more went until only two or three families remained and the big store was empty and grass grew on the hill road. The whole place shouts of tragedy.

We drove on to Malagawatch and a man to whom we gave a lift told us about a colony of blue heron that could be seen not three miles away. He said the long-legged bird had nested there for a hundred years, probably, as old nests had rotted away and been replaced until the rotted material had made hummocks below, and no one had ever gone near to cut down a single tree of the grove as the stench in summer was unbearable. Rotting fish that had fallen from the feeding youngsters, rotten eggs that did not hatch, and decaying youngsters that had died and been pushed out, all combined to produce an odour that could be detected almost the three miles distance. Our passenger also told us about the oysters at River Denys, and said thousands of barrels had been gathered and shipped away. He said that even boys of ten or twelve gathered oysters with a rake to make a few dollars, and urged that we insist on River Denys oysters whenever we were buying such a treat. Then we were at Orangedale, and asked our friend how it came to have such a name. He said there were about seven families in the place and it had no postal address so they called a meeting. It so happened the day was July 12th, and one of the men was an Orangeman. After a long debate in which nothing original had been proposed, the Orangeman rose and proposed they name the place Orangedale and his suggestion was accepted gratefully by the weary pioneers.

"You are really coming to a beauty spot now," announced our man. "I don't think Whycocomagh need take a back seat from either Marble Mountain or Ingonish. And it's got history, too. These places on our left was all Indian reservation, and the Micmacs used that ground back farther than any of their history can tell. They almost had a battle among themselves about the time the first Scots were around. There were two pretty Indian girls then in the village and three young bucks wanted them as wives and were ready to fight to see who would be the winner. Three wanting two made a pretty problem and the old chief wondered how he could prevent bloodshed. Then he had the bright idea of letting the two girls do the deciding. As the tribe gathered in great ceremony he rose and made his announcement. The girls then were asked to act and to the amazement of the Indians each walked over and selected herself a man from those not in the fray. The trio were left looking so dumbfounded that all the other Indians began to laugh, and they laughed the three who had been so determined right out of the field.

When the first settlers had their homes there was only one

who had a frame house. The others were log huts, temporary shelters. But one man had money and he also had a comely daughter and felt she would soon want to marry. He could not consider a wedding in a log cabin so purchased sawn timbers and boards at Sydney and brought them down the lake to Whycocomagh. When his house was ready he moved in and shortly after a neighbour came and said his daughter wanted to be married and to invite all hands but there was no room in the small cabin. Could she be married in the house? Certainly, said the generous Highlander, and the wedding was duly celebrated. This gave the idea to another girl and soon there was another wedding in the frame house that looked like a palace beside the cabins. Then came a third and fourth wedding in the house. There had been no church but services were held under a big tree and our friend pointed out the spot to us. Finally as more and more settlers arrived it was decided to erect a church and one was built by community effort. And the first wedding in it was when the daughter of the man who had brought the framework from Sydney was married.

Whycocomagh is sheltered by hills all around—a delightful retreat. There is a small hotel and we saw two cars from New York parked nearby. Our friend left us and we drove on and turned right at Little Narrows and drove down to Grand Narrows. The village of Iona at Grand Narrows is Scottish to the core, and there is an atmosphere that reminds one of some austere Scottish hamlet. We walked about and found it difficult to engage someone in conversation until we met a man who carried a basket as if it were filled with eggs. Soon he was telling us of his uncle who had been a mighty man of muscle in the old days and who had brought the old claymore from the homeland. Uncle Donald was about six and a half feet tall and when someone came and said a bear was bothering the sheep he seized the claymore and set forth. There was not one bear, however, but three. One was so intent on its sheep-herding tactics that Donald got near enough to deliver a mighty stroke that severed the bear's head. Wiping off the blade with a handful of grass, he charged at the other bears uttering a wild war cry that started ravens croaking a mile back in the forest. One bear simply scuttled for safety but the other rose on its hind legs and when Donald made his stroke the claymore was sent flying by the boxer. However the bear had seen enough and it started to follow its companion, with Donald running along beside until they reached the claymore. Then he seized bruin by the rump and hauled the animal to a standstill. It rose to repeat its boxing effort but this time Donald feinted and kicked a great boot at the same time. The kick in the middle fairly doubled the bear and down swept the steel to decapitate as neatly as before.

One morning Donald wanted to make a trip by boat to Baddeck with a friend who said he would start at seven. Donald lived alone and wondered how he would waken in time, thought of his rooster and fetched him in the house and placed him under a tub. The dawn crow would be all the alarm needed. Donald woke at ten, leaped up and overturned the tub to find the rooster dead from want of air. "And a mighty lucky thing for ye," snarled the enraged Donald.

At a picnic held at Iona in those good old days someone from Sydney introduced the sport known as "pulling the lazy stick." This was a game of the long ago that had many followers and we had heard of many champions during our driving off the main trails. There was huge John Kent of Amherst who had been at Advocate in the old days when a giant negro weighing three hundred pounds, the cook on a vessel loading lumber, pulled all comers. The Advocate men sent for Kent who was six foot four and weighed two hundred and sixty-four pounds, all bone and muscle. Large bets were placed and Kent threw the negro cook over his head three times. Then there was Jehu Mosher of Newport, a giant weighing almost three hundred who picked up an anchor on a bet and carried it thirty feet. The anchor weighed over five hundred pounds and Mosher's boots burst at the seams as he walked, but he won the money. And on a gala day in Halifax he pulled every man who offered by the lazy stick. We thought of the Donald Macdonald they had told us about in Pictou County, who lived at Grant's Lake, stood six foot five inches tall and weighed two hundred and ninety. He had never met a man he could not down and at some barn raising had challenged the two biggest men to wrestle him together. And never had any two of them been able to put Donald on his back. And no one could oppose him with the lazy stick. What a fine sport it would have been to have all these old giants meet at some spot and settle arguments. A boat on a pleasure cruise from Sydney touched at Iona one holiday and among those on board was a huge Swede who had bested Sydney's champion in a lazy stick duel. Soon he was matched with Donald and a crowd gathered. Donald knew nothing of the game. He sat down and gripped the stick, placed fairly above their toes, and was yanked upward a foot or so at the signal "go." Then he saw the trick of the game and, somehow, managed to regain ground. One great heave and the Swede was spread-eagled on the grass, and there was no second pull. The Swede had sprained his ankle with effort as he hoisted Donald the twelve inches.

On we went to Shenacadie and Beaver Cove and Boisdale and Barachois to Leitches Creek. The road is narrow and rough in places but there is no trouble if you take it slowly and you are following St. Andrew's Channel all the way, with wonderful scenery. Here and there we chatted with folk along the way, and all were friendly. We had learned that Shenacadie was an Indian name meaning "place of cranberries," that Barachois had produced some men prominent in provincial affairs, that there was a Game Sanctuary at Leitches Creek. Then we went on to Sydney for the night and found the Isle Royal Hotel tops in every way.

In the morning we drove to Glace Bay on Highway 4, noted for its coal mines and swordfish, and kept on six miles to Port Morien, which was "Cow Bay" in the old days, so named because a man from Sydney purchased a cow at Louisbourg and took her home by boat. At first chance she escaped his barn and headed for home, had reached "Cow Bay" before being overtaken. It was at this place that the French mined coal and a cairn there bears the following inscription:

Canada's Coal Industry. Two thousand feet south-easterly from this place are the remains of the first regular coal mining operations in America, established by the French in 1720. From the modest beginnings of those early days this industry has become one of national and imperial importance.

It was not a super highway we followed around to Mira but any car can get along, and though they call it Mira River it is really an inlet of the sea and many people have fine summer homes there. We talked with a gentleman by Albert Bridge, once called Mira Gut, and he told us of first English settlers finding in the area the remains of a huge French farm. The barn was almost sixty feet in length and had stalls for forty cattle and a great number for horses. The house had been burned but it had been very large and the chimneys and brick showed that it had contained ten fireplaces. All around were scattered implements, spades and axes and bars and mattocks, carts and barrows and sleds.

There are two places on this road twenty-three miles from Sydney. One is Louisbourg, the town that has a thriving fish industry; the other is Louisbourg National Historic Park, slightly over a mile from the town and containing over 328 acres. Two cairns and four tablets mark historic features, and a fine museum houses hundreds of relics unearthed from time to time among the ruins of the ancient French fortification. There is, as well, a relief map showing the place as it was in the days of its splendour. Much work has been done. Old wells have been opened and old cellars cleaned so that the original line of streets of the great walled city can be traced. The vaulted crumbling casemates show how gigantic a task even the destruction of the fortress must have been. One drives through the memory of the Maurepas gateway, over the reedy moat to Rochefort Point and the cemetery where French and British and New England soldiers sleep in peace. The situation of the old fortress is unique; the harbour, its rocky mouth and frontal island; the Atlantic gnashing against gray, gnawn cliffs; grassy marshes and meadows backed by the woods. All this and more may be seen from yesterday's ramparts while the wind is never still, whispering eternally in the long grass, and when mist hangs over the park, lone gulls sail overhead like eerie phantoms of the past.

The first lighthouse on the Cape Breton coast was at Louisbourg. It was built in 1731, the first concrete fireproof building in America. Coal was burned in an iron pan set in a tripod, seen six leagues away. An oil lantern was established in 1736, and was shot away during the siege of 1758. Tablets affixed to the tower read:

Louisbourg. On this site was erected by France, in 1731, the first Lighthouse Tower, constructed of fireproof materials, in North America. Near here the British erected batteries to silence the defensive works erected by France on the island opposite the entrance. In 1745, these batteries were commanded by Lt. Col. John Gorham; in 1758, by Brigadier General James Wolfe.

This tablet commemorates the valour and endurance displayed against overwhelming odds by the French forces, who, in 1745, and again in 1758, garrisoned the defensive batteries on the island opposite the entrance to the harbour of Louisbourg and facing this spot.

By the terms of the Treaty of Utrecht in 1713, Great Britain was given undisputed possession of the whole Atlantic coast of North America with the exception of Prince Edward Island, some islands in the Gulf of St. Lawrence and Cape Breton Island. France saw that a determined effort on her part would be necessary if this island, known to France as Isle Royale, were to be retained. Accordingly, in 1717 the work of constructing the immense fortifications of Louisbourg planned by the engineer Vauban, was begun and was continued for twenty years. Meanwhile the impression grew throughout New England that unless the British had control of the whole coast, the safety of New England was in constant jeopardy. This though their ships traded there constantly and old French records reveal that as many as fifty New England vessels would call there during a single season and carry away goods they secured in exchange for produce. There is also an account of an English frigate going to Louisbourg to claim eighty deserters from the garrison at Annapolis. The story of Louisbourg is one of years of inefficiency, of amazing drunkeness, of graft in all forms, of scanty funds, of smuggling and deceit. The officers in command of the garrison often inherited their commissions without doing as much as a month of drill, and all drew excessive provisions in order to sell to the civilians or use the extra in their own household. The soldiers were on the verge of mutiny most of the time. Some worked at jobs all day and drew the soldiers pay just the same. Some had not done a guard in ten years. Many had shacks in the bush and lived there as the barracks beds were of musty hay and crawling with vermin. The soldiers were under-sized, stupid from excessive drinking, indifferent to discipline and of doubtful quality in action. From time to time officials came from Paris and made reforms that lasted a time. Yet the fortress was finally completed and the island battery made a very strong point. And Swiss soldiers were imported and 200 of the poorer members of the garrison were sent home.

Then in 1745 New England raised a force of artisans, farmers, fishermen and labourers, placed under command of a merchant named Pepperell, and made up an expedition to attack the fortress. It seemed a futile project for the fame of the walled and fabulous Louisbourg was wide-spread and it had cost so much, been talked of so much that King Louis stated that he expected to be able to see its walls from across the sea. The New England force was joined by a British fleet under Commodore Warren. Despite the difficulties, the force got ashore and once they had footing drove the French behind their ramparts. Then the artillery was brought ashore and after a time the island battery was captured. After a siege of forty-nine days the mighty Louisbourg surrendered. Then the French flag was kept flying and numerous French ships with valuable cargoes sailed into the harbour and were captured.

The prize money was divided among the sailors and the New Englanders found that the terms of the surrender stopped them from getting any plunder. Then, to add to their grievance, they were told they had to stay and garrison the place as no regular troops were available. So they stayed and drank rum and before the spring a large number were in their graves and it has been said that almost as many victims of the devil rum are buried there as those who died in battle.

Then came the keenest disappointment when the great fortress was, in 1748, by the terms of the Treaty of Aix-la-Chapelle, handed back to France. However on July 25, 1758, the stronghold once more surrendered to a British expedition consisting of a fleet under Admiral Boscawen and land forces under Major-General Amherst and Brigadier-General Wolfe. It was at the landing Wolfe showed the great courage and leadership that placed him at the head of the forces which were to conquer Quebec, and throughout the campaign his work was outstanding. Two years later orders were given to demolish completely the great fortress and large crews of workers with explosives and crowbars did what they could. Yet there is much remaining and the visitor can stand and easily visualize the walled city at the height of its glory when balls and banquets were the rule of the day and French dandies were dressed as if on the streets of Paris and every French lady of note felt she had to spend a summer at the stronghold.

Fishing was a main industry at Louisbourg from the beginning, and it is interesting to note that after orders were given to allow no trees planted or houses erected within three hundred and fifty "toises" of the fort, an order was issued against building any house within the city more than seven feet high at the post, this in order to have free circulation of air for drying fish. It was also forbidden to cover any dwelling with bark, as the fire hazard was great. The streets were narrow and the records show that though the sheep and goats were under the control of a public herdsman, paid a salary, pigs were allowed to run loose and caused much damage among the drying fish and to poultry. They were finally considered a menace to small children and orders were given that any citizen could kill a pig that was doing damage.

We drove four miles to Kennington Cove and saw there a cairn bearing an inscription reading:

Wolfe's Landing. Here, 8th June, 1758, the men of Brigadier General James Wolfe's brigade, after having been repulsed with heavy losses by the French troops entrenched westward, made their gallant and successful landing. Thus began the operations which ended on 26th July by the capitulation of Louisbourg.

The account of the landing reads:

The British found the French prepared, with three thousand regulars and Indians guarding all shore landings within a five-mile area. These parties were strongly entrenched and supported by artillery. The sea was high and such a surf was running that the British had to wait one day, another and another, until it was the 8th before they resolved to attack, and in all our seaboard history there is no tale more stirring than that of Second Louisbourg. The surf was far too strong. Boats were overturned. Others crashed against one another and staved in sides. Some men swam — others drowned. Some reached shore without weapons. And all the while muskets and cannon blazed at them from the French entrenchments. Yet, somehow, the British got a footing. A handful charged with bayonets. The Indians fled and the French militia followed them. The French regulars, dismayed, were also forced to retreat. They gave ground slowly at first, but General Wolfe was at the head of those who had landed and the British attack was so determined that every French soldier was soon driven within the fortress walls, leaving their supplies and guns along the shore. If no other record survived than the story of Wolfe's landing, Louisbourg would still hold its glamour.

Next we drove along the narrow and stony road leading fifteen miles to Gabarus, on to Framboise, meaning "raspberries," and to Grand River, and then up past Loch Lomond and back to Highway 4 at Big Pond. It is not a drive for those who are nervous on narrow and rough roads, but it is a venture that takes one into a rugged part of the island where everything is rugged, people included, and Gabarus Bay looks like a dangerous and wild water. A man of coarse features and with hair on his neck like a brindle bull came and talked with us in an amazingly gentle voice, asked our mission, and said it was a risky thing to talk about any unusual person in an area where everyone was known. We told him we would not name any locality and soon he was talking about Mary Cameron. "She stood an inch over six feet and weighed a stone more than two hundred but was quick on her feet as a house cat," he said. "There were some rough times at some of our shore celebrations but no one molested the women when Mary was along. She went to school where the big boys attended in winter and learned to hold her own with them by the time she was twelve. When she sixteen there wasn't a young chap in the settlement who dare face her, for she had the strength of two persons. It was a gift and that is sure for her parents were ordinary and she did no unusual work to develop muscle. When she was fifteen she picked a barrel of flour from a sled and carried it one hundred yards to her kitchen. She drove away an ugly bull that had cornered a neighbour, using a short pole she had picked up and when the animal tried to turn on her she staggered it with a blow over the nose, grabbed it by the horns and threw it on the gravel. When it scrambled up it headed to the barn, blatting like a calf. One day Mary went to town and, not noticing signs, put her horse and cart in a "no parking" place. She came from a store just as a policeman was going to move the rig, but a grip on his arm flung him around and she ordered him to keep his hands from her property. With that he started to arrest her but she gave him a shove that nearly put him through a store wall and when he had picked himself up he hurried to the town hall to tell the magistrate his trouble.

Mary moved her rig when a passerby kindly pointed to the parking signs, then followed the policeman and walked into the town hall. She started to ask questions but the policeman got back of a table in quick time and the magistrate tried to bluster and scare her. In a moment she had reached him.

There was a desk in her path but she pushed it aside with a splintering of wood as nails and spikes were torn loose. Another grip wrenched a rail from place as if it were nothing and the magistrate, his knees rattling in fear, pleaded with her to be reasonable. There was no charge against her, and there would not be one, and anything she wanted in town was hers for the asking.

It was said that after she was gone the mayor and others were taken to the hall to observe the rail Mary had wrenched from place and the desk she had uprooted. Soon after she went to Boston and worked in a hotel for a cousin, and, it was said, maintained perfect order at all times.

The drive along Loch Lomond is beautiful. Many men find that lakes hold an inexplicable attraction, a boon of solitude and silence. Rivers and brooks are noisy and the sea is never still. But lakes are silent waters, and silence is the handmaiden of mystery and wisdom, and no man is hardened against the influence of a lake at daybreak when the slow mist rises like a veil and the glassy surface seemingly has no rim. Loch Lomond was like a mirror as we drove along and the reflection of trees and bush and sky made a picture no artist could paint.

Back again on Highway 4, we drove toward Sydney for our friend at Gabarus had told us of a spot we had missed, two of them, in fact, Baleine and Mainadieu.

They are not imposing situations and there is little to suggest either romance or history but if you go there and let your imagination have full sway you can see the actors on the stage and let your sympathy run riot. Away back in the hard old days a ship, *Providence*, left Ireland with eighty convicts for Quebec. But there was bad weather and the ship made slow time so that it was too late by the time the Atlantic had been crossed and the brutal captain decided he was not going to be godfather to his passengers. So he steered for land and hoisted out his yawl and landed all the convicts two miles from Mainadieu, knocking off their irons and leaving the poor wretches without a morsel of food. It was late in the evening and the 11th of December when the last were landed. Seven of the poor souls strayed into the woods and died from exposure. The others, men, women and children, found their way to the few houses of Mainadieu where they were given food and shelter. Fifty went on to Sydney in a shallop where they were cared for the rest of the winter, and fifteen were placed in hospital suffering from frost bite. Despite letters to the Home Government no orders were received for the disposal of the convicts. Sydney was paid for their board and lodging and the poor devils were allowed to go and find employment as best they could.

Sir William Alexander obtained from King James I in 1621, a grant of Acadia including Cape Breton and all country north to the St. Lawrence. America had at this time a New England, and New France and a New Spain, so Alexander thought there was room for a New Scotland. Under the powers conferred on him Sir William offered to grant tracts of land three by six miles on the sea coast "to all such principal knights and esquires as will be pleased to be undertaker of the said plantation and who will promise to set forth six men, artificers or labourers, sufficiently armed, apparelled and victualled for two years." On October 18, 1624, the king announced his intention of instituting an order of baronets for the purpose of advancing colonization in Nova Scotia. The number was fixed at one hundred and fifty and in the course of ten years 111 were created. Not until 1629, however, was any actual settlement made, when four vessels sailed from Scotland to Nova Scotia with upwards of seventy colonists under Sir William's son of the same name.

An attempt was made at this time to plant a colony in Cape Breton. The promoter was a Baronet of Nova Scotia, Lord Ochiltree. His sixty emigrants were in two vessels and were accompanied by fifteen men of war in armour. They arrived at Baliene on July 1, 1629, and cleared land and built a small fort. This whole shore had been given to Alexander but to their surprise some French vessels were fishing in the coastal waters. Lord Ochiltree sent one of his ships to tell them they were trespassing in British waters but could stay and fish and trade with the Indians if they paid Ochiltree ten per cent of their earnings. One Frenchman was loath to pay but arranged to leave three cannon as security though his mate was held as an hostage until payment was made.

Meanwhile a Captain Daniels had set out from France with two shiploads of provisions for Champlain at Quebec. Peace between Britain and France had been declared on May 17. At the Grand Banks, Daniels became separated from his other ships and sailed on alone, saw an English vessel carrying cattle, captured it, was told about the declaration of peace, and let the Englishman go. He went on to St. Ann, Cape Breton, and found there some French who told him about Lord Ochiltree's settlement. Thereupon Daniel ordered fifty-three of his best men to make scaling ladders and announced he would take the place. He arrived at Baleine on September 18th, pretended friendliness, went in the gate of the fort and seized Ochiltree who, he claimed, had pistol and sword in hand. Then his men took the fifteen who wore armour and disarmed all, took down the flag and hoisted the French colour, ignoring all the while Ochiltree's protests that peace had been declared. He also refused to look at Ochiltree's papers confirming his holding but searched the fort, found the mate from the French fishing vessel and freed him, then looted the place. He and his men drank and caroused all night, forcing unfortunate women with the party to cower for shelter under upturned boats on the beach. Next day all the stores were loaded on a ship and all the prisoners taken to St. Ann. There, fifty of his men forced twenty of the ablest male prisoners to assist in the building of a fort, chapel and magazine. Leaving forty men as garrison, Daniel sailed for home on November 5th. Some of his prisoners had been so starved and exposed to cold that they died on the vessel and were thrown overboard, thirteen altogether. Forty-two of the others were landed near Falmouth, and the other twenty taken to France. Ochiltree at once appealed to the Court of Admiralty at Dieppe but got no notice. Daniel went off on another cruise and Ocholtree was finally released. He had lost fifty thousand pounds. He appealed to the king but could not get any recognition. Thus ended the first Scottish attempt to settle Cape Breton, and it is a picture of the lawlessness that existed in those times, of the futility of anyone who had lost their possessions to appeal for help.

The next day we drove to Baddeck on Highway 5 and from there took a cross country drive that is a part of the Cabot Trail. Few use it, however, as the majority enter Cape Breton and turn left on Highway 19 that is paved all the way to Margaree Forks. They there join the Trail and continue up to Cheticamp. The circuit is completed when they reach Baddeck via the eastern side, and from there they go to Sydney. The road we took had many sharp turns through hilly country known as Hunter's Mountain. Then we were at Middle River, known to the Indians as "Little Green Water," and favoured by them as a summer camping place. Then came the drive by the beautiful Lake o' Law, a mirror set in emerald, and with Three Sisters Mountain as the background for this gem set amid greenery. Soon we were in the lovely Margaree Valley with its famous salmon pools and vistas where artists go every year and where many classes have been held during the summer. Here there are sunsets and sunrises that rouse emotion in all but the dullard, and a beauty that has brought visitors back time and time again. Justice L. D. Currie, an eloquent speaker, described the beauty of Cape Breton during an address regarding St. Ann. He said:

I trust you will not regard as extravagant my admiration for the beauties of the little island of Cape Breton. To me there is nothing that can be compared with that spot of loveliness, tucked out there at the edge of the horizon, the actual pot of gold at the end of the rainbow, bearing on all its vistas the loving and caressing touches of the Creator's hands. Scripture says it was on the third day that the earth was made, and I can fancy how towards the close of that day, after He had made all the rest of the earth. He turned to the spot where many waters meet and built there an island upon which He lavished all the glories of His hand; and how as night fell He gazed upon that most perfect act of world creation, breathed upon it the breath of Scotland, "and saw that it was good."

Shakespeare has described England as "this precious stone set in a silver sea;" but he was denied the joy of seeing Cape Breton. Had he been privileged to see and to describe that lovely land with its twilight shadows caught from the emerald of the hills mingling with the blue of the sea, with the silver of her tumbling streams melting into the gold of the setting sun, to watch the mighty arms of Cape North reaching out to seize the rising sun as it leaps from the sea and hurl it on its way to light the world, to stand upon the broad plateau where winds the Cabot Trail, to walk down the lordly glen where the tall trees whisper to each other—then even he, that master of imagery and of words, would have failed to describe adequately that brightest gem in the whole diadem of earthly glory.

There are wonderful people along the Margaree. Perhaps it is that living amid such beauty they have acquired a grace and kindliness beyond the average, and perhaps they have inherited their charm, for a grand people populated these settlements, a folk who know that Gaelic was spoken in the Garden of Eden and that the Scots are the chosen race. We had not joked long with an oldster near one of the crossroads when he recited to us something written by an old Kirk Minister:

> Should Gaelic speech be e'er forgot
> And never brocht to min'?
> For she'll be spoke in Paradise
> In the days o' auld lang syne.
> When Eve, all fresh in beauty's charms,
> First met fond Adam's view.
> The first words that he spoke to her
> Were 'Cia mar a tha thu an diudh?*
> And Adam, in his garden fair,
> When e'er the day would close,
> The dish that he'll to supper teuk
> Was always Atholl brose.
> When man first fand the want o' claes
> The wind and cauld to fleg
> He twisted round his waist
> The tartan philabeg.

*How are you today?

And music first on earth was heard
In Gaelic accents deep,
When Jubal in his outer squeezed,
The blether o' a sheep.

There is a grand place to eat at Margaree Harbour — Duck
Cove Inn, but many know of it and we advise any heading that
way at meal time to be sure and arrive early, else they may
have a long wait. One thing, the food will make it worth the
wait. And as we drove up we saw many cars parked on a hill-
side and wondered what might be going on, then came to one
of the finest spots to buy handcraft, to view Nova Scotia scenes,
to take an unusual picture, that there is in the province. It is
the Paul Pix Shop and they have on display views of Nova
Scotia, every part from Port Royal to Cape North, in colour
and in black and white, in every form from miniature trans-
parencies mounted in a tiny magnifying viewer attached to a
key chain, to beautiful enlargements for framing. The Paul
Pix Shop has the finest assortment of postcard views of the
province that I have seen. Kenneth Hansford is the proprietor
of the shop, and he trained at Banff under Bill Gibbons, the
finest landscape photographer in Canada. Mr. Hansford is also
an expert in leather work and has an unusual display of fine
items of every nature. He has stocked the world famous Cheticamp hand-hooked rugs and has a selection of the finest in
everything from coasters at fifty cents each to rugs thirty-two
square feet in size, and a group of tapestries that excels anything I have seen elsewhere. Everyone in the shop the day
we were there was exclaiming in delight over a portrait of the
President of the United States. It was made in the shop by a
lady specialist who turns out the tapestries, and she demon-
strated her methods of work throughout the season.

There is huge space in the shop and customers can wander
completely around the building, returning to the starting
point, and seeing something different all the way. There is an
extensive line of hand weaving done by the Star of the Sea
experts at Terence Bay. We saw handmade oxen, singly and

in teams, made by a blacksmith in Lunenburg, and hand-wrought iron specalities turned out by an expert in Chester. Then there were displays of blankets and quilts and crochet work and aprons and hand bags and fox furs, etc. The prices seemed very reasonable and the clerks were busy. And there was continual use of the platform outside which allows visitors with cameras to get an exceptionally good shot of the model fishing village. We were amazed when Mr. Hansford said a crippled native of Margaree Harbour had made many of the items. On three different days last summer more than three thousand visitors with cameras made use of the platform look-ing over the model village. And the visitors think Mr. Hans-ford has been thoughtful in adding public washrooms to his establishment, as none were available at the Harbour. We had seen many places selling handcraft and souvenirs around the province but the Paul Pix Shop at Margaree Harbour is in a class by itself.

As we lingered outside we heard an American anxiously asking if there were no road by which he could reach the North Cape Breton Plateau. He was asking an engineer, and we stood near to listen. The engineer said there was no route to the interior as yet but that the area was being probed by geologists whose findings could conceivably convert the massive barrens into industrious mining centres. He said there were six hundred square miles of barrens unknown to Cape Bretoners themselves, and that Professor H. L. Cameron of Acadia University was doing week-end excursions into the plateau lying in the Cape Breton Highlands National Park. He said the strange plateau was mainly tundra which gave it the appearance of territories in the Arctic regions. Peat formed the congested vegetation, and it has such an affinity for water that the swamps bulge like a sponge which will carry a man's weight, and in the middle of the bogs are ponds with water cold and crystal clear. Rabbits, foxes, wildcats and bears roam the plateau, and the greater part has never been trod by man. Stubby, short trees follow the waterways, bushes and moss crowd the flats. It is said, informed the engineer, that back in the old days a herd of many thousand caribou lived in the barrens, but hunters and sickness took a tremendous toll and now they are extinct. He said there were bleached bones everywhere and one pile was ten feet high and thirty feet wide, proof of hunters killing the animals for their hides. His story excited the American more than ever, but no hope was given of arrangements for other geological parties entering the vast barrens.

We wanted more new territory to explore so drove over the hill and found a dirt road rolling down-shore by Whale Cove and Chimney Corner. For some miles we drove right beside the sea and then we were back again on paved Highway 19. If you want a glimpse at the places off the trail in western Cape Breton, take that drive, and you will like it, and if you stop and talk with folks along the way you will like it so much better. An old man with tattoo marks on his arms was repairing a sheep fence, seemed glad that we stopped to ask about an island in sight. He explained carefully that it was Margaree Island, and that he knew it well. In fact there were many places he knew well, such as Sydney and Port Hawkesbury. As a young man he had worked at Hawkesbury, and said he had often heard about the circus that came to that port in 1870 by steamer, and put up the tents. "Half of Cape Breton was there by ten. A balloon was to go up at eleven. Well, they charged high for them times, fifty cents a head. After the first rush began a Macdonald handed in a ten dollar bill for a ticket and got fifty cents back as change. He shouted for the rest of his money and a circus hand come and ordered him to move along. But Macdonald said he'd have his money or go into the box and get it and the ticket seller blew a whistle. Up rushed a big fellow with an iron bar in his hand and knocked Macdonald down with it. Well, that was a mistake, you know. Some more hands came running with clubs but Angus Gillis knocked three of them down before they could hit him and Macdonald's brother nearly killed the fellow with the iron bar. Then the ticket seller drew a revolver and fired, wounding a Gillis. Angus threw a club, knocked the pistol from his hand and then knocked the box over with the seller in it, dragged him out and clouted him silly. The crowd seized the side of the tent and tore it away, overturned the cages and wrecked everything. Monkeys ran all over the place. Clowns and horseback riders went up the hill like they were chased. Camels and elephants just walked around, loose, and both cages of tigers and lions were upset. One man was killed and about twenty hurt before the sheriff got order restored, and the circus people were glad to get back to their boat with what was left. Some wagons were broken beyond repair and two of the monkeys were never caught. Away back over the hill and bridge going toward Port Hastings there were two houses where only one person lived. In one was a scrawny, bow-legged fellow with hardly any forehead, and he was bad friends with the occupant of the other house, an old widow with a savage temper, who kept a number of hens and always put the padlock on the hen-house at night as she said there were thieves around, meaning her neighbour, of course. Well, she knew nothing of what happened at the circus and that night just as she's going to bed about dark there's a clawing on her roof and one of the monkeys looked in her window. Was she ever wild. Next day she went to the Hawkesbury magistrate and told him to arrest Tim Gillis, the scrawny fellow. 'What for?' asked the magistrate. 'Because,' she flamed, 'the dirty old character climbed on my roof last night and looked in at me, him with no shirt an' all.' They had to shoot both the monkeys because they couldn't catch them."

We talked with him for some time and heard a description of Sydney that was not good for tourist advertising, but then he was speaking of a Sydney of 1920. So we left him and within a mile or so saw a lean man with a bald head coming from his field with potatoes in a basket. We stopped and asked about his vegetables and he was very pleased to tell us of his tomatoes and beans and cabbage. We asked about his past and he admitted he had never been off the island, "and don't want to go." He had worked in the coal mines in Inverness for years and had developed a cough but working on his little farm had brought him fair health and he'd not go underground again no matter what wages they paid. He told us about Inverness in the good days of mining and the money spent there on a Saturday night, asked where we were going and advised us to turn left below Inverness and go over to Scotsville and down along Lake Ainslie to Trout River and Highway 5. So we accepted his directions and were glad, for the drive along the lake is one of unusual beauty, and the lake is the largest freshwater, twelve miles in length, seen on the Island. We stayed the night in Whycocomagh, and the moon was wonderful as a carload of young folk sang old songs in great harmony, a most pleasant change from juke box din usual at ice cream parlours. Everyone went walking in the dusk and there was a peace and quiet at day's end that was most enjoyable. It would be nice to spend a week at Whycocomagh in the summer or fall.

There was a heavy dew and as we started along Highway 5 to Glendale and Port Hastings we saw countless funnel webs of grass spiders. It seemed that every square foot of pasture had its huntress sitting at the door of her funnel tube, ready to pounce on the first unlucky insect that came blundering into the trap. Some road work was being done and there was no traffic so we stopped where we saw a rarity, a beech tree. Blue jays were there, feasting on the three-cornered nuts, and opening them by pounding them on the branches. We saw red squirrels storing the sticky cones of the fir tree. Black-capped chickadees inspected us as we tried to get a picture of the squirrel holding a cone, and we saw many maples and birches blazing with colour. Hay-scented ferns were knee-high around the fir stand and pale yellow. The brakes were dead and brown.

A boy came along the road on horseback. He would be about ten and he smiled down at us as if he rode far superior. So we offered him a candy bar and he swung his steed about smartly with much kicking.

"What about school?" we asked. "Don't you go?"

"I've got a sore foot," he grinned. "I stepped on a nail. I'll go again next week."

10

Bears, and Moose, and the Biggest Woman

WE had had so much fun
along the off-trail roads that we studied our map and
turned left from Route 4 at Monastery, down Route 16
to Boylston, then right on a narrow dirt road to Roman
Valley and through Caledonia Mills to St. Andrew's and
back on Route 4. It was one of those warm days called
"Indian summer," and we used any excuse to stop and poke
around. An old road looked very inviting when we saw a
red fox with its head up like a dog, watching us. So we
parked and walked a distance through bush growing up
in what had one time been good farmland. A large black-
and-yellow bumblebee in heavy droning flight circled near
us and came to rest on a ditch bank. There were several
crevices and she vanished into one and did not re-appear
while we were there, so probably had selected the crack as
her winter home. A chipmunk came out and watched us
as we sauntered, finally had courage enough to come within
a short distance to get a peanut.

Then a voice startled us as an old man appeared from
nowhere, carrying a shot gun. "Don't fear me," he called.
"I've been after a scoundrel fox that took another of our
chickens. Makes four he's took in two weeks but I'll get him
yet. He's too bold for his own good."

We explained that we had seen a fox minutes before and the old man did some wary searching, then returned to us, asked our errand, grinned and said we would not find much in Roman Valley. "Not even a Roman," he chuckled. Then he sobered. "Don't go walking far from the road," he advised. "The last year or so we've been hearing of panthers seen in Nova Scotia, and a chap going through in a car the other night said something long and yellow bounced across the road ahead of him. He said he'd swear it was a panther."

"When snow comes," we said, "there are many rabbit hunters and trappers in the woods. How is it they never have found a track of any of these mysterious panthers. Where do they go in the winter?"

The old man agreed we had something there, then gladly accepted a drive up the road to his home, an old house with banking around it so that it looked tamped into the earth. He was determined we should go in and meet his wife who was a charming old lady and when she understood our errand laughed about a Hallow'een party when she was a girl. A husky young woman of the settlement had dressed in her father's clothes and in the dark was readily accepted by a group of lads out to play tricks. Soon they were telling what they intended doing at various places and she slipped away from them and got to her home well in advance. They were going to take her father's old gray mare from the stable and put her in the school house. Soon she was home and hoisting a wash tub to the loft floor above the stable. A few trips to the well with two pails filled the tub with cold water. Then she removed some planks in the loft floor and waited. The lads arrived and after much whispering outside cautiously opened the stable door and pressed inward, bunched closely together to maintain courage. The girl upended the tub and the lads below were drenched from head to foot. They yelled and ran as if the devil were after them and there were no more pranks that night.

Then the old lady showed us a chimney swift's nest that had fallen down her chimney, a bunch of sticks glued together

about the size of half a saucer, and got to talking of swallows
nesting at her sister's place near Knoydart. We said we had
driven that road and they questioned us and found we had
missed a most important cairn that perpetuates the memories
of three Highland soldiers who were "out with Bonnie Prince
Charlie" in 1745, and who lie buried at that spot. We sat
and heard the story of the Prince landing on Scottish soil
and finding the Chiefs despondent through lack of funds
and munitions. But young Ronald MacDonald declared that
though not another man in Albyn drew a sword, he would,
and soon the spark was set to the heather. The story is well
known but we were amazed to learn that the daughter of
that same Ronald MacDonald found her last resting-place
in the old Arisaig Cemetery, almost under the shadow of Eigg
Mountain and not too far from Knoydart Point where the
three soldiers from Culloden lie buried. The cairn, our friends
told us, is twelve feet high and is constructed of native
materials with some stones from the battlefield of Culloden,
and the inscription is a verse from the Gaelic translated
in English:

> Let them tear our bleeding bosoms,
> Let them drain our sweetest veins.
> In our hearts is Charlie, Charlie
> While a drop of blood remains.

Then it was the old man's turn and he told us about a
nephew in a Nova Scotia town. He had gone with a girl for
some time but did not like his job and had gone to the States
for ten years. When he returned he got work in a store and
the girl was still in town and single, waiting him. He told
her he had small prospects working in the store but they were
married in the parsonage and she accepted him "for better,
for worse, for richer for poorer." Then the store was sold
and he had no job. He got work here and there and they
lived in two rooms but times got tougher and at Christmas
she had but two dollars and fifty cents. And outside their
few possessions in the room there was only a huge black trunk

which he had stowed in the attic. The wife asked about trying to sell it but he said it was too big, and of poor material. Christmas Eve came and at noon he said he had a small job for the rest of the day, so she went out for window shopping and was surprised to see a banner strung across the front of a small shop that had been empty. It read: "Come In and Have Your Fortune Told by an Expert. Special Christmas Price. One Dollar per Question."

The girl decided it was worth one dollar of her precious fund to know what was to happen them and she went in. There were small blue lights and a bearded mystic in turban and robe gazing at a large crystal ball. The girl paid her money, asked her question, and after some study of the ball the mystic announced her loved one would return with facts she needed and her future was secure. The girl was so glad she at once spent the rest of her money and at late supper hubby returned with sixteen dollars he had earned and the news that he had landed a job. So they spent much of the money and had a fine Christmas, and the job proved good enough to allow them to put money by and soon he launched into business for himself and did very well. But before they moved from the two rooms he had taken from the big black trunk in the attic a false beard, robe, turban and crystal ball, all of which he buried deeply in an old garden. "And," chuckled the old man, "she doesn't know to this day that he was an expert at the crystal ball back in the States, or that he sneaked the rig out of the house that Christmas Eve to do his stuff. And likely she wouldn't believe it was him talked to her."

We stayed an hour with them, hearing moose hunting stories, tales of old elections and auctions, and then we drove on and saw a boy with bare blond head and a red sweater, wearing a pistol in true Davy Crockett style. He was going through a field with a fine collie, and a man wearing a checked shirt and overalls and carrying a crooked stick was going toward some sheep. When he saw us he came to the fence and asked if we were looking for some place, and we said any place that was interesting. He smiled at the boy, and said. "That lad thinks this is interesting. He was never in the country before. He's from Boston."

Then we talked and discovered that the farm we were at had been purchased by money made in the gold rush down at Goldenville. A lady had walked into the bush and during her rambling found a bright bit of quartz and carried it home. She showed it to a man who went to the spot and soon was getting gold in some quantity. His secret was discovered and a party of men surged to the district. In one day they broke up quartz enough to get four hundred dollars worth of gold, and the rush was on. Soon a building boom was going and a small town mushroomed overnight. And the ancestor had been on the spot and staked out several claims. He had not worked a mine at all but had sold his claims for a handsome sum, and he had also bought lots where the building began and tripled his outlay. So he went home with his profits in his purse and purchased the farm.

Soon we were discussing another topic. Our friends were much concerned about the location of a proposed "Highland village." There were those who wanted it on Cape Breton Island, perhaps near the causeway, but why should it be there when the first Highlanders were in Pictou county long before? Pictou was the Nova Scotia birthplace of Scottish settlements and no one could argue against it. Such a village should be located on the northeast side of Green Hill, famed for its Look-Off and Museum, near two main highways, overlooking an estuary of Pictou Harbour and an area in which the first Scottish settlers made their homes. We were surprised that they had not suggested Antigonish as a site, and said so. But, they smiled, we're from Pictou in the beginning.

We had lunch at New Glasgow and then took Route 6 to Lyon Brook and started off in search of Scotsburn. It was on a fine paved highway and a village of size, in pretty location. We talked with various folk and when in conversa-

tion with one man learned that he was an original member
of the famous North Nova Scotia Highlanders and had been
taken prisoner on D Day plus one when the Highlanders
had driven further inland than any other unit and had been
attacked by four times their strength in German forces. He
talked of being in the woods in boyhood when porcupines
were plaguing the area and killing a lot of trees. As he and
his father pushed through the bush they heard the familiar
complainings of a "porky" on the move and his father
reached for a stick with which to kill the animal. Our friend
was greatly excited and pushed ahead to spot the prickly one.
Instead, he saw that on the next tree was a bear cub, and
before he could shout mother bear came plunging through
the undergrowth. Our friend said he shrilled one word—
"bear!" and went through the woods like a singed cat. He
heard his father yell as he ran and then a great crashing
in the bush behind him. He felt it was the bear in pursuit
and fairly took off but the pursuer came faster and then
passed him. It was his father. "The old man's jacket was
spread out behind him like a sail," he grinned, "and he
cleared windfalls like a deer. I let out a wail as I was sure I
was going to be bear meat, and he just hollered one word:
'Run!' I don't know what he thought I was doing. Anyway
the old bear hadn't chased us at all, and by the time we
were back to the clear father was making plans to borrow
a gun. He got a neighbour, who had a rifle, to go with him
and they went to the tree but mother and child had vanished.
Even the porcupine was gone. But that was the last time I
went in the woods without a gun in my hands."

We drove slowly and stopped again when we saw four
girls in Scottish costumes doing the Highland fling on a
verandah, and soon were told that Scotsburn had some fine
dancers and that Pictou County had a fine girls pipe band. Our
informer told us that Earltown was a first Scottish settlement
in the old days and told us how to get there. Either he was
mixed in his directions or we became mixed after watching

those Highland lassies for we came to a place called Meadow-
ville instead of Earltown and saw a man in a yard working
with some farm machinery. We talked to him and found
he lived alone but was a descendant of first settlers, and very
proud of the fact.

"My great-great-great grandfather wore his kilt the first
four winters he was in this country," he said, "and as he had
no greatcoat he wore a blanket around his shoulders. They
practically lived on potatoes the first year, and fish. Then the
old man acquired a musket and shot a caribou in the fall.
He also learned how to snare rabbits. The Indians taught
him the trick. Mostly the Scots had nothing to do with the
Micmacs but the old man found an aged Indian mired in
a swamp to his waist and cut some poles and rescued him.
After that the Indians brought him moose meat and partridges
and showed him how to set snares. I guess rabbits would be
quite plentiful in those days. There were lots of them out
on Pictou Island."

"Oh," I said. "I've never been to Pictou Island. What's
it like?"

"My father worked there five years when he was a
youngster," said the man. "There are over three thousand
acres and it's good sandy soil. In the old days when first
settlers went there they found it alive with foxes and muskrats
and rabbits. There were no snakes or toads or squirrels. So
it must have been that the rabbits and foxes crossed over
on ice from the mainland. The whites caught and shot the
foxes for their pelts but it was some time before anyone
began living there. In the meantime an Indian who had been
across to Prince Edward Island stopped at the island on his
way back. It was late afternoon and his canoe had been
leaking. He had his wife with him and he disliked her in-
tensely, wanted to be rid of her. So he beached the canoe
and began patching it, and ordered her to go in the bush
and get him some strips of birch bark. As soon as she was
gone he got into the canoe and paddled for home. Arrived

at the camp he told the tribe his wife had died while they were on Prince Edward Island and he had buried her there. The poor woman had got back to the beach to see the canoe far in the distance. And it was late fall. She hastily built a crude shelter of driftwood and such saplings as she could break, tied with withes. Then she set snares as rabbits were very plentiful, and augmented her diet by getting shellfish which were abundant along the beach. She had a good sharp knife and skinned every rabbit she caught or killed, and soon had an enveloping garment made of them. As she got more skins she made a blanket of them, then a second blanket. Next she made a covering for her shelter, and after that added a second garment to keep her warm. She existed through the winter on a diet of rabbits and in the spring some Indians in canoes off shore saw something moving on the island, investigated and brought the poor woman home. So enraged were the relatives that they seized the guilty husband who had so cruelly abandoned her, built a big fire and roasted him alive. In 1814 some Irish moved to the island and built homes there but five years later a Scottish gentleman acquired the land and moved Scottish settlers there. Soon there was strife between the Irish and Scottish which ended in the Irish having to leave. But before they went they set fire to the woods which, it being a windy day, was totally destroyed, leaving no source of fuel supply."

We noticed the grain stubble about and the potato field and asked our friend how he liked farming. "Good enough," he grunted. "This country suits me. I was away five years and saw all I want of the rest of the world." We had to coax somewhat but learned he, too, had been a member of the North Nova Highlanders and in the terrible night attack on Tilley had been with a platoon that reached a forward area and then were left isolated. They were under enemy fire all day as they huddled in slit trenches hastily dug in a wheat field. Several were wounded and at night the survivors had to help them as they got back to their battalion, or what was left of it. We had read the story of Tilley and knew our friend had survived a terrifying experience. We thanked him for spending time with us and drove off without thinking of where we were going and next we knew had arrived in River John on Route 6.

A man in a store gave us mixed directions and the rest of the day we were driving a maze of back roads that took us to West Branch River John and Millsville and Four Mile Brook and Six Mile Brook and, finally, Earltown, rather East Earltown. How we managed to get so lost and get from one tangle to another I do not know. We enjoyed every moment and nowhere else in Nova Scotia did we see so much wild life. We were not many miles from River John on a soft dirt road where the car ran with hardly a sound and first shadows were lacework along the trees. Suddenly a deer was standing at a glade, gazing at us, and as I slowed to no more than five miles an hour a second deer appeared just beside us, snorted and drew back, then lunged into view again. Soon after we came to seven ruffed grouse in a sunny road corner, sitting together as if it were a Ladies Aid of the woods. They did not fly but just scurried among ferns and bushes. Next a red fox ambled onto the road ahead of us, lazily ran off to one side and grinned at us from scant yards away in a pasture corner as we went by. And just ahead was a farm, and hens were in the yard. We turned in at once and a farmer came slowly from the woodpile and said it was a remarkable day for the time of year.

"Yes," we said, "but we came to tell you there is a fox in your field, not one hundred yards from here, and it's likely he's going to try and steal a hen."

"I stoned him off yesterday," said the man dully. "There must be a dozen of them around. I see one nearly every day."

"Why don't you shoot them?" I asked.

He shook his head. "I've had enough of shooting to do me out. We haven't a gun on the place."

"But we saw partridge in the road, just a short distance back?"

"Must be six or seven flocks around," nodded the man. "They've been in my apple trees."

"Aren't there any young fellows to hunt them?" we asked.

"No. There aren't any young fellows around here at all. Just we older folk who won't leave. I doubt there's over half the population there was when I was a young fellow."

"Well I certainly would have a gun if I lived here," I said. "You could have nice partridge stew every night."

"Like I said," came the return, "I've done enough shooting to do me."

He looked old, but I said. "Last war?"

He nodded. "I was twelve years older than the average but I wanted to see other countries, and I did. I was in the North Novies and D Day plus one I crawled on my hands and knees three miles through grain while the Germans plastered us with shells and machine gun fire. Then I was in the attack on Authie on July 8th and got mine there. I was sergeant and we run into a nest of them, and I used a Sten at less than ten yards. I didn't miss many, and they didn't miss me, either. I'm pretty well shot up but I get a pension and I'm glad to be alive."

We could see the memories in his eyes and we drove away without thinking to ask anything about roads. After what seemed three or four sharp turns we took roads as they came, choosing the best ones, not knowing where we were. Then we came to a farm where two women were in the sunshine, taking in some cabbage. We stopped to chat and soon were getting plenty of Pictou County history. The older woman talked as if she had been a school teacher and she pointed to various places where a blazed trail had run and talked of so many settlements we were more bewildered than ever. "Turn right next time," she admonished, "and you can't get lost. And don't forget this county has produced more clergymen and lawyers and doctors and politicians than any other in Nova Scotia."

"You from Halifax?" asked the other.

We admitted we were. "I was there once, to the Exhibition," came the return, "and didn't think much of it. Made me think of my grandmother when she went to New Glasgow. Father asked her what she thought of it. 'Fair enough town,' she said, 'when they get it finished. They're still building some houses.' But what I'd like to know is who thought up that Nova Scotia Tartan? Don't they know you can't have somebody mix up colours and name them what they like? Tartans are a birthright. They belong to the select clans of old Scotland, and they're next thing to sacred. You'll never see any true Scot wearing one of those atrocities, because every Scot has his own tartan. Only English or the like would wear them."

"Must be a lot of English, then," we said. "You see ties and caps and scarves of it in Halifax, and bags, and suits. And most people think it is just as nice as some of your sacred tartans."

"None of them that come as special guests to the Mod will wear it," came the dogged response.

"But hundreds of visitors will take colour shots of Piper Roy at the Border Information Bureau," we said, "and he's wearing the Nova Scotia Tartan."

"What's your tartan?" came the sudden thrust.

"I wore the Black Watch four years," I said, "and had bagpipes for breakfast and dinner and bedtime while we were out of the trenches. Can I get by on that?"

Our friends smiled charmingly. "Ye can," they answered in Scottish, and turned toward the house as a little man with a small moustache appeared.

He walked slowly and wore a dark red vest ornamented with large buttons.

"Why can't I have company, too?" he queried. "Here I am laid up with lumbago and my sisters having the time of their lives. Are you a tax collector or an insurance agent?"

"Neither. We are just explorers finding out where all your Pictou county roads go to, and talking with all the pleasant people we see."

"Sound like you're Irish," was the comment, "or in politics, both of which is bad." He put up a hand. "Don't defend yourselves, and pardon my chatter. It's too nice a day for anything disturbing."

We explained our mission, and he said he was one-quarter MacKay, one-quarter Macdonald, one-quarter Murray and one-quarter Fraser, had all the good qualities of each clan and had mainly discarded the other kind. He talked about pioneer days, about the log cabins and cold winters, the year of the mice, the temperance societies, barn raisings and bear hunts. "I guess you've had such things all the way along," he surmised. "It's the stories handed down to us but we've a distinction. We've an uncle who left here on account of moquitoes. He vowed he'd get some place where he'd be rid of them and he landed in New York, got a job in a shipping company and in twenty years was a partner in the firm. He's dead now but he came home every few years and always in the late fall. He made plenty of money and had a comfortable home, all of which, he used to say, he owed to mosquitoes."

"Are they bad around here?" we asked.

"There are no good ones, friend," came the retort. "The Pictou ones that live in these wooded areas are a bit larger than average, and more savage. The year of no summer killed off the oldtimers, which was a good thing. Some of them down around Four Mile Brook were so large they roosted in trees. A first settler down there crawled under his over-turned big cooking pot to escape them at night. They drilled right through it to get at him but he had a hatchet and pounded their stingers over like rivets. This went on till midnight when so many were fast to the pot that they flew away with it. They're smart you know, smarter than man. Man has studied their habits and life histories and found it's only the female that does the biting. He's sprayed poison over their breeding places by planes and drained swamps and ditches and all that but the mosquito is still here. Man has fought him with every sort of swatter from the Pharoah fan to a *Halifax Chronicle*. He has invented lamps and sprays and nettings but the mosquito still gets him. So he has prepared lotions and ointments to daub himself with and repel that aggressive buzzing female, but there are more mosquitos than ever, and they have an agility their foremothers never had. If you follow nature articles you will note that every living thing from bass to bison seem to go through cycles when their numbers decrease, but the mosquito gets bigger and bitier, and more longwinded. Scientists used to tell that a mosquito never travelled more than six hundred feet from her breeding place. But I've been in the middle of a five-mile lake in a stiff breeze when one attacked me, then called her sisters and they drove me to shore. And they can travel the blackest night made and find the only tiny crack there is in the netting and enter your porch. They can search you out in silence, take a bite and be gone in quiet, but in a bedroom at night one can sound like a jet plane over your bed. I tell you the man that invents a way to beat the mosquito will make a fortune even Hitler never dreamed of, and I've been working on an idea since I was in Labrador."

There wasn't much we could say in the way of comment and then our friend patted the waistcoat and said it was worn by his grandfather on a trip to Boston, and that it had had gold buttons and his grandmother had removed them least they be stolen and replaced them with the bone ones. "She was a dear old granny," he said softly. "Stubborn as a mule when she made her mind up, and her daughters didn't know how to manage her when she got old and they thought she should have a check-up for she seemed to have some inward trouble. But they knew she would scoff at the idea of a doctor so they asked one to come from New Glasgow and said nothing. He came and gave her a thorough check-up, and when he was gone the daughter went in. 'How did you get along, granny?' she asked. 'Fine, dear. That new minister is a nice man.' 'No, no, granny, that isn't the minister. That was a doctor.' 'Oh, well I did think he was a bit personal but then I didn't know about ministers these days."

The two women were giving me glances so I got out of the car to look at some of the cabbage, leaving Ethel to talk with fancy vest. "Don't pay attention to him," whispered one of the women. "He has that lumbago so bad we have to let him have some brandy and he's been taking too much. And if you stay he'll talk that way all the afternoon." We could see how nervous she was about his stories becoming trouble-some and so we said we had to be going, and he waved us a grand good-bye, and almost over balanced against the stone wall.

Many turns and some time later we stopped again and talked with a man who was fixing a gate, telling him we felt we were lost. When he told us we must have come through East Earltown we wondered, and then he said there were three Earltowns and the one he thought we wanted was over near Balmoral Mills. We asked where we were and he said in Millsville, and Four Mile Brook was next. So we got our map and studied it and decided there was no time to go back that night. We told him our errand and he said there was nothing to record about the place but that a paper dated March, 1884, had been discovered in an attic. Its title was *The Monthly Record of the Church of Scotland in Nova Scotia, New Brunswick and Adjoining Provinces,* and it had been published in Pictou. Among the items of interest was the following:

On February 4th a delegation from Church and Dalhousie sections of the congregation of St. John's Kirk, at Roger's Hill, Pictou County, called on Alexander McLennan, Esq. of Roger's Hill. Mr. McLennan has been for thirty years identified with the leading of the congregational music of the said Church, either as precentor or latterly as the leader of the choir. The delegation intimated that the above men-tioned sections of the congregation wished to recognize his eminent service to the church, for so long a period, in a more practical way than usual, and begged his acceptance of a well filled purse, which they had the pleasure of presenting, as a small token of their appreciation of his services. Mr. McLennan gratefully accepted the donation in words which well accorded with the estimation in which he is universally held, both by the congregation of St. John's Kirk and of all who knew him.

We copied the item as we are well acquainted with Charles McLennan of the Brookfield Creamery Company Limited of Truro, he being a grandson of Alexander, the precentor.

Then we went on to Four Mile Brook and again there were forking roads and we drove into a rough ravine and saw a farmhouse high on our right. So I parked the car and climbed the bank and saw a yard in which no fewer than three old-time threshing machines were having a final rest. Going nearer, I saw that one was in good repair and there was evidence that it was still in use. Soon a man came from one of the barns and as he drew near I saw he was of unusual size. He said his name was MacKay and when I questioned him admitted to two hundred and thirty pounds. It was all bone and muscle and he stood over six feet tall and I thought of stories of the old timers. Then I noticed a tunic hanging on the fence, faded and worn but large enough to fit him, and signs of three chevrons on the sleeves.

"Were you overseas?" I asked.

"North Novies," he grinned, and went into the house. He returned with a small box carrying a foreign decoration for bravery at the front, and many other medals. Then I read citations and found I was talking with a man who had been taken prisoner at Authie on June 6th, 1944, deliberately shot in the face and left until other prisoners were rounded up. He had managed to bandage himself and despite loss of blood and great pain had kept up in the march. He was placed in field hospital and as soon as he was recovered to some extent escaped and got back through the lines, rejoined the unit and became a holy terror in the line. On the Scheldt the North Novas were being held up by heavy fire from a strongpoint on the left and MacKay walked down a road unobserved and worked forward and got to the very door of the concrete building. He shot the German sentry on duty and shot an enemy officer who rushed out at the sound of the shooting. The garrison inside the strongpoint had a fine field of fire in front, but no chance to defend the rear and they walked out with their hands in the air and were marched over to the Canadian side. The Diary of the North Novas contains many accounts of Sergeant MacKay in action and few were his equal in battle.

We talked with him until late and made our way back via Scotsburn to Pictou for the night. In the morning we met an oldster as we went to buy the town paper and asked him a casual question about getting to Earltown.

"Go along to Tatamagouche and drive down on Route 11," he advised, then squinted as if he were getting his eyes accustomed to daylight and asked our errand. We explained we wanted interesting items about various places off the main trail and he was most insistent that we make all effort to visit Rockley.

"I was born there," he stated, "and it's packed full of history. First land was granted there in 1811 to Bennie Seaman, and the first frame house built on that grant is still standing and good as the day after it was finished. But families run out and I reckon the Gordons are the only descendants of the first settlers still around Rockley. The first frame house put up was in 1816 and it is still there as good as ever. You want stories about folk. All right, one of the first settlers was a Scottish lad named Archie Campbell. He didn't like the sea but times had been bad at home and he had signed on as crew with an old windjammer. The captain and mates were tough and the hard tack wasn't soft and the pork wasn't fresh so when the ship put in at Pugwash to take a load of lumber Archie watched his chance, got ashore and took off along the shore road. He went far as he could in a day but was mighty tired by night and slept in a barn. In the morning he was hungry enough to eat nails but feared going to a farmhouse lest they report him and a deserter would have a hard time in those days. But his stomach urged him so much that he went up to a farm house and looked in the window. The good wife was making oatmeal porridge and so he knew she must have Scottish blood. In a moment he was knocking at the door and she heard his story and fed him and kept him and that was the home of Angus McLean and the lad stayed there until he went to Rockley and settled on land as his own. Good folks, all of them, in Rockley, and often I wish I stayed there. John Fraser built close by a brook, put a dam in the brook and put in a paddle wheel which turned a saw that cut his wood. Lot easier than bending over a bucksaw. Them's the kind of men we had in the old days.

"You want some human interest story? Sure, they've had every kind at Rockley. There was Mary Harney just over sixteen years of age and a fine plump good-looking girl and a grand help around the house and farm. One day in September it had been rainy and misty and the cows didn't show up at milking time. It was Saturday night and her father had been on an errand to a neighbour's so Mary said she'd fetch the cows. Off she went to the back pasture. An hour or so later it come dark and she hadn't come back so the father went and found the cows but no Mary. They waited and looked and were not much alarmed at first for Mary knew the land round there, and she couldn't get into the woods without going over the fence. But the night passed and no Mary. So the father went over to the church Sunday morning and told the gathering folk about Mary and every man jack in the place joined in the search which went on all day Sunday and all day Monday and Tuesday. But Mary was never found, nor so much as a track of her going. Week's later there was word of a girl's body being washed up on the shore of Prince Edward Island and a piece of the dress the drowned girl wore was sent to Rockley. It was so faded and sea-washed it was hard to tell much about it but it did have the same pattern as the dress Mary was wearing. The resemblance, though, was not near enough to cause any investigation and to this day no one knows where Mary Harney went when she walked into the cow pasture."

Our friend told us about the many turkeys raised in Rockley in the old days, and the great flocks of geese. All have vanished and it seemed to him to be a different community.

A man came along as we stood talking and excitedly told our informant of a discovery of Indian relics near Lowden's Beach. He said Kenneth Hopps had been digging a drain on his property when he unearthed a burial cache that included severel large copper pots, a number of axe heads, some of them huge, many knives and daggers and swords, as well as bundles of hides and birch bark. We got driving directions at once and soon were at the spot. Mr. Hopps had the articles in a shed and visitors were many. A can on a table invited donations to help make the place a museum. An expert from the New Brunswick Museum later examined the cavity and the items, then stated that the place had probably been the grave of a Micmac chief, that burial had taken place between 1600 and 1650, and that the articles had been acquired from French fur traders.

We could see that too many cars were arriving. We saw that soon there would be no chance of getting away unless we left the scene at once. Even then we had to back some distance and ask one car owner to move his vehicle so we might get by. He was a kind young gentleman and one of his passengers was an elderly man with the whitest beard I have ever seen. I halted up by the main road and went back to speak with the old gentleman, found him very courteous and a native of the county. He talked about the old days when he was a boy on a farm near Durham and a man's credit depended on his adherence to his church. No casual visitor was permitted to attend to stay to Sacrament in those days, and only members carrying a token were admitted to the Table. These were the supposed cream of the settlement and being a strict Presbyterian meant there was no need of a note when money was borrowed. The man's word was as good as his bond, and an elder of the church could borrow one hundred dollars without any form of security.

The talk shifted to days when grists had to be taken miles on sleds in the winter, and the old gentleman lamented the fact that most of the old mills had long ago ceased operations and had fallen to decay. Even the old streams seemed to be drying up. He advised us to go to Avondale and see a typical old mill that had served the communities for well over one hundred years. Much of that time the mill had been operated by the Stewart family and it had a reputation for turning out the best oatmeal a Scot ever tasted. Our friend recalled old carding mills and bone mills and tanneries that had been established at various points around the county, and gave us a real surprise when he said he was eighty-six years old.

We drove to Tatamagouche along Highway 6 and turned off to the left over the hill to New Annan and paused by some apple trees where an oldster was taking in the last of the fruit. He placed his basket on the ground and said he had no marketing problems. He knew where his apples were going — into his cellar.

"There are four of us and we wear store teeth," he grinned, "but we can eat three bushels of apples before Christmas, and my wife will make pies and sauces every week. I reckon we've over ten bushels of apples all told, and there won't be a peck of them go bad."

We asked about New Annan and he told us of attending an open-air service of the United Church at Munroe's Corner in August to commemorate the beginning of the New Annan congregation. The spot where the service was held was the site of the old log church, and people from Earltown and The Falls and Tatamagouche Mountain had attended.

"The first settler hereabouts was John Bell from Dumfries-shire," he said. "He came in here some time after 1812 and built a log cabin. After he had some land cleared his family moved in and by 1820 there were five families around. They worked hard in chopping the big trees of virgin forest and in burning the stumps and planting by hack and hoe. They used wooden plows and harrows, made their footwear from hides of their cattle, their clothing from their wool, and were capable smiths and carpenters. By 1861 there were over one hundred and eighty families and they named the settlement New Annan after Annan in Dumfriesshire in Scotland. That year they cut one thousand, one hundred and seventy-seven tons of hay, made seventeen tons of butter, had seventy-six hand made looms that turned out seven thousand yards of cloth that one year. They raised buck wheat and rye and barley and wheat and oats, and made about two tons of maple sugar in the spring. They had some of the finest oxen in the country."

"We've been told the biggest woman in Canada was raised in this area," we said.

"That's right," nodded our friend. "Annie Hanen Swan was born in Millbrook, not far from here. Her father came from Scotland when he was twenty-one but her mother was born in a log cabin in the vicinity of the Swan home. She was a Graham and ordinary in size, same as Annie's father. Annie started to grow like a weed. When she was four she stood over five feet tall and when a stranger was at the home and saw her playing with a doll he thought she was a young woman of the moron class. He said so at another house in the neighbourhood and was amazed when he had the truth. Annie kept on growing and started to school at Byer's Corner in New Annan. She was so big then she couldn't fit into a home-made school desk and the trustees had to build her a special one. But she didn't go to school very long in Nova Scotia. Word of her size had reached New York and P. T. Barnum sent an agent to investigate. When he saw Annie and realized she was the biggest girl for her age in the world he had power given him to make any necessary financial arrangement so in a short time Annie and her parents were in New York where Annie was given a proper education. Then Barnum began to arrange tours for her and everywhere she went thousands flocked to see her. She shot up to over seven feet when she was only fourteen and kept right on toward the ceiling. She was eight

feet one inch tall when she stopped growing and weighed over
three hundred and fifty pounds. Her shoes were thirteen and
one-half inches in length from heel to toe, and she had a skirt
that was decorated with fifty yards of lace. Annie was taken to
England by Barnum and had a great tour of Europe. She drew
crowds wherever she went and had the very best accommoda-
tions and dresses.   Then she met Captain Martin Van Buren
Bates who was an inch shorter than Annie but who weighed
five hundred pounds. They were married in London, and had
two children but both died soon after birth. One weighed
twenty-two pounds at birth. Annie visited Truro in 1882 with
the Barnum and Bailey Museum and it wasn't long after that
when she settled with her husband in a home of their own in
Ohio. The doors of the house were nine feet high, the ceilings
eleven feet, and the furniture was all over size. She died at the
age of thirty-four, and a six-thousand-dollar monument was
erected over her grave."

Travel in those days, for a person her size, was likely very
trying, we said, and our friend reckoned it was the cause of
her losing her health.

"Yes, and it's hard on anybody, even on an animal, to be
looked at all the time," remarked the oldster. "My uncle over
on the Island had a pig that grew so fast everybody in the
place used to go and look at it. It kept on growing till it
weighed over half a ton and then my uncle charged ten cents
for folks to see it. They came all the way from Summerside to
look at it and often there would be more than a hundred
people on a Sunday and you'd think uncle was making money
but he said it took a lot to feed the pig. Then it got nervous
with people staring at it all day and just took sick and died.
Uncle couldn't realize a cent from the carcase."

We offered our sympathy in return for the story and then
inquired the way to Earltown and drove off—with a dozen fine
apples on the car seat. Highway 11 from Truro will take anyone to Earltown and the same route leads from Tatamagouche.
It is a pleasant village of pleasant people, and we had a grand
time talking with three different persons who seemed to have

plenty of time. The first was a stout man with more salt than pepper in his hair and an easy smile. He told us Earltown was settled in 1816 by hardy folk from Sutherland under patronage of the Marquis of Stafford who sent each family a Bible.

"I think some seed grain and tools would have been more practical," smiled our friend, "for those first-comers were very poor. They had to be very saving and as soon as it was warm enough all of them, men, women and children, went barefoot. They weren't used to chopping and the axes of those times were not much good. They had to gather stones and build their own fireplaces and the biggest job in winter was getting enough fuel to keep the fires going. They never were allowed to go out and I've heard grandfather tell that those first settlers would pull big logs into the cabin and push the ends into the fire, then keep pushing the logs in as the lengths were burned. This was quite a task and all hands had to take hold and push. Of course the youngsters would enjoy straddling the log as a seat, but it must have been awkward for mother and grandmother to hoist the long skirts and step over the log as they went back and forth. Yet those people were never too tired to carry on a study of the Bible and the few books they had. In order to save candles they would meet in one cabin and there one would read and expound and the others would offer opinions, and it used to be said of anyone taking part in an argument: 'He sounds like one of them tutored Earltowners.' Sometimes, not very often, a preacher would visit the community, and that caused a commotion as there was only one fine shirt in the place. It was passed around to whichever man was playing host for the missionary. And there were only three bonnets in the place, which were handed around as there was need."

We asked if there were any stories of the old days that were unusual.

"Well, that depends on what you call unusual," smiled the man. "There's one story about a Cameron woman who had to go twelve miles to borrow potatoes in January. Her man was not well and they had almost nothing to eat. So she took a sled and walked by blazed trail the twelve miles through the woods.

She stayed overnight and went back with her load the next day, and wildcats followed all the way, often in plain sight of her. They used to say the governor heard about her and when he visited Earltown a year later he brought her a fine bonnet and gown. She loaned them three times to brides for their wedding day."

It was getting past noon so we parked by the school and ate our lunch. Soon a very thin man wearing an old-fashioned vest came by and asked if there were anything we lacked. He gave us a cordial invitation to go to his house and get a cup of good tea. We thanked him and asked about the history of Earltown.

"There's others know much more than me," he said modestly. "My grandmother knew much about the first-comers but she's long gone and I'm seventy-eight. Her father had a small house and a big family so he built what I figure were the first three-decker beds in the county. He had a ladder up the side and the six boys slept in it. The two in the top deck couldn't sit up straight. Their bed was only two feet from the ceiling. And she used to tell about a chap that went on a trip to Halifax and had trouble getting a place to stay overnight. Finally he found the Three Bells Inn and the man said he could have a place in a three-decker but not till nine o'clock. That was late to get to bed but the man from Earltown had no choice. The landlord said the three-decker had three beds on the bottom tier, two in the middle and one at the top. At nine in come two sailors the worse for drink and they had the other two berths on the lower deck. So the Earltown man had a hard time getting to sleep as the sailors wrangled and muttered till nearly midnight and when they quieted the two in the middle tier snored like steam whistles, waking him half a dozen times. And there was a heavy odor in the room that was most obnoxious. At six in came the landlord and dragged out the sailors and the Earltown man, saying the night was ended. This made the Earltowner very ugly, and he went to a magistrate and made complaint. So the landlord was fetched and said he could explain everything. The three in the lower deck were not allowed to retire until nine because the two in the middle deck were farm women in for the market and they had to get tucked in before the men arrived. And then the men had to be taken out of the room in the morning at six so the women could get up. As for the odor, a Newfoundland seaman had died in the top bunk two days before and the undertaker was on a binge so the body had not been removed. The landlord was fined five shillings for allowing the body to stay in the three-decker, and the Earltown man made sure he got away home that day."

The thin man gratefully accepted a banana and candy bar, then continued thoughtfully, about a hunter who had killed twelve bears in one winter, about a man who had been annoyed by something getting down the chimney and stealing food. He set a trap and caught a marten. He said Earltown had been surveyed by Alex Miller who named it for the Earl of Dalhousie, that the first settler was a MacIntosh in 1813, that other first families were MacKays and Ross and Murray, that most were Gaelic speaking and from Sutherlandshire. John MacKay had established the first grist mill at a waterfall fifty feet high.

"He rigged a good water wheel and had plenty of power but the trouble was to get the mill stones to the spot. They were cut by a mason who lived fourteen miles away and it was decided that a community effort was needed. So a drag of peeled logs was made and the stones lashed to it by ropes. Then thirty-six men gathered and hauled the drag by hand the fourteen miles. They were grand people, those first settlers, and good-living, too. My grandmother was carried to Pictou in her mother's arms to be baptized."

"Were there any big fellows?" we asked, thinking of strong men.

"Ever hear of Maggie's Bill?" he asked.

No, we had not heard of the gentleman. "Was he a valet?"

"Maggie had a tongue like barbed wire," informed our friend. "And she used it on Bill but it never had effect. He was over six feet tall and must have weighed nearly three hundred.

Maggie used to declare he was hollow inside for it took a loaf of bread, ten potatoes and a turnip to provide him a snack along with his meat and gravy. One day he was plowing when he hit a stone and broke the plow share. It was seeding time and Bill had a one-track mind. He put his horses to pasture and walked to Truso and bought a new plow. In his hurry he had not bothered to get his coat and so as he started back the plow rather cut into his shoulder. So he stopped at Bible Hill and bought a bag of bran which he set on his shoulder first as a cushion for the plow. Maggie was mad at him when he got home for she said he was wasteful. They wouldn't need the bran till fall."

It was a lovely drive through the woods beyond Earltown. Twice we saw deer and as we reached a point where there is a spring beside the road a rabbit raced madly across the way in front of us while a squirrel shrieked fear as it leaped from bush to bush in the spot where the rabbit had come from. I was driving very slow and stopped altogether as a tawny flash showed in the undergrowth and the next minute a marten appeared on a branch of squat hemlock. It glared at us as it crouched there and did not move for a full sixty seconds, then doubled back with a marvel of balancing on the narrow limb and was gone like a streak of light. The only time I ever saw a marten in the flesh.

We drove to Route 2 from Onslow and went westward until we reached Glenholme when off we went toward Oxford on Route 4. After some pleasant farm scenes we entered the woods of Folly Mountain and began long successions of elbow turns through a hardwoods area. We only met three cars in twenty miles and the down grade carried us along with very little sound. At a turn we had a picture of a pair of brilliant blue jays working over a bush that was splashed with scarlet berries. What a colour picture it would have been! In a hollow we saw fox sparrows scratching among dead leaves, their foxy-brown backs conspicuous. Big butterfles with orange and black and white markings fluttered in a sunny glade. We saw three ruffed grouse running silently to cover for the birches and maples were mostly bare though quite a few pale yellow leaves remained on the poplars, and witch hazels still sported their yellow spidery flowers. Taller beeches were naked but the saplings retained their leaves.

Presently we arrived at Folly Lake, 600 feet above sea level, with a saw mill at one end, a railway station and many summer cottages on the far side. It is said that a settler named Flemming made a first clearing in the area, which is rocky and not suited for farming. Soon those who saw the place called it "Flemming's Folly" and then, over the years, the Flemming part was dropped and it became known as Folly Lake. More downgrade and we found the gravel road fairly good despite the fact that most of the traffic is trucks. We emerged in the beautiful Wentworth Valley and could understand why there have been so many requests for hard surfacing the road through this district. The small Wallace River flows through the valley, winding leisurely this way and that beside green stretches of pleasant intervale and absorbing many tributary streams. The surrounding hills are beautiful at all times and in the autumn hundreds drive through the valley despite the dust to view the brilliant foliage. And in winter special cars carry parties of young folk to the area for ski parties. They have their food and spend the afternoon gliding down the slopes. The place was named after Sir John Wentworth, Governor of Nova Scotia.

There were two American cars at Wentworth Centre and another by a beautiful picnic spot near the water and away from the road. Then we were at Lower Wentworth and were told about a historic farmhouse that had been the post office for over one hundred years. It is the home of Mrs. Eva Nelson and generations have gone there to post letters and parcels, to receive them from friends abroad. The house was built in 1830 by the grandson of Huguenots driven from their home in the south of France during 1757. The grandparents had been given refuge in England and had been assisted in getting to Nova Scotia where they had settled at Lunenburg. In 1784 the family moved to Tatamagouche, and from there a son made his way to Lower Wentworth and wrenched a farm from the wooded wilderness.

United Empire Loyalists were moving into the district and as he battled the virgin growth he had time to think of romance and he whose people had been driven from their native land because they were Protestants wooed the daughter of a family driven from Vermont because of their patriotic convictions. As no clergyman was yet in the region they went to Wallace and were married by a magistrate. Their first-born was a son, Lemuel, he who built the house that is the post office, and the first big event in his life was the settlement's rejoicing over news of the battle of Waterloo. These Hugue-nots had become strong Methodists and the home was the stopping place of visiting clergy and also a place of worship until a church had been built. When the mail service was extended from Halifax and Truro to include Wentworth on the route to the Northumberland Strait the choice of Lemuel Bigney for postmaster was well received. Stage coaches carried the mail twice weekly when the weather permitted. First penny stamps carried the likeness of Queen Victoria and the shilling stamps bore the royal crown and the mayflower of the province.

Lemuel Bigney became magistrate, and wrote deeds for the majority of the people in the Valley. He also wrote many letters for the illiterate and was good neighbour to all. Finally he constructed a water mill with the old up-and-down saw and hired his crew from the settlement. As Lemuel had no children he adopted the daughter of a relative who died and this girl married and carried on the postal duties. In turn, her daughter, Mrs. Eva Nelson, inherited the fine old home and carries on the good work. The coaches have long since gone with the clip-clop of iron-shod hoofs, the creek of harness and the crack of the coachman's whip, but a car fetches the mail from Wentworth Station and descendants of the original settlers go to the old house to send money orders and letters and parcels just as was done in the beginning.

Turning two sharp corners, the road goes on to Streets Ridge and South Victoria. The first log cabins in that area

were built near the lake but in 1870 the present road came
into being. In 1875 the Methodists of the two communities
built a church at the crossroads by Victoria that is still in use,
while a school was erected at South Victoria which saw service
until 1914. Some lively old gatherings were held under its
roof according to our informant, a man wearing a bright red
shirt and cap and about a week's whisker.

"They tell," he related, "that a farmer nearby who liked the
bottle too well come home late and staggered into the school,
thinking he was home. He fell over a desk and yelled angrily
at 'Jane' for moving the furniture. Just then a big owl sailed
in at the door he had left open and, bewildered, buffeted
about, trying to find the exit. Its wings caught the farmer and
knocked his hat off. 'What's wrong with your lungs?' yelled the
drunk. 'Have your say. Don't just knock my hat off.' The owl
lighted at the teacher's desk and the farmer saw the big eyes.
'Say something or shut up,' he roared and staggered toward the
big bird. Claws tore at his scalp as the owl struck and then
dived out the door and when the farmer woke in the morning
on the hard floor of the school he indignantly felt of his hurts
and declared Jane could claw worse than a tomcat."

We asked about the name of the lake and our man
said some called it "Big Lake" and some called it "MacArthur's
Lake" as the MacArthurs had a sawmill there for forty years.
Then we asked if our man were going hunting and he said it
might be but there was no real urge as he still had plenty of
fresh meat on hand.

"Neighbours share it," he shrugged. "There aren't many
months in the year when a man doesn't get fresh meat from
somewhere."

We were curious about a road leading to the left from
South Victoria and were told it led to Westchester and Greenville, so off we went, exploring. It was our good fortune to find
Mrs. J. H. Webb of Westchester Station who gave us the story
of the area. First, in full view of her home, there is Stevens
Mountain, settled by pre-Loyalists and joined later by settlers
from Westchester County, New York State. Many old clearings

and cellars can still be found on the hill slopes where those
firstcomers fought the forest. One William Blockley was the
first to make a home on the mountain. He walked there from
the North Shore carrying his axe, some seed grain and a few
implements for clearing land and building. He lived in a bush
shelter until he had constructed a small log hut, hunted and
fished and lived well enough, walked to Great Village to buy
meal and flour and sugar. There was no road of any sort, not
so much as a horse path, but the man came and went with
ease until a relative came searching for him, found him and
after much talk persuaded him to go back whence he came. He
was never back in the area but where he had his hut is still
called Blockley Corner.

Jeremiah Moore was a first settler who cleared land and
stayed on it. It must have been a healthy location as he raised a
large family and the majority of them lived to be well over
ninety. Joshua Stevens came from New Annan and built
higher up on the mountain and gave it his name. His son
built the first frame house up the slopes and was last to leave
the area. A family named Hughes lived on the mountain and
one year luck ran against them and winter found them with
no other conveyance than a veteran billygoat and tobaggan.
Two teenage sons would harness the goat and drive over the
mountain to buy much-needed supplies. One bitter cold day
they started out when a storm came up and they had to take
refuge in an old log hut. They huddled against the goat for
warmth but before morning one lad had his foot and leg
frozen. When he reached home he fell in a fainting spell and
his father thought he had died and hurried to a neighbour's
to borrow burial clothes. When he returned he found the boy
much alive and then kind friends took the lad to Greenville
where a surgeon amputated the leg which was properly buried
in Eagle Hill Cemetery but, it was said, sometimes raced up
and down the hill madly at sunset. Years later the boy, fitted
with a wooden leg, returned to the district riding a donkey
and carrying a violin. He called on all residents, gave them a

tune for a few coppers and so made his way through the country.

There is nothing like mountain air, it seems, as far as health is concerned. All the Moores lived to be nearly a hundred, and William Warks, another who lived on the Mountain had eighteen children, as spry nippers as ever was seen. Warks was going through the woods one winter day with his old muzzle loader and dog, looking for some fresh moose meat, when the dog began digging at an opening under large tree roots. The frantic barking denoted something unusual so Warks went to investigate and found himself looking into the sleepy face of a large bear that had been rudely wakened from its winter sleep. Warks suddenly remembered he had nothing but shot in his gun so hastily thrust his iron ramrod down the muzzle of the weapon and pressed the muzzle against the bear's shoulder as he pulled the trigger. Then he started for home in high gear hoping the gun's blast had so dazed bruin it would not be able to follow him.

He reached a neighbour's house and told his story, and the neighbour loaded his gun and they started back to the tree. The bear was there, a few feet from its den, quite dead, with the badly-bent ramrod firmy embedded in its body. The old muzzle loader became a family treasure and is still in the possession of one of the sons of the sturdy pioneer. Twenty families made their homes on Stevens Mountain, and all finally acquired frame houses in place of the first log cabins. One farmer had over five hundred bushels of buckwheat in one crop, and all threshing was then done by the flail. Buckwheat pancakes were a stable article on the menu, and when served with fresh maple syrup made a breakfast fit for a king. Potatoes and turnips grew in abundance and potato bugs were unknown. Strawberries and raspberries and blue berries grew in all the clearings and were gathered by the pail. The settlers petitioned the government for a road and one was constructed from the Acadia Iron Mines to Greenville. Today cars and trucks still drive up the old route through the berry and hunting seasons. In those days the Iron Mines wanted charcoal and every farm had its coal-pit. Traces of them can be seen today when one explores the Mountain and surrounding area. Life was good and no one realized he or she had been born sixty years too soon. The women had quilting bees and mat hookings as excuses to get together, while the men had logging bees and building frolics. Prayer meetings and sing-songs were held at the various homes in turn, and the younger folk had their fun with such games as Blindman's Buff and Puss in the Corner. In the long winter evenings the flax wheel sang its merry song and as candles flickered and the winter wind moaned around the eaves father would tell tall tales of Indian prowlers to bug-eyed youngsters who knew in their hearts they were listening to fiction but thrilled to it just the same. We listened with wonder as Mrs. Webb told us the story of the Mountain, and regretted that with the passing of the demand for charcoal the settlers upped stakes and left for more prosperous regions. The fields that once yielded good crops have been logged over in recent years and the visits to the area today are by those picking mayflowers or fishing in the Roaring River, visiting a sugar camp or picking berries. Always the flowers survive and many go up to view the lilacs in full bloom or the profusion of columbines around old cellars. Two farmers went up the mountain looking for lost horses and found hundreds of white narcissus in bloom. Some old relics of the first settlers still remain in Westchester, such as a wooden churn brought from Holland in 1765 and an iron arrangement similar to a pestle and mortar used for crushing wheat. There are sieves with varying sizes of mesh and old dishes that were used over a century and a half ago.

In the year 1785 lots of five hundred acres were surveyed north of the Londonderry boundary lines and nearly all who settled on that ground came from Westchester County of New York. Land was cleared and cabins erected and slowly the settlement grew. In those early days rum was considered essential by the same element which today kills thousands on the highways and talks about personal freedom and "learning how to drink." Wives and mothers had hardships doubled by drinking bouts of sons and husbands and some of them had courage enough to do something about it. One man had the rum brought in small casks which he placed outside the house in the shade. When the men were absent his good wife took an auger, bored holes in the casks and let the liquid run into the cellar whence it escaped by a drain. The drain led to low ground that was a goose pasture and the geese began sampling the dark potion that formed in pools beside them. Soon they raised their voices in wild squawkings, as do humans after imbibing, and the men rushed from the field sure that a fox was attacking the geese. They saw the big birds wobbling around and pitching helpless on the grass. Some were on their sides, kicking and hissing. The gander was backward in a low bush, helpless to extricate himself, giving loud voice with fullest vigour. Then the odor reached the noses of the men and there was a rush toward the casks. The old account merci-fully draws a veil over what happened thereafter.

In 1832 immigrants from Perthshire, Scotland, who had landed at Wallace wanted good farming land and sent two members to do some exploring. The pair reached Westchester and what they saw was good so the Scottish folk moved in to take over wooded grants and make homes in the wilderness. The first road was made by someone who simply moved over high ground across low ground to other high spots regardless of the steepness of the hills. Hikers and riders followed the trail but when vehicles began to be used the grades were too difficult and the government was asked to make a road over which cart traffic could pass with some speed. Two brothers, Henry and Gabriel Purdy, were appointed road commissioners and as one was Liberal and the other Conservative the roads received good attention no matter which side was in power and soon a fairly good highway came into existence along which the coach drawn by four horses passed daily, and a daily mail became possible. The good folk realized the need of education and constructed a school house and hired a teacher. The three R's were taught in this primitive school until the free school system came into force and many youths went from the first building to conduct business as competently as those who later received regular training.

It may have been that the Micmacs gave the first settlers reasons to dread as the community came into being but in later years the redmen were citizens of Westchester and highly regarded. Dr. Frank Cope was one of these, perhaps the only Indian herb doctor in Canada, and his extensive practice took in patients from every county in the maritimes, from other parts of Canada and from the United States. He got to be so well-known that cars were always parked near his house, and after one call the patients were in the "mail-order category." He had other Indians for miles around gathering herbs and barks and shipping them to him. These he dried and mixed and used in medicines and liniments and salves. Patients in almost helpless arthritic condition were able to resume regular duties after a few months treatment by Dr. Frank J. Cope. People driving past would sometimes ask if a funeral were in progress as they would see from twenty to thirty cars parked along the roadside. Mrs. Webb said that one day when visiting the doctor a nurse from one of the most modern hospitals in the United States arrived and wished to see his methods. The doctor welcomed her warmly and she enjoyed to the full the unforgettable, aromatic medicinal vapors wafting from kettles of herbs in the process of steeping. Much was explained to her and as a lively program of dance music emitted from the office radio the doctor asked the nurse if she danced. The answer was "yes" and soon the pair were doing the grand and Cope was as light on his feet as Freddy Astaire. The cream truck was seen coming down the road and the housekeeper suddenly remembered she needed butter so rushed to the office door and hailed the driver. The very large dog belonging to the doctor, excited by the music and dancing, lunged forth barking while the doctor's wife and daughter and visitors cheered on the dancers. The startled truck driver saw all in a glance and simply stepped on the gas and fled the scene.

Mrs. Cope's father, Stephen Hood, and his sons, George and Tommy, lived with the doctor, but all moved to Shubenacadie when Father Plenty, the Department of Indian Affairs, centralized the Micmacs there and provided them with fine modern homes, electricity and concrete basements. George Hood was an excellent violinist and was always in demand at gatherings. Tommy Hood was noted for having the strength of two men. He could take a large spike and bend it double in his bare hands, perform feats of strength that no man, no matter his size, could duplicate. Tommy possessed artistic talent and made beautiful bracelets of porcupine quills, creating many intricate designs. Steve Hood was an expert in putting splint bottoms in old slatted ladder-back chairs, using ash as his favourite wood. He was a wizard in all wood-working, using a drawing knife and a "crooked knife." The Indians told many tales of their burial grounds, of their moose hunts and sports. Moose were plentiful in Nova Scotia in the long ago and ticks did not cause any deaths as there was always a large acreage of burnt lands and the moose would roll in the ashes and something in the ash content destroyed the ticks. An important election was being fought some twenty-five years ago when several Indian families were camped in Westchester areas and every member was placed on the enumerator's list. On the big day sturdy open cars crowded to capacity, with others standing on the running board, rolled to the polls, and the Indian supporters of the popular party were greeted with prolonged cheering as they dismounted, entered the booths and made their marks in the proper places.

We were most grateful to Mrs. J. Harris Webb for the information she gave us of the area round about Westchester. The first settlers were a family named Eagles and they were refugee United Empire Loyalists. One day in the early 1800s, while the heavy crust was still hard enough to make for easy travelling, he and his wife came through the forest from West-chester Mountains, each dragging a long home-made toboggan on which were their worldly possessions. Mrs. Eagles had a precious load, two little children and all the clothing and bedding the family owned. Mr. Eagles had food supplies and seed and axe and saw and spade and other tools to be used in erecting a cabin. They located on the hill just above the CNR station and later relatives followed them and made clearings alongside. Mrs. Webb pointed out the spot where their old cellars are still visible.

When Gabriel Purdy came he found a clearing of a few acres in a heavy stand of pine, with stones in heaps showing the land had been cleared for planting. There was an old log cabin, abandoned, and a spring of fine cold water. Purdy made enquiries and found an Embree family had started to make a farm there and had a cellar of sorts under the cabin. One day when Mr. Embree went away several bears prowled near and at nightfall they came closer and closer until at last the big animals nudged an opening and got into the cellar. The terrified woman and children on the floor above listened to the bears growling and moving about and would not stay in the place. Mr. Embree had to pull stakes and go to another location but Purdy was not afraid of anything in the woods. He was a very religious man and had good education. These firstcomers chose well for there is no lovelier spot in the fall when the foliage turns colour. Not far from Westchester is Rose Post Office, once a thriving settlement but at Scotch Hill the once fertile farms have become blueberry fields that are sheets of white when in bloom, a whiteness that carries as far as the eye can see. Then the fruit ripens and the country is a blue of varying shades. Now we were to see the fields after a first frost had struck the plants and the colouring of the leaves is a vast mixture of reds and purples. It was on one of these forgotten farms that Henry Bliss lived, uncle of Sir Charles G. D. Roberts and Bliss Carman. Those early pioneers were God-fearing and held prayer meetings around the homes. Gabriel K. Purdy was gifted as a speaker and as a prayer leader. During one meeting the audience was quite enthralled by Purdy's eloquence and as he ended a listener was so overcome he rose to his feet and cried out: "If I could pray like Brother Gabriel I'd never work another day!"

A great many Westchester men have entered the employ of

the CNR, and it is said there are more employees from the
district in the railway service than from any other community
of like size in Canada.

Mrs. Webb pointed out the "old post road," which a few
years ago was thickly settled and now has no residents. There
are three lakes in the area, Isaac, New Found and Little lakes,
and moose, deer, bear, wild ducks and ruffed grouse now
populate the zone. There, once, lived a man named Rushton,
and one evening when his cows did not return at milking time
from the pasture which stretched to a remote brook area, he
called his dog and son to go with him and locate the animals
before dark. At the back pasture they saw what they thought
was one of the missing cows standing beside a windfall. Rushton set the dog after it to start it homeward when he was
startled to see it was a large cow moose and that her calf was
nearby. The moose lunged savagely at the dog and the boy
was near so Rushton shouted at the lad to climb a tree. The
lad went up the nearest one and, unfortunately, it was not a
very large one. Meanwhile the father quietly moved behind a
very large tree which had no lower branches he could grasp, so
that his only hope was to remain unseen. The moose swung
from the dog to attack the tree as she saw the boy scrambling
among the branches and her charge almost dislodged him. But
the youngster hung on grimly and there were more charges
which became more fierce until the tree seemed likely to be
pushed over. The father, watching, wanted to shout to his son
but knew the moose would at once locate him and he would not
have a chance. He wanted to tell the boy to urge the dog
against the cow moose. The lad seemed to understand and
suddenly began shouting encouragement. The dog had had
several narrow escapes from pile-driving hoofs but it gamely
went back to the attack and so scared the calf that it ran off
into the woods. The cow lashed out wildly, saw that her calf
had vanished and began to give ground. The dog barked like
a crazed thing and drove in with rushes that made the cow
dizzy and at last the victory was won. The cow moose turned
and followed her calf into the woods. The boy came down

the tree so fast he almost dropped and he and the dog headed for home as fast as legs could carry them. The father followed as fast as he could and at the barn yard found the cows which had returned by another route. Mr. Rushton lived to the age of ninety-five and always declared that he never saw another animal as ferocious as that cow moose.

There are fine views from the crossroad at Westchester as the mountains are the Cobequid range and motor visitors who do not reach this region are missing much. The highest points of the hills are Sugar Loaf and High Head. Sugar Loaf has a tower on it with a scenic road leading up, but High Head is too steep for a vehicle. It must be a healthy place to live — Westchester—for Mrs. Webb mentioned folk who worked very hard and lived to be nearly one hundred, and in the village at present is a grand old lady in her hundred and first year, and another in her ninety-fifth year, both possessing excellent memories of by-gone days when candles gave light in the evening and the fireplace was the cookstove, when bears and moose were seen in the pasture and the Indians were numerous. Mention of bears made Mrs. Webb remember when on the Wentworth road a father and son saw a large bear trying to catch a young colt in the pasture. The father grabbed the old muzzle loader and the son picked up the axe and they rushed to the rescue of the very frightened foal. The bear turned on them at once and the father fired. The shot struck the bear fairly in the head and shattered the jaw but the charge was not heavy enough to send the bullet into the brain and the savage animal charged at them. The son tried to strike with the axe but the bear reared and with one blow sent the axe flying into some bushes. The father had no time to reload and had to fight with the clubbed musket. His blows could not beat back the bear which closed in and with one great stroke broke the father's arm. The father was made of the stern stuff that was featured by the pioneers and stayed in the battle as the son returned with the axe. He succeeded in closing in, receiving bad slashes in chest and head, but grabbed the bear's tongue which has hanging from the dreadful wound and this hold enabled him to swing the brute around, thus putting it off guard as the son struck a mighty blow which broke the bear's spine. Then both attacked, the father with only one arm not being able to do much, and the son getting mauled as he went in too close in an effort to deal a finishing blow. The bear was killed but both men had to receive medical treatment for a long time and both carried scars to the grave.

We asked Mrs. Webb if there were any persons who were not the ideal pioneer type. She smiled and admitted that occasionally there had been a settler not up to the mark but his kind were few in the strenuous days. They were not noticed until a community had been established and had become a going concern. Then the odd loafer would appear and exist for a time until he could not obtain anything more on credit. One such lad was notorious for his scheming to get something for nothing and the merchant of this account, in Westchester, was exceedingly wary and never let the idler have anything he could not pay for in cash. The battle of wits went on a long time and the shyster was often in the store and the merchant was friendly enough with him. One day a shipment of clothing arrived at the store as the loafer sat around. There were suits for men and as they were unpacked the lad saw a "pepper and salt" that was his exact size. He examined it with care and asked the price. Then sat and talked with other customers and kept an ear turned toward all that went on. He heard the merchant tell someone he had to go to town the next day and would get away on the morning train. After some time the idler got up again and had a look at the suit. Finally he told the merchant he had decided to buy it and would go to a person who owed him money. He was afraid the suit might be sold during his absence and could it be put away for him, with his name on it to make identity certain. The merchant agreed at once, thinking it nice to have a cash sale, wrapped up the suit, placed it on a back shelf to await the return of the no-good. The next day when the train had gone the merchant's wife was in charge. In came my lad and blandly exclaimed he had bought a suit the previous day but had not been able to take it with him as he had an errand up the hill. The good wife searched, saw the parcel with the no-good's name on it and handed it over without question. Then the lad vanished for six months and the merchant had to grin and bear it. When next he saw the "pepper and salt" it was not worth seizing and they ne'er-do-well had the last laugh.

We headed away to Oxford via Victoria and as we drove felt that if visitors to Nova Scotia could reach the area where we had been and talk with persons like Mrs. Webb some of them would surely decide they could write a book about the country. And Oxford is an interesting little town, and has a fine paper, the *Oxford Journal*. The town was first known as "Head of the Tide," as it nestles in the River Philip Valley at the confluence of the River Philip and Black and Little Rivers. At the time the first settlers arrived the tidal waters of the River Philip almost reached Oxford. We went into a store and asked how the place got its present name and were told that the firstcomers used to wade their oxen across the stream at low tide and began calling it "ox-ford," then soon used the name in memory of the old city in England as the first settlers along the River Philip Valley were Yorkshiremen. First homes were located on knolls beside the brooks and streams and in the beginning spring freshets often marooned the villagers so that canoes and rafts and boats were used. First log bridges were washed out frequently and one old-timer constructed a bridge and then anchored it with heavy chains so it could swing around but not depart during high water.

The storekeeper, a pleasant man and a native, went to his office and brought us an anniversary copy of the *Journal* to which he referred as we asked questions. Much material was in a series of articles an old-timer had done and chiefly dealt with his experiences as a boy. Then the main feature for the boys in summer was an ideal swimming hole near the woollen mill yard. The Oxford Woollen Mills has been an industry that helped put Oxford on the map and its product ranks with the best. The boys divested shirt and pants in jig time and jumped in the water but as more homes were built the swimming hole was too public and so another was chosen above the railway bridge and this had a sandy beach. Once more the growth of the town caused a move and this time it was to a deep hole at the bend. There the lads enjoyed themselves to the full and the best fun was to get one of the planks that were always escaping the lumber mill and use it as a raft. There was a good machine shop, and a grist mill, a broom handle factory at Stonehouse's Brook, even a hair store that turned out switches and bangs. Sawn deal were rafted downstream to Pugwash, and hardwood lumber from Windham was used in the furniture factory.

The old-timer related that his boyhood was far more fun than that of the boys of today. On July 1st the country folk moved in by buggy and cart and on foot, and games were played and sometimes a parade staged. It was the time of mutton leg sleeves and hoop skirts and bustles, and men wore whiskers and long boots that required boot jacks to remove them. The marvel of boyhood was baptisms in the river after ice had set in. Holes would be chopped and the preacher would wade in without a tremor but often his converts would shake and shiver like short-haired puppies. There was also a different sort of entertainment for a coloured family resided in a corner of the town and did much scrapping among themselves but never bothered others. Woe betide the lad, however, who might tease one of the youngsters; he had the family on his neck in no time. Reuben Johnson, the father, was a tough and hardy citizen who worked hard and asked no favours. One evening he happened to be standing with others near the Salvation Army barracks when some rogue placed cayenne pepper on the hot stove within just as those who had held a service outside were returning. Police were called and it was declared that Reuben had played the trick. It was no use for Reuben to declare he had not done it, and it is doubtful that he even knew when the trick was played. Two policemen, the town force, took him to jail despite his protests and struggles, and it was stated he would be sent to Amherst for trial.

He would be taken by train and next day the mail team was taken to the jail and the policeman led Reuben out. The leading policeman was a rotund chap known as "Shivery," and he saw that Reuben's family were assembled but paid no particular attention. This was his undoing. Reuben let go a haymaker that felled him and Mrs. Reuben, Mandy, the husky daughter, Herb, Free'm, Art, Howe and the dog joined in merrily. It was a struggle royal and half the town gathered to watch the fray. The two policemen could handle Reuben and finally they got him in the wagon but decided to take the family as well for resisting the law. It was a wrong decision. Mandy wrapped herself around Shivery and, somehow, a foot in the way tripped him and down he went with Mandy in his arms and on top, and she got a firm grip on his beard that made things very difficult indeed. Reuben was standing in the wagon watching and when he saw Mandy's success he suddenly wrenched free and went overside straight into the crowd. It parted instantly to let him through, closed just as suddenly to hinder his pursuer. Then someone fell against the horses and started them, and the driver lost strength and could not hold them, and the train whistle blew at the Junction and Shivery knew the day was lost. He managed to arise and saw that his comrade in blue had lost the foot race with Reuben, that all the family was ready to continue the battle and that public sentiment was solidly with them. So he quietly and carefully staged a retreat and Reuben and his loyal crew were not troubled further.

We wandered around Oxford, saw the swimming holes, saw where the battle had been staged, where the first homes were built, and then were told that the plaster mill had been quite an institution in its day. So back we went to ask at the store and were shown a clipping which read:

The rumbly mill and the rustic kiln waited beside the lake. The loaded scow, with the barrow atop, waited beside the rude wharf. Week after week no one came or went. Nothing but the rippling stream beneath the weathered dusty mill showed any signs of restlessness. Two long delivery spouts, like bony arms in mute appeal, stretched from the side of the mill toward the roadway. Thus, in apparent neglect, stood the old plaster mill throughout the sunny days of harvest. But the miller would come, in time—if not today, tomorrow. He had never hurried. Years ago as a young man he had uncovered the soft white gypsum rock and visioned its use. In time, he had stayed the course of the little salt brook with a dam which formed a lake and waterway. In time, he had hewed the long timbers, laid the flume and set the water-wheel. In time, he had framed the mill, matched the wooden gear wheels and placed the rude grinding machinery. In time, he had fashioned the wide low scow and its primitive paddle. All these had yielded to the firm patient moulding of his strong brown hands. Between seedtime and harvest he had quarried the white rock at the head of the lake, filled the broad scow and slowly ferried the load to the wharf at the mill landing to be made ready for burning. Seedtime and harvest had been markers of his many years of pleasurable work and accomplishments. Amid the fruits of his labour he smiled as he worked—breaking the white rock, trundling the filled barrow, firing the kiln, filling the mill hoppers.

These were self-appointed tasks for he was neither merchant nor manufacturer; he was a tiller of the soil and gathered his needful substance from the warm brown earth. But in the valley the builders had come to depend on the white harvest he gathered. They would come to empty the bins of the flour of this crop from nature's storehouse—garnered, winnowed and measured. The homes in the valley, as long as they endure, will carry within their plastered walls a token of this mill, the miller and his powdered white crop.

Today, ungarnered, the white rock still glistens in the quarry sunshine, waiting. The restless stream yet trickles beneath the dam which still remains, but the old weather-worn mill slowly slipped into decay, waiting for the restoring, brown hands that came no more. Beyond the pines in the lovely silent acre, overlooking the lake, all that we once knew as the tiller and the miller awaits the beckoning hand of the great Giver of Life and the token: "Well done, thou good and faithful servant."

We saw just one American car in Oxford for they are afraid of the gravel road leading from Amherst, but they could come via Springhill on pavement, if they would. We drove on paved

road up the River Philip to Pugwash, a nice drive in quiet sunshine, with crows lazily cawing from fence tops and not
troubling to fly as we drove by, with lambs in the pastures
trying to look as grown as their mothers, and sheep laurel a
blaze of colour along worn-out patches that were once fine
farms. We saw Rockley that the old-timer at Pictou had talked
about but did not stop and continued through Port Philip to
Pugwash and on to Wallace Bay. A man wearing a grin that
showed three missing teeth was coming from a shop handling
farm machinery and we began asking him about about the
settlement. He said the first white man in the place was a
Major Forshner who had served in one of the hired Hessian
regiments that helped the British during the American
rebellion. He was given a large grant of land by a grateful
government and settled his sons on the holding. One operated
an inn at which the Amherst-Pictou stage coach stopped to
change horses. One of the first tragic happenings was during a
heavy July storm when a settler was killed by lightning and
three cattle killed in a nearby pasture. Our friend pointed out
some old pines and said they had been standing by the mill-
side for well over a century. He said the mill dam was just as
old and in a perfect state of preservation, with some of the
original pickets still in place, while just below the dam a
number of old logs are bedded crosswise as a foundation of the
flume.

Our friend had sandy hair and blue eyes and looked to be
almost any age between forty and seventy. He grinned when
we questioned him and said we were two years short, he having passed the alloted time in 1953. He kept young, he said,
by fishing in summer and playing croquinole in winter. Then
he grinned more and began telling of an Englishman who
settled at the Bay and decided to raise cattle in the forest. He
said if moose and caribou could thrive in the wild there was no
reason why a steer could not survive. So he put his herd back
in the bush and let them forage for themselves but when he
went to get a pair of steers for winter beef he found only the
skeletons. All his cattle had died, and then his daughter died.

A baby was born and both infant and mother died and were buried beside the daughter in a spot on the farm. Our friend said it was marked today by a growth of wire birch. We asked about the father and he said the man had handed his son over to a neighbour, got into an old boat and rowed down the creek. He was not seen again.

"But mostly all who settled around here were the right sort," continued our friend. He told us about a McFarlane who settled between the Bay and Gulf Shore and raised a family of four sons and four daughters. One year he raised five hundred bushels of wheat all of which was cut with sickles and bound with bands of straw. Then the sheaves were taken to the barn and the winter spent in swinging flails as the entire amount was threshed by hand. "Try getting some of these young fellows today to work that hard," grinned our man. "They don't know what work is. You can't get them at anything before eight in the morning, and the old-timers would have had two hours' work done by that time. And they want to quit around five in the afternoon, while they were working it was just half effort."

We went along to Gulf Shore, ten miles in length, along Northumberland Strait and a really beautiful drive. Herring were caught by the first settlers, and today lobsters are a seasonal catch and much of the catch is shipped alive to the United States. A man with a deep tan and "humor wrinkles" at the corners of his eyes told us of many lobster factories built in the place, of first fishermen working from old-time skiffs, of the later sail boats in use when he was a boy, and then the move to forty-foot boats run by high-powered car engines. We said it seemed a fine spot for tourists and he pointed out cabins that had been built and said many visitors to Pugwash drove out in the evenings to enjoy the scenery. First settlers found Acadian cellars and old wells and apple trees so the French had liked the area away back in the beginning. One of the Gulf Shore settlers built a first threshing machine, a huge affair to be operated by either oxen or horses. But grain and chaff were left together and the fanning had to be done as when a flail had been used. First sieves used in the machine were made by removing wool from a sheepskin and stretching the raw hide over one end of a deep wooden hoop, then, when the hide was dry, holes were burned into it with a hot iron. And there were many sieves, as different ones were used for each type of grain. Shipbuilding was carried on and the MacKay shipyards were employing a number of men when the call for rum became insistent. So buckets of the refreshment were served and soon the old story had been repeated. Rum had ruined the industry. Its cost had been too high. Workers had lost their usefulness. There was plenty of food in the early days as herring were easy to catch and each family salted several barrels for winter use with potatoes grown on the burnt land. They had potatoes and fish for breakfast and fish and potatoes for dinner, then reverted to potatoes and fish for supper. But now and then a moose was killed and fresh meat changed the menu. And there were always large flocks of wild geese and ducks to help out the diet in those early days. One feature was that each of the first "Clans" in the area had its own burial ground. So there are seven cemeteries at the Gulf, from MacLeods to Robertsons. When the Ship Railway was being constructed at the Isthmus near Amherst, stone needed in the construction was purchased at the Gulf Shore Quarry operated by MacDonalds and Smith. All went well for two years, then the project was halted and today big cut stones still lie there on the beach.

We drove back to Highway 4 via the Middleboros to Wentworth Centre. Old maps show the district marked as "Hillsborough," and at that time Wallace was "Ramsheg," names long forgotten. The first grant at Middleboro was made in 1787 to John Pugsley, and was surveyed by Charles Baker who noted it was wooded with birch, maple, spruce, black birch, elm and pines. This much we had read and as we drove along the winding road which looks over a lovely rural scene we saw a man fixing a gate and so stopped to pass the time of day. He was a find, a local historian who had every detail on the tip of his tongue from the year of the mice to the present.

He told us of an amazing settler who battled the year of no summer, the mice and bear plagues to eventually become well-to-do, yet he had not gone to school a single day. He was known as a master of figures, could write shorthand, read Greek, compose any legal document, make anything of wood or metal, conduct a meeting or speak in a debate. There were many clever persons in the Middleboro section. One had no learning and knew nothing about grist mills yet determined to build one. So he built a dam and cut the stone and soon the Stevens Water Power Mill became a reality and at a time when the settlers were weary of grinding grain in a handmill. Mr. Stevens had never worked in a shipyard but he went on board a vessel for two days and asked all manner of questions, then came home and built a two-master and sailed it to Quebec with a load of lumber sawn at his mill.

"The women were smart as the men," concluded our informant. "My grandmother told me of six of them riding horseback to Truro by blazed trail, and she said they could handle some horses the men were scared to saddle. And once when there was to be a social gathering at North Middleboro the six women rode through the woods by a short cut and each, in turn, jumped her horse over a pole fence near the farm as the astounded folk gathered watched their arrival."

Back we went to Oxford and then to Little River and Mansfield and on to Salem and through Brookdale into Amherst. It is a drive through small rural communities and if you like the country everything is interesting. We did not see wild life as we had in some sections but twice we stopped and had interesting talks with farm folk. Then we were back to where we had started and had more miles to our credit than if we had followed the main highways. We knew we could never put on paper adequate descriptions of the countless small coastal areas we had visited or of the many inland settlements each with its own inimitable character. Such tourings as we had done makes one comprehend that in many places along the lobster-claw peninsula life goes on much as it did fifty years ago. Men follow the sea as did their forefathers, and have inherited the lore of lobster trapping and hand lining, and the reading of the day's weather.

We had discovered once more that the people are the richest possession of Nova Scotia, that in the little out-of-the-way places characteristics of the past still dominate, that a particular combination of history and coast and state of mind instils a feeling of a "different" country. Those secondary roads had taken us from the dizzy, rushing world of today into a serene, old-world setting of yesterday. And memories warmed in our thinking until we could close our eyes and hear many of the old-timers talking unhurriedly, telling quaint tales and beliefs, each and all, from the tired shopkeeper in South Maitland deploring the vanished prosperity of shipbuilding days down to the pensive and gentle-voiced old lady off-trail on the South Shore making perfect bird calls and chatting of her treks into the bush. We thought of the wonderful afternoon and evening we had spent with the old couple in Pictou County, and the spell of the past they had spun about us until it seemed, when we were in their "spare chamber," resting on a spool bed more than a century old, with sleepy country sounds lulling us to dreamland, we were back in days they had known with a candle by the bedside, a sheepskin on the floor kindly to cold feet, and hearing the spinning-wheel still whirring below stair as granny finished her evening's stint.

It was easy to remember the scrap books we had seen, the treasured bits that old folks keep to read and read again, to recall the precious things handed on from mother to daughter like Italian doll dishes known to four generations, grandfather clocks that came with the Loyalists, relics brought back from the seven seas by loved ones who had become sailormen. There is so much to see and know and feel in those obscure hamlets that are symbols of patience and endurance and courage! And to those who wish to know the whimsical and old-fashioned folk who have been the backbone of these places we say come soon or you will miss them. Time and again we sat and gazed at grassed-over cellars and forgotten orchards, at gray old homes dying amid a jungle of weeds and matted timothy and almost-smothered flowers. Nearby might be a farm where the old folks still survived, living out their days on pensions, the farm taxes paid by the son or daughter in a far-off city who want to keep the old homestead respectable while the parents live. Time marches on and it is sad to see the change. These fading communities made a strong and virile countryside once but now the forest is slowly absorbing the acres won by sturdy men and women who found a full life and independence through the practice of a frugality and persistent endeavour unknown to the rising generation.

Nova Scotia is old and rugged and bears the scars of long battling with the cruel sea but her latch string is ever out for those who wish to know her byways and it is in the smaller places that visitors will get nearest her heart.

INDEX

Acaciaville, 98
Acadia Mines, 27, 29, 30
Advocate, 11, 12, 243
Albany Cross, 117
Albert Bridge, 245
Amherst, 1, 3, 6, 243, 301, 303, 306, 307
Annapolis Royal, 91, 94, 99, 101, 118, 119, 124, 146, 197, 200, 247
Antigonish, 227, 231, 234, 235, 266
Apple River, 10
Arichat, 236, 237, 238
Aspatogan, 141
Aspen, 225
Auburn, 69
Avondale, 53, 280

Baccaro, 172, 186, 187
Baddeck, 243, 254
Baleine, 251,252, 253
Ballantyne Cove, 232, 233
Balmoral Mills, 275
Barachois, 244
Barney's Brook, 232
Barrington, 172, 174, 186, 188, 192
Barss' Corner, 113
Bass River, 28, 29
Bayport, 145
Bayswater, 143
Beach Meadows, 157
Bear River, 94, 96, 97, 98, 100, 101
Beaver Cove, 244
Belmont, 34
Big Pond, 249
Big Tancook Island, 165
Birchtown, 171
Blandford, 140, 141
Blomidon, 62, 63, 65, 84
Boisdale, 244
Boudro Point, 57
Boylston, 262
Bras d'Or, 239
Brickton, 83
Bridgetown, 87, 91, 118
Bridgeville, 214, 215
Bridgewater, 112, 113
Brier Island, 128, 129
Broad Cove, 153
Brookdale, 307
Brookfield, 111

Brooklyn, 53, 171
Burlington, 50
Burntcoat Head, 40
Byer's Corner, 281

Cabot Trail, 254, 255
Caledonia, 109, 213
Caledonia Mills, 262
Canada Creek, 69
Canning, 58, 60, 62
Canso, 149
Cap la Ronde, 238
Cape George, 227, 232
Cape Negro, 172, 175, 181
Cape North, 256
Carleton, 192, 193
Centreville, 68, 125
Cherryfield, 115
Cherry Hill, 153
Chester, 165, 196, 200, 201, 202, 257
Cheticamp, 254, 256
Cheverie, 46, 47
Chimney Corner, 258
Cleveland, 239
Clyde River, 188
Coffinscroft, 172, 186
Collingwood Corner, 21, 23
Colpton, 110
Crystal Cliffs, 235
Cumberland Bridge, 25
Cunard's Cove, 146

Dalhousie Road, 194
Dalhousie West, 117, 119
Dean Settlement, 208, 209
Debert, 31, 32
D'Ecousse, 238
Deep Brook, 99
Deerfield, 192
Delap Cove, 87
Delusion, 83
Digby, 119, 121, 123
Diligent River, 15
Doctor's Brook, 227, 232
Downing Clear, 25
Dublin Shore, 151

Eagle Head, 157
Earltown, 267, 268, 275, 277, 282, 283, 284, 285, 286
East Dover, 134
East Earltown, 270, 275
East Ferry, 128

311